Perfecting the Constitution

Perfecting the Constitution

The Case for the Article V Amendment Process

Darren Patrick Guerra

LEXINGTON BOOKS
Lanham • Boulder • New York • Toronto • Plymouth, UK

Published by Lexington Books
A wholly owned subsidiary of The Rowman & Littlefield Publishing Group, Inc.
4501 Forbes Boulevard, Suite 200, Lanham, Maryland 20706
www.rowman.com

10 Thornbury Road, Plymouth PL6 7PP, United Kingdom

British Library Cataloguing in Publication Information Available

Library of Congress Cataloging-in-Publication Data

Guerra, Darren Patrick.
Perfecting the Constitution : the case for the Article V amendment process / Darren Patrick Guerra.
pages cm
Includes bibliographical references and index.
ISBN 978-0-7391-6838-7 (cloth : alk. paper) -- ISBN 978-0-7391-8386-1 (electronic)
1. Constitutional amendments--United States. 2. Constitutional law--United States. I. Title.
KF4555.G84 2013
342.7303'2--dc23
2013010876

™ The paper used in this publication meets the minimum requirements of American National Standard for Information Sciences—Permanence of Paper for Printed Library Materials, ANSI/NISO Z39.48-1992.

Printed in the United States of America

To my parents
Pat (1941-2007) and Joyce Guerra
For their years of love, sacrifice, and support

Contents

Preface

This work grows out of a deep interest in American Constitutionalism and its preservation of ordered liberty for over two hundred years. As I began to encounter numerous scholarly arguments in favor of abandoning Article V as the sole mode of constitutional amendment, I became increasingly interested in the place of Article V in the larger constitutional architecture. Since its colonial origins, the unique American experiment in ordered liberty has always embraced written documents as the legal foundation of society and government. Covenants, compacts, and constitutions have been a distinctive American way of structuring politics. It seemed apparent to me that a written constitution logically demands a formal amending process, and I found it curious that such an obvious point was in serious dispute. In seeking to understand the situation, I wanted to explore the design and purpose of Article V and better understand its relationship to the larger constitutional order. Furthermore, I wanted to explore the arguments against Article V that have been mounting by a number of prestigious and notable scholars of the Constitution. The more I explored these themes, the more I realized that Article V required a vigorous defense from scholarly critics. Political scientists, like medical doctors, have a duty to diagnose and suggest treatments for the health of the body politic. Most criticisms of Article V are born out of a vision of responsive democracy that is in opposition with the Founders' commitment to written constitutionalism and liberal democracy. The Founders sought to secure rights by guarding against tyranny by the few as well as the many, and rather than simply making government responsive to the impulses of popular majorities they sought to "refine and enlarge" public opinion through constitutional structure. Instead of an expendable appendix to the Constitution, Article V is revealed as a perfecting mechanism of the Constitution and a vital element of a dynamic yet stable constitutional system. If Americans want to preserve their written Constitution, they must first preserve Article V.

I would like to acknowledge the support and guidance of my former professors Ralph A. Rossum, Joseph M. Bessette, and Jean R. Schroedel, who provided valuable guidance and direction in my graduate studies and read large portions of early drafts of this manuscript in another form. I am thankful to my undergraduate mentor and friend Dr. Dennis McNutt who has always inspired me to think deeply and critically about all issues. I owe a debt of gratitude to my dear friend and colleague Jeffrey H. Anderson, for together, we have challenged each other to think more deeply about great issues in American Constitutionalism. Without his careful eye and keen insights this book would be much for the worse. I also owe thanks to friends and colleagues who have read drafts of chapters, helped me think through arguments, or simply provided general moral support in various forms. These people include Margot Anderson, Kevin Walker, Rachelle Walker, Scott Waller, Ravi Roy, and my Vanguard University History Department colleagues John Wilson, Mike Wilson, and David Jon Marley.

I am also thankful for my trusted and talented Research Assistants: Jasmin Botello, Patrick O'Brien, Maria Torres, Daniel Waite, and David Vazquez. I also wish to thank the Gary L. Taylor Fund for providing financial support for a course release to work on this project and the fund's benefactor Vanguard University President Carol Taylor. In addition, I am thankful for the general academic support provided by the Vanguard University Provost Jeff Hittenberger and his office represented by the genial and talented Julie Cowen as well as the tremendous general administrative support over the years by the indispensable and fabulous Cheryl Jensen.

Furthermore, friends and family are always a backbone for such ventures. I wish to thank the families in our "life-group" in Fullerton, California for their love and support. As for family, I thank my brother Dustin for his companionship while doing hours of research and writing, listening to my thoughts on this topic, and helping edit several chapters. I also wish to acknowledge my mother Joyce, grandmother Beverly, brother Dennis, his wife Stacey, and their children Dyson and Grace, all of whom have provided valuable support in one form or another over the years of this project. Their unconditional love has been invaluable. I also want to thank my wife's family for their prayers and encouragement: parents Vic and Lily Dayco, sister Maryanne Dayco, and my favorite couple living in Australia—brother and sister Matt and Josephine Lock. Last but certainly not least, I cannot express enough how much my loving wife Catherine has been a deep source of encouragement and inspiration as well as a skilled editor and confidant. She has spent many hours listening to my ideas and editing my writing. If not for her, I would still be working on this book. The importance of her love and support for me is beyond measure or description. Most importantly, I wish to thank God Almighty who makes all things possible.

PART I
The Creation of Article V

Chapter 1
Perfecting the Constitution

> Like all other human productions, it may be imperfect; but most of the imperfections imputed to it are ideal and unfounded, and the rest are of such a nature that they cannot be certainly known but by the operations of the Constitution; and if, in its operation, it should in any respect be essentially bad, it will be amended in one of the modes prescribed by it.
>
> James Bowdoin, Massachusetts Ratifying Convention[1]

> In questions of power then, let no more be heard of confidence in man, but bind him down from mischief by the chains of the constitution.
>
> Thomas Jefferson[2]

This book is a reminder of how democracies are often seduced by their immediate desires at the expense of forms and formalities designed for their safety, stability, and happiness. The American political order is certainly not immune to this innate democratic weakness. Yet despite such democratic tendencies, Americans also seem to intuitively know that their rights and happiness are dependent upon the health and stability of the United States Constitution. They know that it is vital to maintain the integrity of that document if the people are to delight in their natural rights to life, liberty, and the pursuit of happiness.[3] Indeed, the Constitution has been described as the "safeguard of our liberties" and "the sole source and guaranty of national freedom."[4] Yet, who controls this vital document? Who has the authority to amend the United States Constitution? The simple and most legitimate answer to this question is that "the people" utilizing the Article V procedure outlined in the Constitution have the authority to amend that fundamental law embodied by the United States Constitution. This answer was echoed by prominent figures in American politics such as George Washington, who argued clearly that the Constitution should be amended in "the way which the Constitution designates"; or James Madison who wrote that it should be "altered by the same authority only which established it"; and Abraham Lincoln, who stated that amendments should be made by the "modes prescribed in the instrument itself."[5] Indeed, Article V's claim as the exclusive means of amending the Constitution has gone largely unchallenged; that is, until recently. This seemingly simple and straightforward question is now in doubt among important and influential scholars. Noted legal scholars now openly argue that Article V is not the only way to amend the Constitution; and furthermore, that national referendums or informal adaptation of the Constitution by the normal branches of government can serve the same purpose. The latent assumption is that Article V is not important to the overall structure and history of the Constitution—that while the Constitution may well be the "safeguard of our liberties," the manner of its amendment is of little importance to its overall health and stability.

It may seem obvious, but these debates over constitutional amendment have potentially profound implications. Theoretically, if constitutions serve as fundamental law that restrains tyranny and preserves liberty, then whoever has the power to alter them has immense implications for political life. Indeed, the American Revolution was fought in large part over such issues. That is to say, the American Revolution was in important ways fought over who was allowed to alter the constitutional arrangements between England and its American colonies. The American colonists found themselves in a situation where they believed the terms of the English constitution had been usurped and unilaterally altered by Parliament in a manner inconsistent with the ancient constitutional traditions, the rights of Englishmen, and the natural law. From the American perspective, the terms of the English constitution had been changed. The problem was that, due to the informal nature of the English constitution, the colonists did not realize this change had taken place until "Redcoats" were shooting Americans and enforcing Parliamentary power at the end of a bayonet. In this light, the Boston Massacre and the shot heard round the world at Lexington and Concord were rather late and forceful notifications of constitutional alterations to the English constitution made unilaterally by Parliament some years prior.

Being unwritten and evolutionary, the English constitution provided no means for formal amendment; as a result, the distribution of powers in the constitution had transformed over time without the full awareness or agreement of all the parties (most notably the American colonists). Consequently, these informal shifts in power resulted in disputed claims over the legitimacy of the changes; which in turn produced cavernous disagreements over constitutional limits on Parliamentary power. Americans appealed to traditions and customary constraints on Parliamentary power; while in contrast, Parliament insisted on their newly asserted supremacy over the English constitution. Thus, it was through the struggles of the Imperial Crisis that American colonists learned that the English constitution was, in some important respects, more a matter of *accident* and *force* rather than *reflection* and *choice*. The Americans began to see they had become victims of informal, inexplicit constitutional changes to the English constitution, and as a result, they rejected the unwritten constitutionalism of their mother country. One lesson learned by the colonists from the pain and struggle with England was that governments needed to be formally restrained in law by written constitutions. In addition, amendments to those constitutions needed to be formally made so that all parties were clear on when, or if, the inevitable need for alterations to the fundamental law were made. The formality of written constitutions and explicit amendment procedures would better preserve the balance of governmental power; it would also provide the people with the ability to alter their constitutions of government whenever they wished; and it would allow them to do so in a regular manner that would help limit usurpation and avoid the need for bloody revolution. By the time of the United States Constitutional Convention in 1787, this need for formal amendment of the Constitution took shape in the formal process outlined in Article V of that document. Article V allowed the people to calmly and soberly alter their constitutional arrangements, via deliberative bodies, only after those seeking change had built national coalitions and established a clear national consensus for the desired change. When viewed in contrast with the blood and confusion that characterized power struggles over constitutional authority under England's unwritten constitution, Article V was seen as a valuable means of *perfecting the Constitution* over time and a valuable advance in the science of politics.

The Odyssey and Article V

> 'So far so good,' said she . . .'and now pay attention to what I am about to tell you—heaven itself, indeed, will recall it to your recollection. First you will come to the Sirens who enchant all who come near them. If any one unwarily draws in too close and hears the singing of the Sirens, his wife and children will never welcome him home again, for they sit in a green field and warble him to death with the sweetness of their song. There is a great heap of dead men's bones lying all around, with the flesh still rotting off them. Therefore pass these Sirens by, and stop your men's ears with wax that none of them may hear; but if you like you can listen yourself, for you may get the men to bind you as you stand upright on a cross-piece half way up the mast, and they must lash the rope's ends to the mast itself, that you may have the pleasure of listening. If you beg and pray the men to unloose you, then they must bind you faster.
>
> The Odyssey, Book XII

Homer does not give us certain details of those fateful moments where Odysseus and his crew had to pass the island of the Sirens. One can well imagine that

Odysseus, lashed to the mast and struggling to be free was, in the passion of the moment, irate with his crew as they refused to yield to his immediate impulses. Odysseus well might have heatedly recanted the strategy to bind him and cursed the very chords that lashed him to the mast. Yet, once the danger had passed, Odysseus was likely grateful for the discipline of the crew and the wisdom of the plan to bind him; for in the end, he had experienced the Sirens' song, yet escaped the dangers it presented. The dangers of the Sirens were unique; for their victims were seduced by a sweetness that corrupted their will and their judgment. While under the Sirens' spell, Odysseus was unable to distinguish his true interests from his perceived momentary interests. The only way for Odysseus to continue his journey and still experience the satisfaction of the Sirens' song, was for him to devise external restraints on his own will until the danger had passed. Obviously, the key for Odysseus was to paradoxically *authorize* a restraint upon his own *will*; to commit, while lucid, to restrict his own desire during its momentary corruption. As such, Odysseus's decision to bind himself was an exhibition of self-discipline, prudence, and wisdom.

At the time of the American founding, the history of human civilization had rendered a mixed verdict on the efficacy of democratic politics. The *Siren song* of democracy—while alluring and sweet—had too often proved to be a path of instability, excess, chaos, and destruction rather than prosperity, stability, and security.[6] Thus, to avoid the perils of democracies that preceded them, the founding generation of Americans, in their wisdom, sought to take precautions to avoid democratic excess and collapse. Just as Odysseus bound himself to the mast so that he might hear the song of the Sirens, without surrendering to their seductive tones, so too did the American people bind themselves to a written Constitution. They bound themselves so that they might experience the sweetness of democratic government, while still resisting the seductive siren song of democratic excess. They bound themselves to the Constitution as the fundamental law; and *as law*, it would impede the excessive tendencies of the *demos*—it would help the people resist the passions of the moment. Indeed, the very word "law" derives from the Latin term "ligare" which means "to bind."[7] The Constitution *as law* is meant to guard against governmental tyranny by binding and limiting it. But even more than that, it is meant to bind the sovereign American people themselves to certain forms and formalities so that they might avoid the error and the terror of majority tyranny. The forms and formalities of the Constitution are meant to bind the people in the very moments that their majority impulse is telling them to throw off those very same restraints. It is in these moments, as with Odysseus, that the bindings must be kept in place—indeed perhaps they need be tightened—until the danger is passed. The difficulty rests in the fact that this type of danger is rarely recognized for what it is; for the immediate impassioned desires of the majority—as opposed to its sober and deliberative choices—will sound very sweet, unassuming, and intoxicating. It is a longstanding dilemma in politics—dating at least as far back as the execution of Socrates—that democratic majorities tend to tell themselves that their immediate desires are sound and just, and those who resist are outsiders, naysayers, and the like. For this reason, the Constitution was never meant simply to be subject to the impulse of the raw will of the majority; for the moment majority impulse controls the Constitution, then the Constitution no longer *binds*. When it no longer binds the people against their own immediate unrefined impulses, then it ceases to be a constitution in any meaningful sense of the word.

Not only must the Constitution guard against the abuse of power by the many, but it must likewise prevent the abuse of power by the few against the many, or in the name of the many. To avoid usurpation or demagoguery, the Constitution formalizes the use of power by elites in government. Offices are defined, powers are given, limits are demarcated, and forms are prescribed to allow for the legitimate, open, and safe use of governmental power. In the words of Madison in *Federalist No. 51,* "In framing a government which is to be administered by men over men, the great difficulty lies in this: you must first enable the government to control the governed; and in the next place, oblige it to control itself." Thus, written constitutionalism is a device meant to bind the government as well as the people upon whose authority it rests and in whose interests it serves.

A vital component of the United States Constitution is Article V, which outlines and establishes a formal amending procedure. The fifth article of the Constitution provides for the proposal of amendments by two-thirds of Congress or a national convention called by two-thirds of the state legislatures; amendments can then be ratified by three-fourths of the state legislatures or conventions in three-fourths of the states. This amending procedure allows the American people in their sovereign capacity to alter and amend their Constitution. Just as the Constitution empowers the American people by providing structure and boundaries to democratic politics, Article V similarly empowers the American people by providing structure and form to a potentially chaotic process of constitutional change. Yet while empowering the people by providing clear procedures and institutions, it also *binds* or limits the American polity to its several amending options. It would allow the people to perfect their Constitution over time but do so soberly and deliberatively.

Article V was carefully designed to maintain the sovereignty of the people over their government, all the while still restraining their raw unrefined impulses. Among other qualities, Article V ensures that constitutional changes are explicit, authentically democratic, deliberative, and in keeping with the traditions and character of the American polity. Once alterations to the Constitution become untethered from Article V, the Constitution becomes subject to whatever new forces direct its alterations. If simple majorities direct the adaptations or alterations, then the Constitution no longer binds the raw power of the people in the manner it was designed. For as the Constitution becomes less binding, then it no longer protects the people from their own temporary delusions and misguided judgments. On the other hand, if the alterations to the Constitution become the province of the few, then the very democratic nature of the Constitution is severely undermined. To avoid the *Scylla and Charybdis* of these extremes, Article V was designed to both remove constitutional change from direct popular majorities and to prevent elite usurpation or adaptation.

Now, imagine an alternative narrative of *The Odyssey*. In the alternative narrative, the crew is divided over whether or not to loosen the bindings on Odysseus. The source of the division can be traced to the fact that some of the crew have removed the wax and have fallen under the spell of the Sirens. As Odysseus signals to be loosened, some of the crew urge their shipmates to untether him so he may follow his immediate desires over and against his sober wishes expressed prior to his binding; still others contend that they must maintain the original plan. They argue to sustain and even tighten the bindings on Odysseus, since these actions represent the most faithful commitment to the well-being of Odysseus and the vessel. In the balance of this dispute between the crew members hangs the fate of Odysseus and the entire ship. This alternative narrative, in some important ways, describes the current situation in scholarship regarding constitutional amendment. Some notable and important scholars question the efficacy of Article V and its claim as the exclusive means of amending the Constitution. In effect, they argue to loosen the bindings of Article V, and by logical extension, the binding nature of the Constitution. In contrast, other scholars maintain that Article V be adhered to as the only legitimate means of amending the Constitution.

In the outcome of the debate surrounding Article V hangs the future shape of American Constitutionalism. As we will see, not only was Article V carefully designed, but its function is crucial to maintaining the integrity of the constitutional system. If the American polity were no longer bound to Article V, then in turn the Constitution becomes less binding; for if the Constitution can be altered by means other than those explicitly provided, then the Constitution becomes subject to the whim of whoever can exert enough informal power to alter it. In other words, a constitution that is not subject to formal amendment edges away from its character as *law* and shifts towards becoming a mere implement of *power* unrestrained by law. For law not only binds, but law adheres to form.

Not only are the democratic and prudential forms of amendment jeopardized by abandoning Article V, but the entire logic of written constitutionalism is undermined. The need for, and the logic of, a written constitution has a force all of its own. Tinkering with the series of premises that provided the logical structure of a written constitution can potentially threaten the stability of the entire structure. In the American system, the Declaration of Independence declares the reality of unwritten natural laws, upon which the natural rights of American citizens rest. According to the Declaration the purpose of governments are to "secure" these natural rights. These natural rights demand a limited government. A limited government is achieved via a written constitution which outlines the government's powers and its limits. As the mechanism that empowers and binds government, a written constitution is the fundamental law of the land. As the fundamental law, it has authority over the normal arms of government such as the executive, legislative, and judicial powers. Thus, for one of the branches to exert dominant power to alter or adapt the Constitution is to turn the logic of a written constitution on its head. Not only is the Constitution, as fundamental law, meant to exert authority over normal branches of government, but it is also meant to restrain the immediate impulses of democratic majorities. In accord with these purposes, Article V is similarly designed to restrain such impulses; for it would not make sense to design a constitution meant to restrain the immediate, unreflective impulses of democratic majorities and then allow those same majorities the power to alter any part of that very constitution. Therefore, it is clear by the logic of the Constitution, that Article V must bind normal arms of government from altering the Constitution and it must also bind the people in their sovereign power from exertions of unrefined democratic excess, all the while still providing procedures that empower democratic majorities—albeit in deliberative and prudent institutional settings—to amend the fundamental law. This binding of the sovereign power of the people is a crucial part of the Constitution, and Article V seeks to empower the people's sovereignty even as it binds it. In this sense, Odysseus had nothing over the American Founders.

Attacks on Article V

Despite Article V being viewed by the early generations of American citizens and statesmen as a prudent and efficacious means of correcting imperfections in the young Constitution, by the turn of the twentieth century Article V came under attack by Progressives for being too difficult and undemocratic. Due to its formality and supermajority requirements, Article V was described as "rigid" and there were fears that it was putting pressure on the undemocratic courts to alter and adapt the Constitution.[8] There were many proposals for altering Article V via the existing amending process, yet these efforts all ultimately failed in turn. Ironically, Article V soon provided an outlet for Progressive ideals such as the direct election of Senators, the income tax, and women's suffrage. The fact is, Progressive activists built national coalitions to push through six amendments in twenty years—an unprecedented amount of amendments in such a short time. Article V had become a favorite tool of the very Progressives that had derided it.

However, the New Deal Progressives would face new challenges. After early Progressives chastised the use of the courts for constitutional change as undemocratic, ironically latter progressives soon turned to the courts as an alternative to Article V. This turn to the courts revealed the underlying pragmatism of the Progressive movement. This pragmatism led Franklin Roosevelt to undermine Article V's status and authority during what some scholars term the New Deal "revolution" in judicial power and practice. For some scholars, one of the results of the New Deal was the attempted installation of the Supreme Court as the final arbiter of constitutional meaning and the alteration of the Constitution through judicial rulings and "transformative appointments" to the Supreme Court. For example, one scholar argues that, "New Dealers rejected the traditional form of an amendment; instead, they relied on the New Deal Court to elaborate their new activist vision through a series of transformative opinions."[9] For Roosevelt, it was "wrong to codify the New Deal transformation through forms sanctioned by Article Five," but he thought it better to "rely instead on the appointment of new judges to give new meaning to the Constitution."[10] In subsequent decades, the New Deal ethos led Presidents and Congress to use such methods to "revolutionize" the "fundamental doctrines" of the Constitution.[11]

A key part of the efforts to replace Article V with judicial review have involved the careful language used by political actors and judges to couch such judicial "amendments" in the language of "interpretation." Through expansive "interpretations," new transformative meanings are assigned to an ever-evolving document. For example, Justice Brennan was one outspoken champion of this use of judicial power to affect constitutional change: "the genius of the Constitution rests not on any static meaning it might have had in a world that is dead and gone, but in the adaptability of its great principles to cope with current problems and current needs."[12] Brad C. S. Watson, in commenting on Brennan's outlook, "Although the Constitution is in some degree a 'structuring text' marking out the bounds of government, it is, more fundamentally, a visionary document demanding ever more democracy . . . Brennan sees the judge's job as articulating its meaning as that meaning reveals itself in time."[13] Another proponent of a constitutional alteration by judicial transformation was Thurgood Marshall who quipped, "the Constitution was not fixed in Philadelphia or anywhere else."[14] For Marshall, "Constitutional interpretation involves perceiving and clearly articulating the direction of evolutionary change for an organic document that serves the need of an organic state."[15] Under this new Progressive approach, "Adaptation to the 'ever-changing conditions of national and international life' is the *sine qua non* of constitutionalism, and the navigational system of this organic process, if not its motor, is the judicial branch."[16] Another scholar put it this way,

> It may be concluded that contemporary constitutional theory is preoccupied with a constitutional text not regarded as historically compelling, meaningful per se, representative of a multigenerational historical consensus in the American polity, or symbolic of a wider constitutional experience. Rather, it pursues the idea of a general blueprint, the details of which must be filled in on a continuing ad hoc basis, combined with an 'addiction' to judicial government. Such an approach effectively enthrones the judiciary as a kind of constitutional monarchy, overthrowing the republican form of government instituted at the Founding.[17]

It should be observed that the New Deal "revolution" did not directly attack Article V, rather it simply ignored formal amendment whenever it became inconvenient. In this sense, then, Article V has not been the subject of a full frontal assault, but rather the victim of a swift and sweeping judicial blitzkrieg that swung around its flank and kept on rolling towards open fields in pursuit of Progressive policy conquests. While the judicial blitzkrieg may have bypassed it, nevertheless Article V has never been conquered, and it has stood behind the lines of advancing judicial power as a stubborn reminder of the still enduring American commitment to written constitutionalism and limited government. That is to say, despite the notable successes of the narrative of the evolutionary "living constitution," the old constitutional norms still persist. The logic of a written constitution and the existence of Article V still provide a stumbling block to unrestrained and improper use of judicial review:

> The infrequency of amendment has often been explained on the basis that judicial review rendered most change by amendment unnecessary and comparatively difficult, thus unattractive. Yet judicial review has been a problematic device for obtaining constitutional change. It proved incendiary in Dred Scott v. Sanford, reactionary and provoking in Pollack v. Farmers' Loan & Trust, painfully slow to achieve results in Brown v. Board of Education, and startling and unconvincing to many in Roe v. Wade. Judicial review has been difficult for many Americans to accept, hard to implement, and subject to ongoing challenge and reversal. Judicially imposed constitutional change, whatever its other merits or flaws, is distinguished from amendment by its lack of a democratic imprimatur.[18]

Constitutional norms die hard and a written document and formal amending mechanism still stand as living testaments to the Founding Constitutional order that is still well and alive and still seems to capture the allegiance and imagination of the American citizenry. The Founders' constitutional tradition will not yield very easily as such open claims for obvious instances of judicial adaptation are still "often met with outrage" by conservatives and liberals alike.[19] While scholars may debate the efficacy and authority of Article V, the American people still embrace the Constitution.[20] However the people have also embraced many of the products of judicial adaptation. There is then a tension and incoherence just below the surface of the public mind that must be and will be resolved in time. Thus, even though much of this debate is currently confined to the halls of academe, it is still important to address the scholarly assault on Article V in a direct manner; for in time, it could well influence more popular and public deliberations on such matters.[21]

Open assaults on Article V come largely from a new cadre of legal scholars, who in the last twenty years have renewed efforts to fully and openly de-legitimize Article V. Much of the above constitutional "revolution" has been attempted under the linguistic cover of "interpretation" and with elaborate legal theories that seek to legitimize constitutional changes outside of Article V, while still maintaining that such change is consistent with the written constitutional order and Article V. In other words, the game has been played with new rules while publicly pretending to largely play by the old ones. However, maintaining the democratic legitimacy of judicial adaptation of the Constitution has been difficult and the enduring nature of the original constitutional norms have limited just how far judges can really go. For example, a noted scholar and critic of Article V, who is comfortable with "adaptations by judicial interpretation" concedes that, "such informal methods" are not "always available" and "one might still object to the lack of transparency attached to the use of some of these informal methods."[22] He notes that, "The degree of fundamental change is often covered up by being rationalized in incomprehensible legal jargon that requires inordinate faith in the lawyers and judges writing the opinions. If one believes that transparency is an important part of . . .'Republican Form of Government,' then the use of the judiciary as . . . a 'continuing constitutional convention' has real costs."[23] So even advocates of judicial adaptation of the Constitution admit that the text can only be stretched so far and the ensuing lack of clarity is not optimal. However, what if the judiciary could openly "amend" the Constitution? Would that not alleviate some of these difficulties? Would not the power to "amend" the Constitution openly, via judicial ruling, release the Court from having to shamelessly stretch or ignore the plain constraining language of the Constitutional text?

As long as scholars and courts claim that extremely permissive interpretations of the constitutional text are indeed interpretations, then at least in name, there is no open challenge to the amending process and such interpretations are subject to debate over their validity and faithfulness to the plain meaning of the constitutional text. That is to say, as long as courts claim to merely interpret the Constitution, the operative question is: "Is this ruling a fair and faithful reading of the constitutional text?" In answering this question, there are linguistic boundaries—debatable boundaries, to be sure, but boundaries nonetheless—to how far a given court can stretch the plain meaning of the constitutional text. However, once scholars and courts begin to openly proclaim that a permissive interpretation is actually an amendment, then there is a separate debate to be had. If courts—or legal scholars on their behalf—openly claim to be informally amending the Constitution through their rulings, then the linguistic boundaries on the court's power disappear and, in time, so does the written Constitution and the clear and direct democratic control over the nature, size, and scope of government power. Indeed, if courts are allowed to openly and informally amend the Constitution, the implications of such a development would have profound implications on the American polity's ability to maintain liberal democracy.

Contemporary Critics: Responding to Imperfection

While the New Deal reformers shied away from openly challenging Article V's status, today's scholars show no such restraint. For example, in the introduction to a leading collection of essays on constitutional amendment, the editor Sanford Levinson confirms this essential challenge to Article V:

> a central focus of several of these essays concerns the *exclusivity* of Article V as a method of bringing about amendment. Everyone concedes that Article V sets out *a* way by which the Constitution can be changed. Is it also *the* way? Or are there alternative means of achieving fundamental change within the American constitutional system?[24]

What rationales are offered for denying the exclusivity of Article V? For some, informal change is simply a natural part of the evolution of law; for others, the Constitution is deeply flawed at a fundamental level and creative approaches to change are necessary for the health of the political system.[25] Still others attempt to locate informal constitutional change at the very roots of the American political order.[26] While the arguments and nuances may differ, the common thread is that they all seek to undermine Article V as the exclusive means of amending the Constitution.[27]

What do they seek to offer as alternatives to Article V? Some call openly for a democratic *coup d'état* by the House of Representatives; others settle for majoritarian national referendums; while still others call for less open procedures, such as informal adaptations by the courts or the political branches allied with the courts buttressed by the electoral process.[28] Most of these scholars usually challenge Article V's exclusivity by blurring the lines between formal amendment and informal adaptations or alterations. For these scholars, there is little to no difference between Article V's formal democratic deliberative procedures versus mere "functional shifts achieved by judicial construction, unchallenged legislative initiative, or unchecked presidential embellishment."[29] In short, if they aren't offering *popular referendums* as an alternative to Article V, then they tend to elevate *informal adaptation* over *formal amendment*.

For example, Sanford Levinson argues that the most important constitutional changes have taken place outside of the Article V process and that the Article V process has produced changes that may better be termed as "interpretations." According to Levinson, we should reserve the term "amendment" to reflect broad and fundamental changes to our governmental system and not just changes to the constitutional text.[30] Bruce Ackerman points to defining historical moments where the American people legitimately circumvented the Article V process via what Ackerman calls "structural amendments." In this manner, he does not recognize Article V as the exclusive means of amending the Constitution, seeing Article V as "a" means of amendment but not "the" means of amendment. Akhil Reed Amar claims that the American commitment to popular sovereignty allows the American people in their sovereign capacity to ignore Article V in favor of a national referendum; and as such, Article V does not have a firm claim on being the exclusive means of altering the constitutional text.[31] Still another, Stephen Griffin argues that Article V is a critical part of the outdated "rule of law" constitutionalism, which is not compatible with modern society. For Griffin, the Constitution must be more flexible than either Article V or "rule of law constitutionalism" allows; thus by Griffin's logic, the Constitution must be open to change from sources other than Article V.[32] By rationalizing non-Article V amendments to the Constitution, these scholars all, each in their own way, undermine the written Constitution. While their carefully crafted prose and nuanced legal arguments downplay the impact of abandoning Article V, the logical implications of such a change are indeed potentially staggering. If informal adaptation replaces the formal amendment of Article V, the written Constitution will recede into the swirling waters of court opinions, Congressional statutes, and Executive orders. The power and force of the words of the constitutional text will slowly and certainly depreciate until at some point in the future they cease to have anything other than rhetorical impact on the real daily operations of the government. In short, an abandonment of Article V will severely undermine the edifice of ordered liberty that is secured by a fixed written constitution and its attending norms. In its place will be the persistent emergence of an organic evolutionary unwritten constitution that neither binds the government, nor will it bind the people against their own temporary delusions. In the end, if these scholars are successful, then with regard to the rejection of an unwritten evolutionary constitution, the constitutional effects of the American Revolution will be finally undone.

Defending Article V

In their haste to abandon Article V, critics seem to imply that Article V is not a vital part of the constitutional order, that it is expendable or unnecessary. They tend to downplay the essential role of formal amendment in the structure of the constitutional system, and they tend to ignore the role formal amendment has played in the American constitutional tradition. Part I of this book will seek to counteract this tendency by briefly tracing the history of ideas that led to Article V's creation and its place in the constitutional order. Chapter 2 will show that the American colonists had long utilized written documents as fundamental laws and this experience formed a unique tradition that was certainly related to, but still in important respects distinct from, the unwritten English constitution. As the Imperial Crisis festered, Americans lost faith in the unwritten constitution of England. As they broke from England, most colonies turned to written documents for their fundamental laws and, in turn, many (but not all) experimented with various forms of formal amending procedures. Article V was a natural outgrowth of the American constitutional tradition as it was rapidly developing during the Imperial Crisis, the American Revolution, the State Constitutions, and the 1787 Constitutional Convention in Philadelphia. The historic and theoretical link between written constitutions and formal amending procedures and their mutual dependence can be clearly seen.

In addition, we will see how the unique design and structure of Article V was meant to fit the logic of written constitutionalism, to secure the natural rights of American citizens, and to fit the federal texture of the American polity. Chapter 3 will trace the specific development of Article V at the Constitutional Convention and its vital role in the constitutional ratification process. Chapter 4 will pull together the Founding consensus on Article V and will illustrate how Article V's exclusivity and design are unique structural features of, and supports for, the architecture of the constitutional system. According to the Founding generation, the binding nature of the Constitution as written law depends upon an adherence to Article V as the explicit, authentic, and exclusive means of constitutional amendment. Article V was seen as a perfecting mechanism of the new Constitution that would allow the people to address the Constitution's imperfections by amending it in a prudent, democratic, and legal manner.

Part II will defend Article V from an array of attacks. Such attacks became common during the Progressive era and have continued in various forms unabated since the turn of the twentieth century. Article V will be defended against charges that it is too difficult, undemocratic, and too formal. Chapter 5 will introduce the intellectual shifts and currents that came with the Progressive movement and their impact on legal thought and culture that, in turn, resulted in undermining the confidence of Progressives in Article V and still provides much of the basis for contemporary attacks. Chapter 6 will examine the charge that Article V is too difficult. We will examine that charge from a variety of angles and test it against some basic measures of Article V's historical performance. Chapter 7 will take on the charge that Article V is undemocratic. Such charges usually focus on the supermajority requirements and are rooted in basic disagreements with the Founders over natural rights versus responsiveness and democratic governance. Chapter 8 responds to contemporary arguments that seek to legitimate informal adaptation of the Constitution at the expense of Article V's exclusive authority over constitutional amendment. The sub-text of such arguments is a critique that Article V is too formal to appropriately reflect the evolutionary nature of constitutional change and, as such, Article V should be abandoned for more informal adaptation.

Perpetuating Political Institutions

Comparisons between America and Rome have become common. The Roman Republic lasted for over 500 years before degenerating into an authoritarian empire. As America sits a mere 200 years into her existence, one wonders what Romans thought about their republic a mere 200 years into its existence. Could they anticipate the demise of their republic 300 years into the future? Were there steps they could have taken to preserve their political institutions? One is humbled by the immensity of time that the Roman Republic did exist before succumbing to internal division and strife, only to degenerate into empire.[33] Can Americans feel sanguine about the status and future of the American Republic, which has successfully sustained itself for over 200 years? America has been a functioning democracy for two centuries now, and the American promotion of freedom and democratic values abroad are worthy and admirable accomplishments. Yet in light of ancient histories like Rome's, one gains a certain perspective. Surely in such light, one can see that the liberty and stability of the American Republic is a rare and delicate thing in human history.

The frailty of governments and of institutions is noted as a point of caution against a contemporary hubris that may regard the stability and effectiveness of the American experiment as a given, merely because it has endured thus far. It is the job of political scientists to examine such potentially unsettling questions and confront the possibilities of disquieting futures in an effort to guard against them. Political scientists must understand the political system and its relative health and potential, much as a doctor must examine a patient and anticipate the unpleasant realities of poor habits or disease. Insulated from popular pressure, political scientists should be free to examine such matters with a critical eye, not colored by the fear of charges of pessimism.

Thus, sobered by the historical record and recognizing the natural frailty of governments, it is important for political scientists to understand the impact of institutional change or even the impact of proposed changes. When changes to political institutions are proposed, it is incumbent upon political scientists to evaluate the possible impact of those alterations on the ideals and principles those institutions were created to serve. It is the same with the amending process. Article V was created to serve certain ideas that are fundamental to the nature of the American regime. What impact might there be if Article V is replaced or rendered obsolete? What ideas gave rise to Article V, and what ideas were meant to find security in its institutional stability?

In his Lyceum address, Abraham Lincoln addressed this question of "the perpetuation of our political institutions." He sought to provide guidance as to how the American people might perpetuate the existence of their stable, sound government, and the relative freedom that they enjoyed. In this speech, Lincoln outlines what he sees as the dangers facing the young American nation and the task of all Americans to perpetuate their political institutions and protect them from the inevitable erosion that time inflicts on all human endeavors.

> We find ourselves in the peaceful possession of the fairest portion of the earth, as regards extent of territory, fertility of soil, and salubrity of climate. We find ourselves under the government of a system of political institutions, conducing more essentially to the ends of civil and religious liberty, than any of which the history of former times tells us. We, when mounting the stage of existence, found ourselves the legal inheritors of these fundamental blessings. We toiled not in the acquirement or establishment of them—they are a legacy bequeathed us, by a *once* hardy, brave, and patriotic, but *now* lamented and departed race of ancestors.[34]

Lincoln's statement could easily be made to apply to American citizens in the twenty-first century as well as Americans of the nineteenth century. For the citizens of the United States have inherited a very powerful and free nation, a nation crafted by generations that have gone before. These are facts that few, if any, would dispute. Lincoln lays out these facts as a precursor to the question of what is the responsibility of the current generation to perpetuate this beneficial political situation. Lincoln makes clear that the task of the founding generation was far different than the task left to latter generations of Americans. For the founding generation, "Theirs was the task (and nobly they performed it) to possess themselves, and through themselves, us, of this goodly land; and to uprear upon its hills and its valleys, a political edifice of liberty and equal rights."[35] For subsequent generations of Americans, " 'tis ours only, to transmit these, the former unprofaned by the foot of an invader . . . undecayed by the lapse of time and untorn by usurpation." Preventing foreign invasion, *decay*, and *usurpation* is a solemn task and one not to be taken lightly for; "This task gratitude to our fathers, justice to ourselves, duty to posterity, and lover for our species in general, all imperatively require us faithfully to perform."[36]

In a poetic passage familiar to many, Lincoln declares that Americans have more to fear from institutional decay and usurpation than from the invasion of foreign armies. In addressing Americans' duty to maintain their political institutions, Lincoln remarks,

> At what point shall we expect the approach of danger? By what means shall we fortify against it?—Shall we expect some transatlantic military giant, to step the Ocean, and crush us at a blow? Never!—All the armies of Europe, Asia and Africa combined, with all the treasure of the earth (our own excepted) in their military chest; with a Bonaparte for a commander, could not by force, take a drink from the Ohio, or make a track on the Blue Ridge, in a trial of a thousand years. At what point then is the approach of danger to be expected? I answer, if it ever reach us, it must spring up amongst us. It cannot come from abroad. If destruction be our lot, we must ourselves be its author and finisher. As a nation of free men, we must live through all time, or die by suicide.[37]

Lincoln is warning against the tendency sewn in human nature to become complacent regarding the political institutions of a society. While he has confidence in the American people to unite against a clear foreign enemy and to prevail in such a fight, he is, however, less hopeful and more cautious about the internal dangers of "decay" and "usurpation." Decay and usurpation are dangers to be constantly guarded against:

> But, it may be asked, why suppose danger to our political institutions? Have we not preserved them for more than fifty years? And why may we not for fifty times as long? We hope there is *no sufficient* reason. We hope all dangers may be overcome; but to conclude that no danger may ever arise, would itself be extremely dangerous.[38]

These words seem not to have a date of expiration; there is no reason why Lincoln's warning is only applicable to his contemporaries. His caution is equally applicable at fifty as well as two hundred years. Complacency will prevent the American people from recognizing potential instances of decay or usurpation, thus they must be on guard at all times and engrain a reverence for the law that will not waver. But what does Lincoln mean by decay and usurpation? In what way do they threaten a government? While he does not expound upon these in his speech, it is worthwhile to explore them briefly.

Decay in the constitutional context may occur when subsequent generations cease to adhere to the established constitutional procedures, customs, legal precedents, or accepted understandings of the Constitution and its boundaries. In the case of *decay,* there is no assumption of unscrupulous ambition or intentional tearing down of political institutions; rather, the natural passage of time results in fading memories and new methods that may not be consistent with the pre-existing political practices or institutional arrangements.[39] *Usurpation* may exist when leaders willingly exercise power that they are not legitimately granted by the Constitution or by the laws of the country. It is an attempt to advance one's political agenda at the expense of established rules and norms of the Constitution. *Usurpation* is not necessarily attached to nefarious or mercenary motives; rather, it is merely a willful disregard for established customs and constitutional constraints. Thus, some may *usurp* America's political institutions even if in service of benign and benevolent intentions. Now certainly all change does not fall into the category of either decay or usurpation; some change may be seen as *progress*, or positive development. The substantive difference between progress and decay is the subject of political debate. In a democracy, the people should ultimately make judgments between what constitutes decay versus progress. This is why governing institutions must be held democratically accountable. Furthermore, if the people are to judge between decay and progress, they must be empowered by institutions to overcome the natural difficulties inherent in such democratic decision-making. The people must be empowered to utilize their reason over their passions.

The central dilemma of this book is the decay or usurpation of Article V. As we have seen, contemporary neo-Progressive scholars have challenged Article V as irrelevant and superfluous, arguing that other means of altering the Constitution have evolved over time. Challenges to Article V are not surprising or unexpected, for it is the gateway to altering the fundamental law. The stakes are high for such an important guardian of the constitutional text. Like a key fort at the mouth of a narrow bay, Article V seeks to guard the rest of the Constitution from hasty or overzealous alterations. As such, Article V makes an attractive target for those seeking to gain unbridled control over the fundamental law. In the end, the purpose of this book is to understand how Article V has played a key role in perfecting the Constitution and why preserving Article V is vital to preserving a written constitution. If Abraham Lincoln is right, our political institutions embody a "temple of liberty," a temple that is held aloft by "pillars, hewn from the solid quarry of sober reason." Reason, in turn, "must furnish all the materials for our future support and defence" and "be moulded into" new pillars of: "*general intelligence, sound morality*, and in particular, *a reverence for the constitution and laws.*"[40] Let it be the task then of this volume to show why such reverence should extend to Article V as a perfecting apparatus of the written Constitution; reverence directed towards what is indeed a vital pillar in the American "temple of liberty."

Notes

1. Jonathan Elliot, ed. *The Debates In the Several State Conventions On the Adoption of the Federal Constitution, as Recommended by the General Convention at Philadelphia, in 1787*, vol 2., (Philadelphia: J. B. Lipincott Company, 1901) 84. Cited in the American Reference Library [CD-ROM]. Orem, Utah: Western Standard Publishing Company, 1998. Hereafter cited as *Elliot's Debates*.

2. Thomas Jefferson, "Kentucky Resolutions," *The Papers of Thomas Jefferson, Volume 30: 1 January 1798 to 31 January 1799* (Princeton, New Jersey: Princeton University Press, 2003), 536-43. http://www.princeton.edu/~tjpapers/kyres/kydraft.html (accessed March 13, 2012).

3. According to the Declaration of Independence the people's rights are rooted in "nature and nature's God" and only "secured" by government.

4. The first quote is Abraham Lincoln, *Speech at Kalamazoo, Michigan*, August 27, 1856; the second quote is Calvin Coolidge, Address *Accepting Nomination as Republican Candidate for President*, Washington, D.C., August 4, 1924.

5. George Washington, *Farewell Address*, 1796, Yale Law School Avalon Project, http://avalon.law.yale.edu/18th_century/washing.asp (accessed December 20, 2012); Marvin Meyers ed. *The Mind of the Founder: Sources of the Political Thought of James Madison* (London: University Press of New England, 1981), 361; Abraham Lincoln, *First Inaugural Address of Abraham Lincoln*, March 4 1861, Yale Law School Avalon Project http://avalon.law.yale.edu/19th_century/lincoln1.asp (accessed September 1, 2012).

6. See Federalist No. 9 and No. 10 for an example of how key founders viewed democracies of the past.

7. See Thomas Aquinas *Summa Theologica, Question 90. The Essence of Law.*

8. Woodrow Wilson, *Constitutional Government* (New York: Columbia University Press, 1908), 193.

9. Bruce Ackerman, *We the People: Foundations* (Cambridge, Massachusetts: The Belknap Press, 1991), 51-52.

10. Ibid., 52.

11. Ibid.

12. Brad C. S. Watson, *Living Constitution Dying Faith: Progressivism and the New Science of Jurisprudence* (Wilmington, Delaware: ISI Books, 2009), 4.

13. Ibid.

14. Ibid., 5.

15. Ibid., 6.

16. Ibid., 5.

17. Robert Lowery Clinton, *God and Man in the Law: The Foundations of Anglo-American Constitutionalism* (Lawrence, KS: University of Kansas Press, 1997), 22.

18. David Kyvig, "The Road Not Taken: FDR, the Supreme Court, and Constitutional Amendment," *Political Science Quarterly*, Vol. 104, No. 3 (Autumn, 1989), 464.

19. Sanford Levinson, *Our Undemocratic Constitution: Where the Constitution Goes Wrong (and How We the People Can Correct It)* (New York: Oxford University Press, 2006), 163.

20. Ibid., 163-164

21. Sanford Levinson, "Our Imbecilic Constitution," *New York Times*, May 28, 2012.

22. Sanford Levinson, *Our Undemocratic Constitution*, 164.

23. Sanford Levinson, "Introduction: Imperfection and Amendability," in *Responding to Imperfection: The Theory and Practice of Constitutional Amendment*, ed. Sanford Levinson (Princeton: Princeton University Press, 1995), 7.

24. See essays by both Levinson and Griffin; Sanford Levinson, "How Many Times Has the United States Constitution Been Amended? (A) <26; (B) 26; (C) 27: Accounting for Constitutional Change," in *Responding to Imperfection: The Theory and Practice of Constitutional Amendment*, ed. Sanford Levinson (Princeton: Princeton University Press, 1995); and Stephen M. Griffin, "Constitutionalism in the United States: From Theory to Politics," in Levinson *Responding to Imperfection.*

25. Bruce Ackerman and Akhil Reed Amar are examples of this approach: Bruce Ackerman, "Higher Lawmaking," in Levinson, *Responding to Imperfection*; also Amar "Popular Sovereignty and Amendment" in Levinson, *Responding to Imperfection*; see also Bruce Ackerman, *We the People: Transformations*, (Cambridge, Massachusetts: The Belknap Press, 1998).

26. I use the term "normalize" because such approaches usually identify "Constitutional irregularities" or even acts termed "illegal," but rather than repudiating such inconsistencies, they are often embraced as legitimate; the effect of which is to make such irregularities normal and accepted. For an example of this see Bruce Ackerman's take on the New Deal and Reconstruction as illegal, yet still legitimate acts of "extra-constitutional" lawmaking. For the full argument see Ackerman, "Higher Lawmaking" in Levinson, *Responding to Imperfection*; or see Ackerman, *Foundations*.

27. Kyvig, *Explicit & Authentic Acts*, x; Kyvig sums up the current state of scholarship on the amending process fairly well: "In recent years scholars of constitutional law, politics, and philosophy have tended to discount or ignore altogether differences between formal constitutional alteration through the amending process and functional shifts achieved by judicial construction, unchallenged legislative initiative, or unchecked presidential embellishment."

28. For the House coup and referendums see Daniel Lazare, *The Frozen Republic: How the Constitution is Paralyzing Democracy* (New York: Harcourt Brace & Company, 1996) 293-294; for referendums also see Akhil Reed Amar, "The Consent of the Governed: Constitutional Amendment Outside of Article V" *Columbia Law Review*, Mar. 1994, 457-508; for structural amendments see Ackerman, *Foundations*.

29. Levinson, *Responding to Imperfection*, 26.

30. Amar, in Levinson, *Responding to Imperfection*, 89-116.

31. Stephen Griffin, "Constitutionalism in the United States: From Theory to Politics" in Levinson, *Responding to Imperfection*, 40-61.

32. One does not have to ignore the oligarchic features of the Roman Republic to still draw a valid comparison between the "republic" and the "empire."

33. Abraham Lincoln, "The Perpetuation of Our Political Institutions," Address Before the Young Men's Lyceum of Springfield, Illinois, January 27, 1838, in *Abraham Lincoln: Great Speeches*, ed. Roy P. Basler and John Grafton (Dover Publications, 1991), 2.

34. Ibid.

35. Ibid.

36. Ibid.
37. Ibid.
38. Ibid.
39. Decay is distinguished from progress or the positive change of political institutions. The word decay suggests an objective standard from which to judge changes. Reasoned deliberation on how changes relate to the principles of the Declaration of Independence, for example, and other enduring principles, should determine what changes are positive and progressive versus which ones are negative or are evidence of decay.
40. Lincoln, *Lyceum Address*, 6.

Chapter 2
Constitutional Revolution

> The power of parliament is uncontroulable[sic], but by themselves, and we must obey. They only can repeal their own acts. There would be an end of all government, if one or a number of subjects or subordinate provinces should take upon them so far to judge of the justice of an act of parliament, as to refuse obedience to it. . .Therefore let the parliament lay what burthens[sic] they please on us, we must, it is our duty to submit an patiently bear them, till they will be pleased to relieve us.
>
> James Otis[1]

> Happily for us, that when we find our constitutions defective and insufficient to secure the happiness of our people, we can assemble with all the coolness of philosophers, and set it to rights, while every other nation on earth must have recourse to arms to amend or to restore their constitutions.
>
> Thomas Jefferson[2]

On May 15, 1776, the Continental Congress issued a resolution that John Adams referred to as "an Epocha, a decisive event" and "the last step" capping the decade long dispute with Great Britain.[3] The resolution was a vital step in the road to independence and a seminal event in the development of American Constitutionalism. The resolution urged the Colonies to take practical political steps severing their ties to the Crown, declaring:

> [I]t is necessary that the exercise of every kind of authority under the said crown should be totally suppressed, and all the powers of government exerted, under the authority of the people of the colonies, for the preservation of internal peace, virtue, and good order, as well as for the defence[sic] of their lives, liberties, and properties, against the hostile invasions and cruel depredations of their enemies.[4]

Beyond "suppressing" the authority of the Crown, the Congress sent a clear exhortation to the Colonies to take affirmative steps towards creating their own constitutions of government, that "where no government sufficient to the exigencies of their affairs have been hitherto established, to adopt such government as shall, in the opinion of the representatives of the people, best conduce to the happiness and safety of their constituents in particular, and America in general."[5]

Clearly these Congressional resolves of May 10 and 15 are a crude precursor to the Declaration of Independence, which would follow two months later. While lacking the historical notoriety, theoretical depth, and written eloquence of the Declaration, the May 15 resolution of the Continental Congress helped unleash a wave of constitution making the likes the world had never seen.[6] The Colonies literally became laboratories for a "new science of American politics" and the continued evolution of American Constitutionalism. American Constitutionalism had developed steadily for over a century, and now was the moment in which the collective historical experience of the Colonies would come into play.[7] In the cauldron of war the colonies scurried to create constitutions for government that accurately reflected and implemented the political ideals that had evolved over their history or emerged from their imperial dispute with Britain. The issue of constitutional change played an important role in the Imperial Crisis and the constitutional debates surrounding the crisis provide an important context for an examination of early American state constitution making.

Why is this narrative relevant to Article V? Critics of Article V often attack Article V for being difficult, undemocratic, and too formal. They believe constitutional change should allow for improvised adaptations or alterations in addition to formal amendments. Implicit in a number of the critiques is a desire to prioritize the evolutionary informal elements of social change over and above the formal legal elements of the U.S. Constitution. The critics seem to prefer an evolutionary unwritten constitution over the formal written Constitution that was drafted in 1787. What such critics seem to forget is that the founding generation explicitly rejected the unwritten constitution of England in favor of written state constitutions. Contemporary critics seem to ignore much of this early history and the conscious decision by the American people to bind themselves to a fixed written constitution and to the formal amending procedures contained in Article V. Such measures were intentionally meant to impede and control the very "evolutionary" politics that these contemporary scholars embrace. Because of their experience with England, the founding generation viewed unwritten constitutions as unstable threats to the rights of citizens over the long run. Thus, it is important that we review this early history to remind ourselves why American constitutionalism embraced the very constitutional structures, forms, and formalities they did and to underscore the Founders' ultimate focus on unalienable natural rights secured by written constitutions and constitutional forms; forms that served as bulwarks against unstable evolutionary adaptations of the fundamental law.

An understanding of the debate over the British constitution will provide a helpful context for understanding the embrace of written constitutions and of formal amending procedures in many of the states during the Revolutionary era. Discovering the array of amending procedures in the states prior to the Federal Convention of 1787 will also illuminate the range of options and models open to the framers at the Philadelphia convention. What should be clear by the end is that the founding generation was focused on creating an amending process that reflected their core beliefs in the sovereignty of the people and the belief that written constitutions were the best means of constraining the tyrannical use of governmental power. Written constitutions were to be viewed as "higher law" or "fundamental law" that could not be changed by ordinary legislative means but only by the manner prescribed in the constitution itself. This reliance on written documents to limit and shape government had evolved out of a century of American self-rule, and as we will see the debates of the Imperial Crisis, and the experiments in the early state constitutions would have a great impact on the eventual design of Article V.

The American Colonial Constitutional Tradition

It has been said that, "the American people, building upon their British heritage and their own experiences, invented modern constitutionalism and bequeathed it to the world."[8] Indeed in 1787, the only written constitutions in the world were in America and now today nearly every nation sees the wisdom of having one.[9] By 1787 the American constitutional tradition had fully matured and it provided the framers of the U.S. Constitution in Philadelphia deep wells of experience and political theory to draw from in their deliberation and their creation.

While in many respects American legal and politics were deeply indebted to the traditions and political experience of England, it is still important to recognize that the American constitutional experience was from the very beginning very different. The English constitution was a complex and organic assemblage of custom, laws, and institutions subject to change by the raw power of politics and threats of force from time to time by different combinations of the Lords, the Crown, and the Commons. By contrast the American constitutional tradition was from its very beginnings tied to written documents of some sort. This American constitutional tradition was an amalgam of early documents such as the Pilgrim Code of Law, the Mayflower Compact, political and church covenants, and colonial charters.[10] This emerging American Constitutionalism also drew upon the diverse influence of the Judeo-Christian tradition, English Whig thought, English common law, the European Enlightenment, Classical thought, as well as political events leading up to, and after independence.[11]

Whether the devices were religious covenants, more secular compacts, or commercial charters, Americans were very used to organizing their societies and their governing structures with written documents of some shape or form. Such documents—each in their unique way—provided clarity on numerous elements that are fundamental to any political community. As "constitutions" in function, if not by name, these early documents did what constitutions are supposed to do; they defined citizenship, established the authority of the regime, allocated powers and offices, and they sought to place limits on the government.[12] This early tradition displayed firm commitments to radical popular sovereignty and formal written expression of government limits, powers, and responsibilities; elements that would continue to develop and direct the framing of the 1787 Constitution that still serves the United States today.

By the time the Imperial Crisis heated up in the 1760s the American constitutional tradition was over one hundred years old. In fact the American constitutional tradition was so firmly established and reached so far back in history that it predated the thought of one of its clear philosophical benefactors, enough so that Donald Lutz suggests that, "it makes more sense to call Locke an American than it does to call America Lockean."[13] The point is, that American Constitutionalism, while much indebted to English thought and tradition, also had developed and matured on its own out of the necessary isolation from, and sometimes neglect of, the mother country. This unique and strong American tradition of formal written constitutionalism would meet the English tradition of informal evolutionary constitutionalism head on as the Imperial Crisis between Great Britain and her colonies gained lethal momentum.

The Debates over the English Constitution

In significant ways the American Revolution centered around a dispute on the nature of the English constitution and whether it did, or could, constrain the power of Parliament with respect to American liberty.[14] The nature of this dispute further influenced the rather developed notions of American Constitutionalism that existed at the time. Through their dispute with England, Americans would learn important lessons about the nature of government; lessons on the precarious nature of an unwritten constitution, and the importance of institutional arrangements that give practical effect to abstract notions of government. They learned that abstract notions such as popular sovereignty, representation, fundamental law, etc. required institutional expression and reinforcement, for political leaders could not be trusted to adhere to the stringent requirements of such notions when they conflicted with other immediate political ends. The constitutional debate with England bolstered and refined America's unique brand of constitutionalism; and in doing so, it helped Americans articulate the constitutional principles that would drive and direct the creation of constitutional forms in the new colonial governments.[15]

The great issue over the British constitution centered around the scope of Parliamentary authority, the institutional expression of popular sovereignty, and the binding nature of fundamental law on government action. While Americans had gained extensive experience with written documents as the basis for outlining the structure of government and its powers, the English constitution, in contrast, had developed over centuries of struggle between competing segments of society:

> In England the constitution was the complex of institutions, laws, customs, practices, and principles by which the people conducted their political and governmental life. In theory the constitution derived from established principles of reason and justice, its purpose being to promote the common good and achieve a proper balance between liberty and order. Although certain historic documents such as Magna Carta possessed special significance, the constitution was not a written instrument but an organically evolving assemblage of statute, belief, and institutional practice.[16]

As an "organic" assemblage of custom, laws, and institutions the British constitution was often subject to change by the raw power of force however it may be exerted from time to time. For example, the British Aristocracy basically "extorted" King John into signing the *Magna Carta* in 1215. In the 1640s, the Puritan revolution of Oliver Cromwell saw Parliament's power increased and powerfully enforced by Cromwell's army and the execution of King Charles I. During the Glorious Revolution it was the mere threat of force by the armies of William of Orange and the loss of domestic Tory support that forced James II to flee, thus establishing Parliamentary authority more solidly than ever. Parliament offered William of Orange the crown on certain conditions; namely that he agree to a "Declaration of Rights," the basic rights of the Englishman, and the reality of the King being bound by the Common law; the result of which was to secure Parliament's preeminence in British politics.[17] Thus, the relative balance of political power and military force amongst competing groups and institutions in Britain were often key factors in the transformation of the English constitution over time.

Constitution of Customary Constraint

At the time of the American Revolution there were essentially two competing theories on the nature of the British constitution.[18] The first was the belief in the *constitution of customary constraint*, which held that Parliament's power was limited by the fundamental law of the English constitution; which is to say, it was limited by, "Custom, by the trust the sovereign people of Britain placed in its conservators, by the constitutional contract that lay at the foundation of all governments, by the balanced constitutional government of king, Lords, and Commons, and by the rule of law."[19]

This belief in the constraining power of the English constitution on Parliamentary authority was prevalent among most colonial lawyers and even many of their British counterparts and it animated many of the colonial arguments against the aggressive use of British authority in the colonies.[20] For example as a prominent attorney in Massachusetts and the leading colonial advocate against unjust British legislation, James Otis argued against Parliament's authority to tax in the colonies in his influential pamphlet *The Rights of the British Colonies Asserted and Proved* published in 1764. Otis took the lead in defending colonial merchants from Parliamentary excess. More importantly perhaps for our purposes he couched his arguments in the language of the *constitution of customary constraint*: "Every British Subject born on the continent of America, or in any other of the British dominions, is by the law of God and nature, by the common law, and by act of parliament, (exclusive of all charters from the crown) entitled to all the natural, essential, inherent and inseparable rights of our fellow subjects in Great-Britain."[21] These rights, rooted ultimately in nature as well as common and positive law also bound parliament, "Among those rights are the following, which it is humbly conceived no man or body of men, not excepting the parliament, justly, equitably and consistently with their own rights and the constitution, can take away."[22] Otis argues that Parliament is bound both by natural law and the English constitution as expressed through common law and the customary rights granted any other English citizen. Here one can see the appeals to some form of *fundamental law* that is superior and prior to the statutory laws of Parliament. Otis proceeds in his argument to list the specific limits on Parliament:

> *No legislative, supreme or subordinate, has a right to make itself arbitrary.*
> *The supreme legislative cannot justly assume a power of ruling by extempore arbitrary decrees, but is bound to dispense justice by known settled rules, and by duly authorized independent judges.*
> *The supreme power cannot take from any man any part of his property, without his consent in person or by representation.*[23]

When Parliament exceeds its authority it is in violation of the constitution and of the natural law. In this way the legitimate authority of Parliament is circumscribed by the English constitution as an embodiment of fundamental law. For Otis, Parliament logically must be constrained by the higher law of the constitution, "To say the parliament is absolute and arbitrary, is a contradiction . . . Parliaments are in all cases to *declare* what is for the good of the whole; but it is not the *declaration* of parliament that makes it so: There must be in every instance, a higher authority, viz. GOD."[24] Since Parliament is merely an agent of the natural law as embodied in the English constitution, Parliament could not be beyond challenge, "Should an act of parliament be against any of *his* natural laws, which are *immutably* true, *their* declaration would be contrary to eternal truth, equity and justice, and consequently void."[25] For Otis, then it followed that Parliament was constrained in the manner it taxed the colonists, for ". . . by this constitution, every man in the dominions is a free man: that no parts of his Majesty's dominions can be taxed without their consent: that every part has a right to be represented in the supreme or some subordinate legislature: that the refusal of this, would seem to be a contradiction in practice to the theory of the constitution."[26]

Here one can see the appeals to the limits placed on Parliament by the English constitution and the natural law as *fundamental law*. This fundamental law was supposed to restrain the authority of Parliament with regards to basic rights and liberties of British citizens. It is this fundamental law limiting the scope of Parliamentary—and hence governmental—authority that caused even Otis to remark in the same pamphlet, "The British constitution in theory . . . comes nearest the idea of perfection, of any that has been reduced to practice."[27] These appeals to constitutional limits on Parliamentary authority, however, were just that, they were only *appeals*, for they had no teeth, no institutional means by which Parliament could be held accountable for its perceived violations of the constitution. Only Parliament could restrain itself for there was no formal process in place that would allow the colonists to hold Parliament accountable, and similarly no means by which the people in their sovereign capacity to could act outside of Parliament. While Parliament was bound to the limits of the British constitution and the will of the people in *theory*, there was no institutional method of expressing the will of the people outside of Parliament in *practice*. Even Otis acknowledged this painful reality of eighteenth-century English constitutionalism:

> The power of parliament is uncontroulable[sic], but by themselves, and we must obey. They only can repeal their own acts. There would be an end of all government, if one or a number of subjects or subordinate provinces should take upon them so far to judge of the justice of an act of parliament, as to refuse obedience to it. . . Therefore let the parliament lay what burthens[sic] they please on us, we must, it is our duty to submit an patiently bear them, till they will be pleased to relieve us.[28]

Thus even under the view of *customary constraint* Parliament was the judge of its own powers under the constitution. No institutional mechanism existed to directly challenge the decisions of Parliament or alter the British constitution in a manner that might proscribe the powers of Parliament. Despite the lack of any institutional means of addressing constitutional violations, or altering the constitutional *status quo*, most believed that Parliament would adhere to custom and the dictates of fundamental law laid out in the constitution.[29] The likes of Otis hoped that Parliament would recognize any folly or injustice that might result from ill-considered legislation and it was every Englishman's right to petition Parliament and question the justice or equity of its actions: "Every subject has a right to give his sentiments to the public, of the utility or inutility of any act whatsoever, even after it is passed. The equity and justice of a bill may be questioned, with perfect submission to the legislature."[30] Yet in the end, the citizen must simply accept the results of a petition that is ignored, "Reasons may be given, why an act ought to be repealed, and yet obedience must be yielded to it till that repeal takes place."[31]

In the end, there was no direct way to challenge or alter unjust or questionable acts of Parliament and citizens were only left with the option of engaging Parliament in debate in an effort to get that body to see the error of its ways. Despite the lack of an institutional enforcement of the constitution, there was the belief that there was fundamental law that existed above and outside Parliament and its will: this view stands in stark contrast with the competing view of *Parliament's sovereign command.*

Parliament's Sovereign Command

The view of *Parliament's sovereign command* held that Parliament had established institutional sovereignty after the Glorious Revolution in 1688, during which William of Orange agreed, with Parliament, to a conditional acceptance of the Crown, thereby essentially fusing the Crown and Parliament. The vanquished James II had attempted to reassert Royal authority as the preeminent force in British politics, consequently, when William of Orange landed with his army and took control of the throne he did so only under the provisions outlined by Parliament, who had sought his aid against James II. Therefore, the Glorious Revolution effectively tamed the English Monarchy. The new king, though still powerful, was forced to work through parliament to exert his will. As *king-in-parliament* constituted the sovereign power in the realm, Parliament held "absolute and unrestrained power and therefore governed by command."[32] Exercising this sovereign power, in effect, gave Parliament authority to alter the English constitution at will. For instance, Lord Mansfield, held that the British legislature "represents the whole British Empire, and has authority to bind every part and every subject without the least distinction."[33] None other than Sir William Blackstone articulated the sweeping scope of Parliamentary authority as viewed by those holding to the theory of *parliament's sovereign command*:

> The Power and jurisdiction of parliament, says sir Edward Coke, is so transcendent and absolute, that it cannot be confined, either for causes or persons, within any bounds. . . . It hath sovereign and uncontrollable authority in making, confirming, enlarging, restraining, abrogating, repealing, reviving, and expounding of laws, concerning matters of all possible denominations, ecclesias-

> tical, or temporal, civil, military, maritime, or criminal. . . It can change and create afresh even the constitution of the kingdom and of parliaments themselves. . . . It can, in short, do every thing that is not naturally impossible; and therefore some have not scrupled to call its power, by a figure rather too bold, the omnipotence of parliament. True it is, that what the parliament doth, no authority upon earth can undo.[34]

Because of this unfettered power, Blackstone urged the utmost care in selecting such members for Parliament. Members of Parliament "as are most eminent for their probity, their fortitude, and their knowledge," should be chosen to serve, for "if by any means a misgovernment should any way fall upon it [parliament], the subjects of this kingdom are left without all manner of remedy. . . ."[35] Furthermore, Blackstone addressed Locke and "other theoretical writers" who argued for a supreme power that still resides in the people, upon which they can draw if their trust is abused by Parliament. While he concedes that in theory this popular power to reconstitute the government may exist, it cannot be true in practice:

> But however just this conclusion may be in theory, we cannot adopt it, nor argue from it, under any dispensation of government at present actually existing. For this devolution of power, to the people at large, includes in it a dissolution of the whole form of government established by that people; reduces all the members to their original state of equality; and, by annihilating the sovereign power, repeals all positive laws whatsoever before enacted. No human laws will therefore suppose a case, which at once must destroy all law, and compel men to build afresh upon a new foundation; nor will they make provision for so desperate an event, as must render all legal provisions ineffectual. So long therefore as the English constitution lasts, we may venture to affirm, that the power of parliament is absolute and without control.[36]

This is a prime example of *theory* lacking any *institutional* expression or force. Blackstone implicitly acknowledges the just nature of Locke's theory whereby the people retained their sovereign capacity to alter their forms of government; yet there existed no regular institutional means of exercising this authority within the existing constitution. The lack of any real institutional mechanism then, rendered such abstract theories—of supreme popular authority outside of Parliament—impotent and of little more than rhetorical value. To alter the existing constitutional arrangements the people would have to throw off the existing constitution and return to a state of nature in which all law was destroyed. Such a state of potential anarchy seemed worse than the potential overreach of a Parliament that was partially accountable to the people through elections. It was this view of Parliamentary sovereignty that seemed to be taking hold in the power centers of the British Empire. One set of authors summarized the situation well:

> In the seventeenth century Parliament established its legislative supremacy. By the mid-eighteenth century the doctrine of fundamental law had lost much of its

> intellectual appeal and delimiting force in English political life. Considering Parliament's claim to sovereignty, and the fact that its enactments were by definition part of the constitution, how could there be any limits on its power? Although theorists might say that Parliament was obliged to follow principles of right reason and natural justice in its actions, it was difficult to see how the English constitution restrained government in the interest of liberty.[37]

Scholars dispute the exact time that such a sweeping view of Parliament's authority took firm hold in the British Empire, but clearly by the 1770s, American colonists began to believe that just this notion of unbridled parliamentary sovereignty had become the *modus operandi* of the British government.[38]

As Parliament began to exert itself ever more forcefully in the colonies, Americans slowly came to the conclusion that the constitution of customary constraint no longer restrained Parliament and in effect the protections traditionally guaranteed to them as British subjects were no longer institutionally enforceable. The colonists were reluctant to come to this conclusion but the trajectory of British policy seemed to them overwhelming evidence that their liberty was now subject to the arbitrary whim of Parliament.

During the Stamp Act Crisis in 1765 the colonies appealed to the customary constitution as a restraint on unequal, and therefore unjust, taxes in the colonies. Long standing custom had held that the Crown would ask colonial assemblies for voluntary contributions when revenue was needed.[39] Furthermore, the customary constitution required that taxes be distributed equally across the realm, unless some local taxes benefited a given region.[40] The Stamp Act sought to solely impose a tax on the American colonies, and as such, the Americans believed this obviously and gravely violated the established customary constitution. While the Declaratory Act repealed the unpopular Stamp Act, it still forcefully asserted that Parliament nevertheless had the power to legislate and tax the colonies as it saw fit. In this way the Declaratory Act served to illustrate how dominant the belief in Parliament's sovereign command was in England. With the passage of the Declaratory Act of 1766 Parliament asserted that it "had, hath, and of right ought to have, full power and authority to make laws and statutes of sufficient force and validity to bind the colonies and people of *America,* subjects of the crown of *Great Britain*, in all cases whatsoever."[41] While this was a very clear and forceful statement of Parliamentary sovereignty, the colonists were reluctant to press their disagreement on this particular point since the larger act itself was basically a concession to colonial concerns.[42] However, this bold assertion would not lay dormant for long, as upon passage of the Coercive Acts in 1774, some eight years later, Parliament finally gave teeth to the principles of Parliamentary authority asserted in the Declaratory Act.[43]

The four Coercive Acts were passed by Parliament in the spring of 1774. The Boston Port Act closed the port of Boston until the East India Tea Company had been repaid for the losses it suffered from the Boston Tea Party. The Administration of Justice Act empowered the Governor of Massachusetts to transfer officials and soldiers accused of a capital crime against the colonists out of the colonies for trial. The Massachusetts Government Act altered the Massachusetts charter so that the council was no longer elected by the House of Representatives and town meetings could not be held without the written approval of the governor. The Quartering Act allowed the governor to quarter troops among the citizens by his own authority.[44] These Coercive Acts confirmed the worst fears of the colonies, and convinced colonial leaders that Parliament had indeed slipped the bounds of the English constitution, with the intent to tyrannize over the colonies and "enslave America."[45]

> American anxiety about parliamentary tyranny now materialized; soldiers streamed into port cities. The actual exercise of arbitrary power, not amorphous fears about unconstitutional exercise of power, drove Americans to revolution. When, in the American Whig view, Parliament turned unconstitutional principles into sustained, unconstitutional, and oppressive political acts, Americans rebelled.[46]

By the time political wrangling morphed into armed conflict many Americans believed that there were no longer any practical constitutional restraints on Parliament and no means of altering the constitution peaceably; thus leaving them no choice but to take up arms. In their mind the unwritten evolving constitution of custom had failed to secure their liberty and as such the American colonies must move in a direction that would better secure the rights of the citizens by binding government more clearly and providing the people a means of altering or perfecting their government should the need arise.

Summary: Five Lessons from the Imperial Crisis

In the minds of many Americans, the tyrannical intentions of the British Empire were revealed and nothing more than a break from the English constitution was in order. The long debate over the English constitution was nearing its logical conclusion and the Americans were forging key governing principles in the cauldron of real political conflict. A distinct American Constitutionalism would continue to mature as lessons learned from the Imperial Crisis would blend with enlightenment, classical, and biblical ideas, as well as the decades of practical experience using written documents such as compacts, charters, and constitutions which had developed during the century long colonial experiment in "home rule." We can then identify five key lessons learned by the colonists in their dispute with Britain.

The first lesson learned by the colonies was the *natural frailty* of all governments of men. The Imperial debate resulting in the Coercive Acts had shown the English constitution to lack the stability and protections of liberty they once believed that it contained. The "collapse" of the customary constitution and the emergence of the Parliament of sovereign command had not only deprived them of their liberties as Englishmen, but it had also deprived them of the protections and institutions contained in their own home grown written "constitutions" embodied in their colonial charters; thus most American colonists effectively witnessed the demise of two governing constitutions in a very short time and as a result they gained a real appreciation for the frailty of human government.[47] In this way they realized the inherent frailties of constitutions in general and unwritten evolutionary constitutions in particular.

This would also heighten their concern with designing political institutions as the practical expression of political ideas. Their experience taught them that political leaders and political circumstances change, and when those in power find their political interests adversely affected by adherence to abstract notions of political tradition and custom, it is the short-term political interest that seemed to take precedence. Thus, colonists would come to view properly structured institutions as important mechanisms to give weight and force to key constitutional principles and to restrain governmental power. Experience had taught that individuals or even bodies of individuals cannot be trusted to restrain themselves or be restrained by mere tradition or custom.

Thomas Tudor Tucker—brother of the jurist St. George Tucker—in his arguments over the South Carolina constitution of 1784, showed just how far removed from the English conception of constitutionalism the Americans had come. In his pamphlet *Conciliatory Hints, Attempting by a Fair State of Matters, to Remove Party Prejudice* he gives a good example of republican thinking of the time. His writing is a good example of the extent to which Americans consciously sought to ground their constitutions on grounds much firmer than that of the English, and how in his view the English constitution was inherently frail with regards to protecting rights: "Their constitution is established only on precedents, or compulsory concessions. . . upon a compromise of differences betwixt two or more contending parties, each according to the means it possesses, extorting from the others every concession that can possibly be obtained, without the smallest regard to justice or the common rights of mankind."[48] If the foundation of the English constitution was extortion and concession, this not a firm footing for securing rights, for such concessions ". . . can be no longer binding than whilst the parties respectively possess the means of enforcing their observance."[49] For Tucker, this "government of contention, in which the opposite parties have been for a length of time by chance so nearly balanced, as not to have destroyed each other" was not a secure footing for liberty for "it may be affirmed that there is nothing of stability in their Constitution, and that almost every new case of importance introduces some new innovation in it."[50]

For Tucker "precedents" or "compulsory concessions" will change as new exigencies arise or the balance of power between the crown, lords, and commons shifts over time, thus there can be no true stability in the English constitution. To illustrate his point Tucker points to Blackstone's explanation of the right of succession "where it may be seen how every fresh incident has given occasion to a different modification of this right."[51] In Tucker's eyes such "rights" merely existed for limited periods of time, there was no certainty or reliability in the rights secured under such an ever-changing and evolutionary constitution.

> What stretch of authority they have usurped and exercised with impunity, is considered as their established privilege; for they hold it as a maxim, that whatever they have once done, however improperly, they have a right to do again. What farther powers they may safely assume experiment only can teach. Their privileges are undefinable, because it is impossible to say, how far they may be extended without rousing the people to a tumultuous opposition or civil war; for with them there is no other remedy against tyranny and oppression.[52]

With an unwritten evolutionary constitution there was little the people could do if the government evolved beyond clear legal popular control. It was clear then for many Americans that all governments are precarious, and even the vaunted English constitution, being of forced concession, did not exhibit the stability requisite to secure the liberties of a free people.

The second lesson learned is directly related to the first. In their experience with the unwritten, evolutionary constitution of England, Americans learned the value of written or fixed constitutions for only a constitution that was fixed could hope to resist the changing political winds that so often consumed a people's rights and liberties.

> If Parliament was sovereign, then the constitution was not really a constitution at all. In protesting parliamentary statutes Americans argued that a constitution, in order to accomplish its purpose of controlling the government, must be fixed. Moreover, it must be separate from and antecedent to government so as to be unalterable by the legislature or other agencies.[53]

Tucker again gives contemporaneous expression to this principle: "the privileges of the legislative branches ought to be defined by the constitution and should be fixed as low as is consistent with the public welfare."[54] Furthermore, the new constitutions should be fixed "on the firm and proper foundation of the express consent of the people, unalterable by the legislature, or any other authority but that by which it is to be framed."[55]

If Parliament could simply assert its institutional sovereignty when the political circumstances allowed, then the constitution did not really limit government. Drawing on their experience with written charters and covenants and compacts in the colonies, many Americans came to view a written constitution as the main way in which to fix and limit the powers of government. To Americans written documents that restrained civil authority were a logical and natural means to be employed.

> The idea of a fixed, normative constitution existing outside of and superior to government represented a significant theoretical innovation. Yet in the Ameri-

> can context it was not altogether unfamiliar. On the contrary, the seventeenth-century experience in founding new governments had prepared the way for this conceptual development. The joint-stock corporation charters, proprietary concessions and agreements, and fundamental orders of the covenant-compact colonies resembled fixed constitutional instruments. Although they never assumed the extra-institutional status that constitutions in the revolutionary era did, they were antecedent to government and were later appealed to as a restraint on imperial authority. In Bernard Bailyn's apt expression, the new American conception of constitutionalism represented experience elevated to principle.[56]

With a record, or an explicit contract between the people and their government, those in power could not claim ignorance of the rights of the people who had put them in power. A written document would turn an evolutionary government—which could dangerously "adapt" into an oppressive government—into a more mechanical government, which would not change unless altered by its creator.[57]

The third lesson learned was that, in order for written constitutions to adequately limit the actions of the legislature they had to assume the status of fundamental law that precedes and trumps the acts of normal or statutory law. The American Revolution drew heavily on the Western tradition of natural law and its embodiment in the English common law and notions of fundamental law.[58] These traditions sought to protect the legal rights of citizens by limiting the legislative power of government; yet in the English constitution these protections rested almost solely on the hope that such customary constraints would be "internalized" in the minds, habits, and practices of governing officials.[59] Colonial Americans became acutely aware of this institutional defect and sought to remedy this by establishing written constitutions that would embody the fundamental law and the moral basis for rights that rested ultimately in the natural law.[60]

As Otis and Blackstone made painfully clear to the colonists, their liberties were merely reliant upon Parliament's adherence to custom, goodwill, or philosophical commitment to restrain itself. When its immediate concrete political objectives came into conflict with long-term abstract political theory—of the rights of Englishmen guaranteed by some customary constitution—then Parliament did not prove to be an adequate institutional safeguard against intrusions on personal liberty. Thus, a written fundamental law, superior and anterior to normal legislative law was in order; a written law that institutionally reflected the higher nature of natural rights and personal liberties. Since those in power would not restrain themselves, there must be institutions and measures in place to impose restraint upon them; enough so to preserve a free society.

Fourth, the Imperial Crisis reinforced notions of the sovereignty of the people under the natural law, and of the importance of institutions that supported such notions of sovereignty within the world of real politics. As Blackstone pointed out, while supreme authority did reside in the people in theory, there was no institutional means of actualizing these principles in the world of real politics within the British system. To Americans the belief in popular sovereignty and the consent of the governed served as the foundation upon which a written constitution could stand as fundamental law outside of the legislative power. Thus, a written constitution with the status of fundamental law served as a powerful institutional expression of popular sovereignty and a critical link to the exercise of real political authority by the people.

Fifth, the combination of finding no alternative means of altering their constitutional arrangements with Britain—other than the means of revolution—and embracing the notion of a fixed written constitution, led some colonial leaders to examine the possibility of a regular institutional means of altering constitutions. Again, as Blackstone pointed out, there existed no institutional means of altering the British constitution, outside of parliament, other than throwing off the existing government and all of its laws thereby forcing the society into a state of nature. In this context altering the constitution outside of the legislative power seemed to be a cure that was worse than the disease. Better to seek political change under the rule of a tyrannical parliament—who was subject to some accountability via elections—than to be plunged into the potential state of anarchy.

To avoid this dilemma, some in America began to explore a means by which a fixed or written constitution could be changed under its own terms via a clearly stated procedure that drew upon the sovereignty of the people. As early as 1776 a Philadelphia writer *Demophilus* put it thus, "after the approaching Convention has met, and settled the grand outlines of a constitution, let the legislature go on with the affairs of government. . . and whatever inconveniences may be found unprovided for, may be candidly advertised to the public, and amended by another Convention."[61] Similarly Thomas Tudor Tucker again gives a good example of the maturing American constitutionalism of the time, illustrating its fixed, fundamental nature, derived from the people, and unalterable except explicitly by them:

> The constitution should be the avowed act of the people at large. It should be the first and fundamental law of the State, and should prescribe the limits of all delegated power. It should be declared to be paramount to all acts of the Legislature, and irrepealable and unalterable by any authority but the express consent of a majority of the citizens collected by such regular mode as may be therein provided.[62]

Writing in Philadelphia in 1776, another colonial writer also sums up American thinking of the time well: he outlines the frailty of government, the need for a fixed constitution, anterior to government as fundamental law, rooted in the sovereignty of the people, and able to be altered by the sovereign people,

> 'yet there is such a thirst for power in most men, that they will sacrifice heaven and earth to wrest it from its foundation; to establish a power in themselves to tyrannize over the persons and properties of others.' To prevent this, let every article of the constitution or *sett[sic] of fundamental rules* by which even the supreme power of the state shall be governed, be formed by a convention of the delegates of the people, appointed for that express purpose: which constitution

> shall neither be added to, diminished from, nor altered in any respect by any power besides the power which first framed it. By this means an effectual bar will be opposed to those enterprising spirits, who have told us with much assurance, that after the people had made their annual or septennial *offering*, they had no more to do with government than their cattle.[63]

In the end, from the American perspective the English constitution degenerated over time to the point that it proved incapable of securing their rights and consequently they pointed to human frailty, its unwritten evolutionary nature and its origins in forced concession as causes of this degeneration. Based on their negative experience with an unduly pliable constitution they sought to avoid the inherent weaknesses of the British system by employing a written constitution, derived from, and accountable to the sovereign people, without which, liberty would always be in peril. Thus, as a sober expression of American thinking on constitutionalism that had developed throughout their "home rule" experience and their Imperial dispute with Britain, the Declaration of Independence serves as an eloquent expression of American ideas that shaped future constitutions, and as the theoretical foundation for republican government in America.

> We hold these Truths to be self-evident, that all Men are created equal, that they are endowed by their Creator with certain unalienable Rights, that among these are Life, Liberty, and the pursuit of Happiness—That to secure these Rights, Governments are instituted among Men, deriving their just Powers from the Consent of the Governed, that whenever any Form of Government becomes destructive of these Ends, it is the Right of the People to alter or to abolish it, and to institute new Government, laying its Foundation on such Principles, and organizing its Powers in such Form, as to them shall seem most likely to effect their Safety and Happiness. Prudence indeed, will dictate that Governments long established should not be changed for light and transient Causes; and accordingly all Experience hath shewn, that Mankind are more disposed to suffer, while Evils are sufferable, than to right themselves by abolishing the Forms to which they are accustomed . . . it is their Right, it is their Duty, to throw off such Government, and to provide new Guards for their future Security. . . and such is now the Necessity which constrains them to alter their former Systems of Government.

Viewed as an expression of American Constitutionalism and not merely a statement of revolution, the foundational principles of constitutional government are outlined and justified in the Declaration. In terms of constitutional amendment the Declaration clearly states that a people have the right to "alter or abolish" their form of government when it becomes "destructive of these ends" meaning their rights to life, liberty, and the pursuit of happiness.[64] As David Kyvig eloquently states,

> All the essential elements of eighteenth-century constitutionalism were present in Jefferson's spare prose: popular sovereignty, constitutions as devices to de-

> fine and limit the powers of government, and the propriety of altering constitutions when conditions warrant. The Declaration of Independence deserves to be regarded as much more than a proclamation of revolution. It was the foundation block of the American Constitution, or as Daniel Webster would call it in 1830, 'the title deed of their liberties.'[65]

Thus, after their political break from Britain it was now time for the colonial leadership to translate such broad political principles into actual working governments.

Amending Procedures in the First State Constitutions

> In all free states the Constitution is fixed; and as the supreme Legislative derives its power and authority from the Constitution, it cannot overleap the Bounds of it without destroying its own foundation.
>
> Samuel Adams[66]

The first state constitutions reflected American thinking about government near the culmination of the long imperial crisis and likewise they served as an experiential foundation for the United States Constitution adopted in 1789.[67] In this regard it is important to examine the first amending procedures in these early documents as precursors to Article V, and as early supports for and expressions of early American commitments to popular sovereignty and written constitutionalism.

The early state constitutions emerged amidst the exigencies of war during the struggle for independence and they drew upon a diverse but well developed tradition of constitutionalism. As independence and war loomed, English governors fled and British power receded, to fill the obvious void of civil authority, Americans moved to establish new governments. These new governments drew upon uniquely American views of republicanism and departed from the English tradition in significant ways, notably by embracing uniquely American notions of constitutionalism and fundamental law.[68] To some influential Americans, the English constitution of tradition, custom, and informally evolving organic law had proved too malleable—subject to the interpretations or whims of political leaders—and too weak to prevent the aggressive advances of Parliament.[69]

There is much to be said on the origins and sources of American Constitutionalism, however when focusing upon the development of constitutional amending mechanisms, one's focus is drawn to a couple of key factors in their creation. The evolving notions of popular sovereignty and the internal logic of a fixed written constitution pushed the issue of constitutional amendment on to the plate of the framers of early state constitutions and demanded some form of amending procedure in the new documents. Formal amending mechanisms were created in response to the need for an institutional expression of the people that stood above normal government—especially the legislature—and the need to refine and refresh the newly written constitutions which were meant to limit and define the role of government in society.

Fixed Written Constitutions

Whereas the English saw monarchical power as the greatest threat to liberty, and the House of Commons and Parliament as a check on that authority; the Imperial Crisis convinced Americans that no arm of government should wield unlimited power over the people.[70] Their experience with an arbitrary and unmovable Parliament convinced Americans that even legislatures were capable of tyranny and they too must be checked. As Parliament ascended to the status of constitutional sovereign it had become an institution that existed above the English constitution. It had escaped the customary constraints of the constitution to wield sovereign authority over the constitution itself. It proved to Americans that legislative restraint would not come from within, it must be imposed from without, namely by the people through the creation of a written fundamental law.

To address concerns over the weaknesses of a purely unwritten evolutionary constitution and its inability to preserve rights, the colonists sought to create fixed written constitutions which were anterior to normal government and therefore could constrain and limit improper advances from the legislature, as well as provide a public record of the contract between the people and their government. It was becoming a firm principle among American thinkers that constitutions had to be fixed and able to limit all government, even elected legislatures. Samuel Adams expressed the general sentiment well, ". . . in all free states the Constitution is fixed; and as the supreme Legislative derives its power and authority from the Constitution, it cannot overleap the Bounds of it without destroying its own foundation."[71]

Adams was not alone in this view as it was quite common among colonial writers. For example, the pamphlet *Four Letters on Interesting Subjects* published in 1776 provides evidence of the growing consensus over the proper nature of a written fixed constitution derived clearly from popular authority rather than an evolutionary fluid constitution under the control of a single legislative body. This Philadelphia writer gave a concise articulation of the emerging thought on constitutionalism at the time:

> A Constitution, and a form of government, are frequently confounded together, and spoken of as synonimous[sic] things; . . . All countries have some form of government, but few, or perhaps none, have truly a Constitution. . . The truth is, the English have no fixed Constitution. . . It is easy to perceive that individuals by agreeing to erect forms of government, (for better security of themselves) must give up some part of their liberty for that purpose; and it is the particular business of a Constitution to mark out *how much* they shall give up. In this

> sense it is easy to see that the English have no Constitution, because they have given up every thing; their legislative power being unlimited without either condition or controul[sic], except in the single instance of trial by Juries. No country can be called *free* which is governed by an absolute power; and it matters not whether it be an absolute royal power or an absolute legislative power, as the consequences will be the same to the people. That England is governed by the latter, no man can deny, their being, as is said before, no Constitution in that country which says to the legislative powers, "Thus far shalt thou go, and no farther." There is nothing to prevent them from the payment of taxes, or which shall give the house of commons power to sit for life, or to fill up the vacancies by appointing others. . . In short, an act of parliament, to use the court phrase, can do any thing but make a man a woman.[72]

The anonymous author deprecates the English constitution for not being "fixed" and remarks that they essentially have no constitution because the people—outside the legislature—no longer have control over their government. It is this notion of popular control that lies at the heart of a fixed written constitution. A constitution in such a form allows the people to understand and control the structure of their own government. The author further argues that a true constitution must control all of government—even a popularly elected legislature—by placing clear limits on its power.

Furthermore, the same author points to the higher law nature of the new constitutions whereby they merely guarantee the natural rights of citizens and are not the source of those rights. Because of this higher law aspect of the new documents, he advocates separating the new constitutions from normal statutory law, "In short, all the great rights which man never mean, nor ever ought, to lose, should be guaranteed, not granted, by the Constitution; for at the forming a Constitution we ought to have in mind, that whatever is left to be secured by law only, may be altered by another law."[73]

Therefore a written constitution that stood above normal statutory law reflected and implemented the idea that rights were not granted by positive law, but that positive law helped guarantee or secure these rights in practical terms. Thus, the origin of rights and hierarchy of fundamental over normal law reflected in a written fixed constitution was a critical aspect of American thinking.

Reiterating his fundamental point in a different context about the form of a fixed written constitution, the author also advocates a fixed constitution not just for state governments, but for the continental government as well, "A continental Constitution, when fixed, will be the best boundaries of Congressional power . . ."[74] Such was the growing intellectual commitment to a fixed written document as a means of giving popular voice to the very foundations of government, and a means of limiting the arbitrary power of the government over the governed by explicitly securing the natural rights of the citizens.

Even in this relatively early document one can see the constitutional logic progressing to the point of requiring some means of maintaining the constitution through some formal institutional process, a process that can withstand the encroachments of a zealous legislature, "Next to forming a good Constitution, is the means of preserving it. If once the legislative power breaks in upon it, the effect will be the same as if a kingly power did it. The Constitution, in either case, will receive its death wound, and 'the outward and visible sign,' or mere form of government only will remain."[75] For this writer the means of preserving a Constitution were easy, "The means here pointed out for preserving a Constitution are easy, and some article in the Constitution may provide, that at the expiration of every seven or any other number of years, a *Provincial Jury* shall be elected," the job of the jury would be to "enquire if any inroads have been made in the Constitution, and to have power to remove them; but not to make alterations, unless a clear majority of all the inhabitants shall so direct."[76]

A constitution that could not prevent the encroachments from normal arms of government was beginning to be seen by some as a "dead" instrument, a hollow shell of the limited government that once was. To prevent such serious breeches of constitutional authority the author advocates a popular body outside of government to maintain the integrity of the constitution. Whether this tract was directly influential in the framing of the Pennsylvania constitution or not, just such a provincial jury was adopted by Pennsylvania in its first constitution. Clearly the notions of constitutional preservation and alteration were closely tied to the fixed written nature of the document as well as its popular origins, for no alterations should be made, "unless a clear majority of all the inhabitants shall so direct."

Also in 1776, a pamphlet entitled *The Interest of America* stated the need for a means of maintaining popular control over the new constitutions once they were created, "Every Province should be viewed as having a right . . . to alter their form of Government in some particulars; As the Government is for the people, the people, when properly represented, have a right to alter it for their advantage."[77] Interestingly, this pamphlet implied the need for a regular formal process that would be above claims of usurpation, for governments should be altered "without being liable to raise a clamour, by some who would be glad to say that it was contrary to the Constitution that they first formed upon; that it was overturning the original plan, and leaving people at uncertainties as to the foundation they are upon, and the like."[78] Another key point, made by this pamphlet was that an amending mechanism would allow the citizens to perfect their constitutions as they went recognizing that they would not be perfect, "As we must (some Provinces at least) in a short time assume some new mode of Government, and the matter cannot be deferred so long as to canvass, deliberately weigh, and fully adjust everything that may hereafter appear necessary, we should leave room to alter for the better in time to come."[79]

If the constitutions were to be fixed, the authority for such documents must clearly be rooted in the principle of popular sovereignty. In the eloquence of the Declaration of Independence, such new governments derived "their just powers from the consent of the governed" and accordingly these new state governments embraced popular sovereignty to an extent yet seen in England.[80] In this way, a written fixed constitution became an important expression of popular authority, for a single document allowed the people to deliberate upon the proper extent of government power, then create and record the sum of these deliberations for posterity. A fixed written document could be read and reviewed by individual citizens; the citizen's sentiments regarding the document could be heard by their representatives and perhaps ultimately impact the direction of government. Unlike the ambiguous English constitution that relied on custom and tradition—both of which could be conveniently forgotten or misinterpreted by those in power—a fixed written document provided a tangible record of the limits of government power and the rights of its citizens. The average citizen could look to a single document that outlined and defined their relationship to the government. With a written contract between the government and the people, the people could more easily hold the government accountable and in check. The power of this cannot be underestimated in terms of radically putting the destiny of government in the hands of the citizens.[81]

Thus, the American people's commitment to popular sovereignty, limited government, and individual rights, led them to discard the ambiguous evolutionary constitution of England and embrace fixed written constitutions.

Tapping the Constituent Power of the People

The new state constitutions would reflect the notion that the people were sovereign and the source of all legitimate political authority. In their efforts the colonies immediately moved to anchor the new documents in the authority of the sovereign people. For example, the North Carolina constitution declared that ". . . all political power is vested in and derived from the people only," and similarly in Maryland, "all government of right originates from the people, is founded in compact only, and instituted solely for the good of the whole."[82] Nearly all of the new constitutions firmly rooted their authority in the people and declared their right to alter or abolish government.[83] While the preambles of their constitutions professed the popular nature of the new state governments, the challenge still remained to determine how sovereignty could best be expressed in practice. What institutional device would actually allow the people to create new governments?

No formal means of creating a popular constitution had existed in England for the people never had the opportunity to *create* their government out of whole cloth rather they had merely *tamed* the monarchy over time through politics and force. In America there was the chance to actually create new governments free from old world entanglements and arrangements, and such governments could be clearly founded on the authority of the people.[84] The freedom to wisely choose a new course for society—relatively free from the limits of the past was readily recognized by many. "But we have opportunity to form with some deliberation, with free choice, with good advantages for knowledge; we have opportunity to observe what has been right and what wrong in other States, and to profit by them."[85] An aging Jefferson, in looking back on the early state experience expressed the unique possibilities that had existed at the time and contrasted the American experience with the emergence of the English constitution,

> Our Revolution commenced on more favorable ground. It presented us an album on which we were free to write what we pleased. We had not occasion to search into musty records, to hunt up royal parchments, or to investigate the laws and institutions of a semi-barbarous ancestry. We appealed to those of nature, and found them engraved on our hearts.[86]

For Jefferson it was noteworthy that the American experience was freed from the baggage of the old English constitution, the Americans were free to create new governments largely uninhibited by problems inherent in the English tradition. Yet, Jefferson equally explains the challenge inherent in the creation of new governments,

> When forced to assume it [self-government] we were novices in its science. Its principles and forms had entered little into our former education. We established, however, some, although not all its important principles. The constitutions of most of our States assert, that all power is inherent in the people; that they may exercise it by themselves, in all cases to which they think themselves competent . . .[87]

Here Jefferson hints at the importance of the state political experiments of the time in terms of gaining practical governing experience. Experience in principles and forms were important and essential for creating good government. Also Jefferson reemphasizes the importance of the sovereignty of the people. Such was the challenge of creating new "forms" and institutions of government. The new states were truly conducting experiments in the science of politics and Jefferson's retrospective statement highlights the challenges and opportunities faced by the framers of the early documents.

Again, the early major challenge for the state leaders was to find an institutional means of creating these documents in a swift manner—given the demands of independence and war—yet still respect the theoretical need for a popular sanction to the new governments.[88] Even before the Declaration of Independence, states began to wrestle with the problem of translating abstract notions of sovereignty into real working institutions. They needed to find a way to draw upon the constitutive power of the people to create new governments and constitutions.

In England, with the emergence of the *constitution of parliamentary command*, the constitutive power and the legislative power had been fused.[89] Given their experience with a Parliament that had escaped the customary constraints of the English constitution, colonists were wary of the potential danger of fusing the legislative and constituent powers and they took various means of trying to delineate the differences between the two. The task for those creating the new state constitutions was to find an institutional means of differentiating and separating these two powers.

The first states to begin the process of creating new governments were New Hampshire and South Carolina, which in the middle of 1775 were without royal governors and needed to replace them. Hesitant to act prematurely and independently for fear of undermining colonial and national unity, both states consulted the Continental Congress on how to proceed.[90] Upon the authorization of the Congress in November of 1775, both states quickly adopted new constitutions that would be in effect until the hostilities with England were resolved.[91] After the resolves of May 10 and 15 which essentially ended hope of reconciliation with Britain—by calling for the suppression of British authority and the creation of new state governments—all of the states began to erect new constitutions under the authority of the Continental Congress.

In creating these new constitutions the states embraced the sovereignty of the people by avoiding the colonial legislatures in favor of provincial congresses and constitutional conventions.[92] As Jefferson points out, it was important to have a clearly defined means of fixing the state constitution in the authority of the people, and in a manner distinct from ordinary acts of the legislature, "The other states in the Union have been of opinion, that to render a form of government unalterable by ordinary acts of assembly, the people must delegate persons with special powers. They have accordingly chosen special conventions to form and fix their governments."[93]

This rejection of colonial legislatures was clearly an attempt to distinguish statutory law from fundamental or constitutional law; in fact, all of the states utilized bodies other than the ordinary legislatures to write the new constitutions.[94] The states utilized either their provincial congresses or specially designated conventions to create their new governments. Provincial congresses were larger, more representative, more powerful than, and not as permanent as the colonial legislatures; furthermore such qualities allowed them to draw more directly on the authority of the people and distinguish the products of their proceedings from regular statutory law.[95] In all but two cases, the provincial congresses held special elections to elect a new congress, which would then be empowered to write the new constitution.[96] Mark Kruman sums up this point well:

> By conducting extraordinary elections, congresses and committees further clarified distinctions between fundamental and statutory law. The votes signified that the provincial congresses and conventions would not be granting constitutions and liberties to the people, as the king had granted charters and privileges to the colonists . . . the congresses explicitly located sovereignty in the people, who, in turn, would instruct a political body to act on their behalf to form governments.[97]

Along with drafting the new constitutions, provincial congresses often exercised broad powers of government during emergency and transition periods; in contrast, constitutional conventions were created solely for the purpose of drafting a new constitution, and thus were a more explicit means of accessing the constituent power of the sovereign people.[98] Furthermore, congresses and conventions were preferable to legislatures in the creation of constitutions because they were temporary political bodies with no vested interest in the new form or structure of government. In all but three states the congresses and conventions were dissolved once their constitutional responsibilities were finished and a new constitution was in place.[99] Only three states turned their provincial congresses into the lower-house of the new government, and in each case this represented a reduction in their power.[100]

Regardless, of the method, the use of both congresses and conventions were an explicit attempt by the colonies to recognize the fundamental law status of the new constitutions.[101] These efforts were the first attempts to create institutional venues for the expression of popular sovereignty for the purposes of creating fundamental law. Such efforts reflected the clear notion that the new constitutions needed to limit ordinary government, and thus the new constitutions must be created outside of government and be created by the raw constituent power of the sovereign people in some form.

How to Change a Fixed Constitution?

By utilizing popular conventions or colonial congresses the early American leaders were attempting to deal with the practical demands of creating a written constitution which rested on the authority of the people. While there were continued critics about the *means* of distinguishing between normal statutory law and fundamental law, the need to make such distinctions was firmly planted.[102] As logic of written constitutionalism progressed in practice, new challenges began to arise. For example one challenge was how or whether to change or replace such documents. If the new constitutions needed alterations should they be made by the people directly? If they were found to be defective, should they just be wholly replaced? Or should the legislatures, as the representatives of the people, act to alter or improve the new constitutions when warranted? These are the questions that confronted those striving to create the new state governments.[103] While avoiding the use of the ordinary legislatures in the creation of constitutions was universally applied, the means of amending or altering the new constitutions did not enjoy such a consensus among the states. States took varying approaches to the problem of how to alter the fundamental law once such law was established. Some did not provide for an amending mechanism at all, while others simply relied on the legislatures for most alterations.[104]

While not all states incorporated an amendment process into their new constitutions, the usefulness and practicality of such a device was beginning to become clear to leading American constitutional thinkers.[105] It was important to avoid the "constitutional box" which Americans had experienced with regards to the English constitution. As noted earlier, Blackstone and most Englishmen acknowledged the right of the people to alter their government in theory, but there existed no practical or institutional means of exerting this authority. Thus, the only options left to the people when faced with a recalcitrant or dangerous parliament were revolution (plunging all government into a state of nature) or humble petition to the sovereign legislature (unlikely to change the mind of a corrupt legislature). This constituted a box where the only choice was between revolution on one hand or subservience to tyranny on the other. In this context colonies began to see the importance of creating some alternative to revolution, an institutional means of changing the fundamental law without throwing off all of government; without resorting to force and the terrible costs associated with that option.[106]

Having a written fixed document only solved half of that dilemma. While the written text produced a record of the contract between the people and their government, it was still important to secure institutional forms that would allow the people continued control of that document. It was becoming clear that giving legislatures unilateral control over the future of the constitution involved problems similar to those experienced under parliamentary sovereignty with England. For example, Thomas Jefferson, in expressing his frustrations over the creation of the Virginia constitution and his contention that it was created via mere legislative fiat, described the problem of having a constitution amendable solely by ordinary acts of the legislature, "On every unauthoritative exercise of power by the legislature, must the people rise in rebellion, or their silence be construed into a surrender of that power to them? If so, how many rebellions should we have had already?"[107] Similarly, in the debates over whether Connecticut and Rhode Island needed to establish new constitutions—rather than just utilizing their existing royal charters—the suspicion of legislative power was clearly on display. A writer in the *Providence Gazette* complained about the power of that state's legislature to change the state constitution, "We should have no remedy left us, but downright rebellion against that power we have vested them with."[108] In Connecticut, Benjamin Gale put it thus, "If we suffer our Representatives to assume powers never committed to their trust unnoticed *once*, we may not be surprized[sic] to have it done a *second time*."[109] Again, another writer stated, "it is a ruling principle, that what is established by the constitution, cannot be altered by the General Assembly."[110] Furthermore, "the people are the fountain of power, and must agree if the mode is altered, the assembly cannot do it."[111] Still another colonial writer put it this way, "As the constitution limits the authority of the legislature, if the legislature can alter the constitution, they can give themselves what bounds they please."[112] Therefore, if the legislature is given unilateral power to alter the constitution, then the people have only acquiescence to tyranny or open rebellion as options, when faced with a tyrannical legislature.

Although many framers assumed that some revision of their work would be necessary, they also believed that constitutions were immune to ordinary legislation. Precisely the same objections to legislatures writing constitutions applied to amending them. A legislature that could amend a constitution through ordinary statutes could claim tyrannical power.[113] The key to escaping the box of either rebellion or acquiescence was to create an institutional means of securing the consent of the governed for alterations to the fundamental law outside the normal bounds of government. What was needed was a peaceful means of appealing to the constituent power of the people, not in the raw form of open rebellion, but in a domesticated orderly institution that would serve the same purpose. David Kyvig makes this point well:

> Unwilling to accept the notion that the terms of government were unchangeable except by revolution yet indisposed to treat the fundamental directives to and limitations on government as ordinary law susceptible to reform by simple parliamentary majority, some states began working out arrangements by which their new constitutions could be changed.[114]

Tapping the constituent power meant requiring the right level of consensus for such important and fundamental changes. Yet how one could tap into that popular authority without unleashing the potentially dangerous forces of untamed popular passion? In general as the state notions of amendment advanced they began to seek a balance between flexibility and stability. For flexibility they built in formal amending procedures and for stability they sought supermajority consent of the people.[115] "Articulating a plan for amendment was increasingly seen as an essential part of defining a constitution as a higher law while avoiding its becoming a rigid and unduly confining structure."[116]

The Laboratories of Government

As the colonies struggled to establish independence all but two created new state constitutions. Connecticut and Rhode Island decided against new documents seeking instead to maintain their royal charters, which already had adequate republican forms—such as the power to elect their governors for instance.[117] Rhode Island affirmed their charter via resolution in May of 1776 and Connecticut's legislature affirmed their royal charter in October 1776. While there were limited calls for replacing them both, the royal charters remained in effect until 1818 (Connecticut) and 1842 (Rhode Island).[118]

The first three state constitutions were written in early 1776 prior to the Declaration of Independence. All three constitutions—New Hampshire (January), South Carolina (March), and Virginia (June)—contained no provision for constitutional amendment. Perhaps the lack of an amending mechanism resulted from pressures to quickly replace vacated civil authority or perhaps they had not yet realized the importance amending measures this early in their constitution making experience. For unknown reasons these early state framers did not provide for an amending mechanism and they illustrate the lack of consensus regarding the importance of, or structure of, a process of constitutional alteration at this point in the development of American constitutionalism. In Virginia Thomas Jefferson criticized the new constitution as "insufficiently republican" because he felt the populace had no role in its adoption and because it lacked an amending procedure.[119]

The next constitution was that of New Jersey (July 2, 1776), which was adopted contemporaneously with the Declaration of Independence. While this early constitution made no direct provision for amendment, it did reflect the distinction between normal and fundamental law by removing some articles from the reach of ordinary legislation. To some this implied that the legislature was empowered to alter the rest of the document, but the legislature's exact authority was ambiguous in this regard. However, over time subsequent legislatures interpreted the ambiguity in their favor and did begin to exercise the power to alter the constitution via ordinary legislation.[120] Perhaps the ambiguity of the New Jersey document is indicative of the rushed nature of its creation, for fear of British invasion resulted in it being framed and adopted in less than two weeks.[121] In the end, while it left the issue of amendment open for debate, the constitution did seek to reflect the fundamental status of the new document. It wasn't until the fall that the next state constitutions were adopted and the first explicit amending procedures would be created.

Delaware's constitution adopted in September 20, 1776 also exempted certain measures from legislative amendment, but unlike New Jersey's ambiguity, it explicitly allowed the remaining portions of the document to be altered by the legislature. In providing for legislative amendment, the Delaware constitution required steep majorities, namely, five-sevenths of the whole assembly and seven of the nine members of the legislative council.[122] This was the first state constitution to explicitly provide for the amendment of the document, and the first to do so via super majorities in the legislature. The requirement of legislative super majorities reflected the notion that the constitution was something set apart from normal legislation, and thus, required a higher degree of consensus than did normal legislation.[123]

Also in September of 1776, Pennsylvania adopted its new constitution, which was widely regarded as the most radical document of its time; its approach to constitutional amendment was no exception. The Pennsylvania constitution provided for a Council of Censors, which was made up of two elected members from each county. The Censors would meet every seven years with the stated duty to, "enquire whether the constitution has been preserved inviolate in every part; and whether the legislative and executive branches of government have performed their duty as guardians of the people, or assumed to themselves, or exercised other or greater powers than they are entitled to by the constitution"[124]

According the document, the Council of Censors was created, "In order that the freedom of the commonwealth may be preserved inviolate forever."[125] For the length of one year, the Council was empowered to conduct the investigations necessary for their purpose. It had the power of subpoena, it could recommend the legislature repeal suspect laws, "enacted contrary to the principles of the constitution," and the Council could call a convention "if there appear to them an absolute necessity of amending any article of the constitution which may be defective." A two-thirds majority of council members were necessary to call a convention. If amendments were found to be necessary, the council must explain why such amendments were, "necessary for the preservation of the rights and happiness of the people." Furthermore, the proposed changes must be made public six months prior to the election of convention delegates so that the people may have the opportunity to properly consider the proposed changes and instruct their delegates.[126]

Pennsylvania was one of the few states to clearly state the purposes of its amendment process, a process that took pains to ensure public participation and deliberation. Some opponents found the process too constricting by prohibiting constitutional changes prior to the seven-year increments required between councils.[127] On the other hand, others complained that such periodic reconsideration of the very foundations of government were disruptive.[128] The very first review conducted in 1783 produced a deadlock on the Council's recommendations and more than a little controversy.[129] While the effectiveness of Pennsylvania's system may have been a matter of debate, one can clearly see the state attempting to secure popular deliberations and authority for any necessary changes in the constitution. Even more than change, the Council of Censors represented an attempt for the periodic recurrence to the founding principles of the state. As such, the process was thus at once, both progressive and conservative, for both change and preservation were within the power of the council.

It is worth noting that the framers of the Pennsylvania constitution utilized a deliberative body directly elected by the people, required timely and explicit public notification of any proposals, and required a super majority of the Council to make proposals. These mechanisms, or forms, sought to ensure that popular sanction and popular deliberation would be a crucial part of any changes to the fundamental articles of government. Such institutional mechanisms would become more common in other contexts and in this sense Pennsylvania's model was a predecessor for later amending procedures.

Later that Fall Maryland adopted its new constitution on November 8, 1776. Maryland took a unique approach to amending its fundamental law by creating a process that amounted to an indirect popular referendum on given constitutional amendments. The complete article was fairly brief:

> That this Form of Government, and the Declaration of Rights, and no part thereof, shall be altered, changed, or abolished, unless a bill so to alter, change or abolish the same shall pass the General Assembly, and be published at least three months before a new election, and shall be confirmed by the General Assembly, after a new election of Delegates, in the first session after such new election; provided that nothing in this form of government, which relates to the eastern shore particularly, shall at any time hereafter be altered, unless for the alteration and confirmation thereof at least two-thirds of all the members of each branch of the General Assembly shall concur.[130]

With amendments requiring two simple legislative majorities interrupted by a new election, the intervening election served as a popular referendum of sorts.[131] It was a means of allowing the people to instruct their representatives as to their will regarding new amendments. Maryland's unique geography and politics also led to the inclusion of the supermajority requirement on amendments impacting the eastern shore of the state. Maryland clearly differed from Pennsylvania in its reliance on normal arms of government and simple majorities, but was similar in its attempts to create modes for clear public notification, deliberation, and general popular sanctioning of any changes.[132] It is also worth noting that the provision requiring two-thirds majority for amendments impacting the eastern shore was the first clear attempt to institutionally protect minority interests with regard to the people's constituent power.[133]

Not long after Maryland, North Carolina adopted its constitution in December of 1776, but that document contained no explicit means of amendment. Its declaration of rights did comment, "That a frequent recurrence to fundamental principles is absolutely necessary, to preserve the blessings of liberty," yet it is unclear how such recurrences to fundamental principles were to occur, given there was no formal institutional mechanism created to serve this purpose.[134]

It wasn't until after the New Year in February of 1777 that the colonies saw the next state constitution adopted down in the state of Georgia. If the methods of Pennsylvania and Maryland weren't divergent enough Georgia took a completely different tack,

> No alteration shall be made in this constitution without petitions from a majority of the counties, and the petitions from each county to be signed by a majority of voters in each county within this State; at which time the assembly shall order a convention to be called for that purpose, specifying the alterations to be made, according to the petitions preferred to the assembly by the majority of the counties as aforesaid.[135]

Here, rather than a regularly scheduled examination of the constitution—as in Pennsylvania—or a top down legislatively driven approach—as in Delaware—Georgia embraced a more grassroots approach to constitutional change. Requiring petitions by majorities, within the various counties, requesting an amendment followed by a convention, the process clearly sought direct popular sanction and input, and allowed change to occur whenever the people were motivated to do so. Like Pennsylvania, Georgia utilized the convention method, but unlike Pennsylvania, potential changes could be called for at any time rather than regularly prescribed intervals. This method of amendment seemed very cumbersome and no effort was made to use it. In fact, when Georgia later wanted to create a new constitution they did not adhere to the mode of amendment outlined in the original 1777 document.[136]

Later in the spring of 1777, New York established its new constitution, but it did not create a means of amending the document. The full reason for this omission is not clear, yet like New Jersey, the war took its toll on the deliberative process, for significant parts of New York were under occupation by British forces and the colonial congress was often on the run.[137] Whatever the reasons for not including an amending mechanism, New York's omission again illustrates that a full consensus had not been reached on the essential need for, or structure of, such measures.

In June of that summer the disputed territory of Vermont was pushing to become its own state, and in so doing created its own constitution, which was modeled closely on the Pennsylvania document. Like Pennsylvania, Vermont also employed a Council of Censors for the purposes of constitutional renewal and change.

After a full year and a half of steady constitution making among the colonies there was a nine month respite, and it was not until March of 1778 that the South Carolina General Assembly decided to replace their temporary constitution of 1776. The new constitution was created unilaterally by the legislature rather than a convention of the people, and as such, the new constitution proved to be very controversial. Despite the controversy over its adoption, the framers did provide for a means of amendment.[138] Given the actions of the legislature in creating the constitution perhaps it is not surprising that the new amendment process also solely utilized the legislature, "no part of this constitution shall be altered without notice being previously given of ninety days, nor shall any part of the same be changed without the consent of a majority of the members of the senate and house of representatives."[139] Of those states actually creating a formal mechanism, South Carolina employed the least stringent requirements for consensus and deliberation. A simple majority of the legislature could amend any part of the document provided they gave public notice ninety days prior to acting. Unlike Maryland or Georgia there was no formal institutional means provided for transmitting popular sentiment regarding the amendments to their legislature.[140]

Notably the lack of an amending mechanism was a "significant Issue" in the need for a new Massachusetts constitution.[141] Yet despite the need, two years would pass before Massachusetts was able to ratify its first official constitution as a state of the union in 1780. The lengthy delay was largely due to the extremely democratic means of creating the new government, which required ratification by two-thirds of the inhabitants of the state voting within their townships. By extending the debate and ratification of the state constitution to such a local level Massachusetts experienced extended delays and the inability to reach a consensus on an agreed upon set of provisions.[142] Once the people of Massachusetts finally did ratify the constitution it included an amending mechanism that reflected the commitment to popular participation inherent in the ratification process. With regard to alterations, the constitution called for a popular referendum every fifteen years on whether or not to hold a constitutional convention which would then be empowered to propose changes to the document. As one of the leading states the Massachusetts model was influential in American Constitutionalism as it provided a less destabilizing model by making amendment politics optional in contrast to Pennsylvania's mandatory Council of Censors.[143]

Four years later, New Hampshire—like South Carolina—replaced its original constitution in 1784 and this time it did create a procedure for constitutional amendment. In the new constitution, the General Court was required to call a convention in seven years and any products from that convention needed approval by two-thirds of the qualified electors who voted.[144] It is worth noting that both New Hampshire and South Carolina reversed their earlier action of not including an amending mechanism in their original documents, by creating formal amending mechanisms in their new constitutions. This seems to suggest that the need for formal amendment was becoming more widely recognized among the new states.

Summary: Lessons from the States

In the end, by 1784, seven of the thirteen states had adopted some form of amending mechanism while six did not: two states (New Hampshire and South Carolina) quickly added amending mechanisms when they adopted new constitutions. Of the six who did not adopt amending procedures prior to 1784, only two did not have mitigating circumstances. Two states (New York and New Jersey) were plagued by military threat and war during the framing process which somewhat hampered their deliberations; whether they would have included amending procedures absent such harassment one can only speculate. Still two more states (Connecticut and Rhode Island) never even created a new constitution so they did not have a chance to accept, or reject, the notion of an amending mechanism. That leaves only Virginia and North Carolina as states that did not have clear mitigating circumstances—impacting their ability to create amending mechanisms—or did not reverse such omissions in relatively short order. Even then, Virginia's lack of an amending mechanism drew significant criticism most notably from Thomas Jefferson.[145]

Furthermore, four of the six states that created new constitutions—but did not include an amending mechanism—were the first four states to create such documents and all were created in the six months just prior to the Declaration of Independence.[146] Thus, it was the first initial wave of constitutions that did not have formal amending mechanisms, and after the first burst of early constitution making nearly all of the rest included some form of amending mechanism. Therefore, while clearly no universal consensus existed regarding the best means for constitutional amendment, it seems clear that the trajectory of opinion among the states was moving towards the notion that some formal process was helpful—perhaps even necessary—in a written fixed constitution resting on the authority of the people. Furthermore, the steady acceptance and adoption of amending procedures over time seems to indicate that while the new and radical beliefs in popular sovereignty and written constitutionalism demanded such procedures, it took time for these new ideas to sink in. That is to say, it took time for the framers to realize the implications of creating new governments that embraced such principles, and time for them to design institutions that would reflect these principled demands. It is important to examine the relationship between the new ideas of actualized popular sovereignty and written constitutionalism and the new amending mechanisms and the exact form of those procedures.[147] For while they all differed in form, some basic tendencies in their design can be identified and linked to the abstract principles they were meant to actualize. In other words some basic ideas about what constituted a proper amending procedure were beginning to emerge even though such ideas would not be refined until the design of the federal amending procedure in 1787.

There were a number of notable developments in the ideas surrounding amending procedures worth mentioning here. First, amendment provisions should be *explicit* and clearly defined. As more and more states began explicitly recording formal procedures for constitutional amendment, such actions reflected the belief that the new documents were legal in nature, but they were law that should be clearly accessible to the people. Not providing for change explicitly would risk weakening the new constitutions by allowing those in power to alter them through informal or ad hoc means, thus replicating the unacceptable situation the colonists experienced under the English constitution. Therefore, if change were not explicitly provided for, the new constitutions would be decidedly less popular, for the simple fact that the people could not have direct input or control over changes unless they actually were aware of the process by which such change could be effected. Furthermore, such procedures must be public to be legitimate law. For example, Blackstone notes that the basic legitimacy of law requires it to be a public matter, and easily open to public inspection, unlike "Caligula who . . . wrote his laws in a very small character, and hung them up upon high pillars, the more effectually to ensnare the people."[148] Procedures that were not explicit ran the risk of de-legitimizing the legal nature of the document, by removing such changes from the public eye, much as the "high pillars" of Caligula effectively removed any real public knowledge of the law from the people. If a legitimate law must be adequately public, it necessarily follows that such laws *must be explicit in order to be public* and therefore *legitimate* law. As a fundamental law created by the people any changes in the new documents were required to be done explicitly and in the open, and to be recognized as amendments. Consequently, to recognize the legal and popular nature of these new documents, the states created formal procedures for amendment. Several state constitutions demanded various methods of public notification so that any proposed changes to the documents would not escape the notice of the people who created the documents and would include their input in some form.

Second, amending procedures needed to reflect the fundamental nature of the new constitutions. If the constitutions stood above and existed prior to normal government, then surely this demanded institutional mechanisms that would reflect this theory in practice. States sought to reflect this notion in their constitutions via extra governmental bodies such as Council of Censors (Pennsylvania and Vermont), various methods of popular ratification (Massachusetts, Georgia, and Maryland), and super majorities in the legislatures or conventions (Delaware and New Hampshire). Certainly such early procedures were not always the most effective or prudent, yet they all represent early attempts by the framers of state constitutions to reflect the fundamental legal nature of the new documents. The principle reflected in these efforts is that the constitutions should be above normal government and normal statutory law. Again, to achieve this fundamental status the constitutions were created via extraordinary bodies, so it stood to reason that changes must also require some extraordinary process.

Third, the new procedures had to draw upon the constituent power of the people. In other words they had to be sufficiently popular mechanisms for change. Sufficiently popular procedures would ensure that changes were genuine in the sense of truly reflecting the consent of the governed. Accordingly states invented methods such as popular conventions (Massachusetts, Pennsylvania, Vermont, New Hampshire 1784), special elections (Maryland), and local petitions (Georgia) to initiate or ratify changes to the new constitutions. Again while such approaches varied widely, they all attempted to access the popular will to secure the consent of the governed and in doing so gave institutional expression to theoretical concerns.

Fourth, for the most part the states sought to ensure that popular participation in the amending procedures was deliberative and thoughtful. They did this by using legislatures, conventions, and councils that were directly elected by and accountable to the people, yet they were small enough to provide an environment conducive to public and reasoned debate and decision-making. Again, councils, conventions, and legislatures were all designed to be deliberative bodies in some form. Clearly the commitment to deliberation was real and meant to harness popular sentiment without unleashing its more dangerous tendencies.

The Articles of Confederation

Like several of the state constitutions, the Articles of Confederation were also drafted amidst the strain of war. In the final plan for confederation the framers of the Articles rejected Ben Franklin's suggestion for amendment based loosely on his Albany Plan of Union from 1754, which called for a majority of state assemblies as the necessary standard for accepting amendments to the confederation. Franklin's plan for revision was too radical for the Continental Congress at that time as they settled upon the unanimous consent of the states as the standard for amendment of the Articles of Confederation. The mood was for *any* confederation for the purposes of executing the war, rather than a *perfect* confederation. The inherent problems of the Articles and the need for revising them were "an unspoken necessity." Many of the states had reasons to reject the Articles, some of which included issues regarding amending procedures. For instance, South Carolina specifically objected to the requirement for state unanimity in the revision of the Articles and it recommended requiring only 11 states to agree on changes. Despite these and other reservations, South Carolina instructed its delegates to ratify the Articles with or without the proposed changes.[149]

The Articles were approved by Congress on November 17, 1777 and declared sufficiently ratified (excluding Maryland) on September 8, 1779. Even without Maryland the Articles began to function, but were in constitutional limbo without the unanimous consent represented by Maryland's hesitancy to accept them. Maryland finally agreed to ratify in 1781, but just prior Congress had actually discussed calling a national convention to reconstruct the confederation before the Articles could be formally put into effect. This discussion of a convention was prompted by early dissatisfaction by some with the Articles.[150] In the end, the Articles implemented a means of amendment that would later become too constricting for the young republic and its limitations would be a topic for debate at the Federal Convention of 1787 in Philadelphia.

Conclusion

In the end, the Imperial Crisis and the wave of state constitutions during the American Revolutionary period show a firm American commitment to fixed written constitutions and a rejection of organic evolutionary unwritten constitutions. This embrace of written fundamental law was driven by a desire to preserve the natural rights of American citizens as articulated in the Declaration of Independence. A written constitution was seen as a practical means of limiting the powers of government, founding that government in the authority of the people as sovereign, and in turn limiting the people to the precepts of their constitution unless they should exercise their sovereign authority to "alter or abolish" their constitutions. In contrast, unwritten constitutions hid the powers of government in a swirling and confusing mix of precedents, traditions, decisions, and fragmented documents; all of which were susceptible to unseen or inexplicit evolutionary changes or usurpation by elites in power. By writing down the core powers and limits on government the people would have access to the contract between them and their government. Furthermore, popular majorities would be bound by the forms and formalities of the fixed written documents. We have also seen how the embrace of fixed written constitutions led to the increasingly common reliance on formal amending procedures. The natural rights of citizens would be protected by fixed written constitutions and formal amending procedures would in turn help ensure that those constitutions were respected as law; for laws should not be ignored or informally altered, thus a formal means of altering the fundamental law was increasingly seen as necessary to maintain constitutional government. Each state addressed this need in their own unique way and they served as helpful laboratories to the Framers of the U.S. Constitution as they gathered in Philadelphia in the summer of 1787: it is to these deliberations we will now turn.

Notes

1. James Otis, "The Rights of the British Colonies Asserted and Proved" from The Rights of the British Colonies Asserted and Proved, 1764, in *Colonies to Nation 1763-1789: A Documentary History of the American Revolution*, ed. Jack P. Green (New York: W.W. Norton & Company, 1975) 32.

2. Thomas Jefferson letter "To Msgr. Dumas, Paris, 10 September 1787," *The Writings of Jefferson: Monticello Edition Vol 6.* Deposited in the Department of State and Published in 1853 By Order of the Joint Committee of Congress (Washington, D.C.: Thomas Jefferson Memorial Association, 1904–1905) 294-295, cited in the American Reference Library. [CD-ROM] (Orem, Utah: Western Standard Publishing Company, 1998).

3. John Adams, letter to Abigail Adams, May 17, 1776, Butterfield, ed., Family Correspondence, I, 411; as quoted in Gordon S. Wood, *The Creation of the American Republic:1776-1787* (New York: W.W. Norton & Company, 1969) 132.

4. "Toward the Creation of Independent State Governments: The Resolves and Recommendations of Congress," May 10, 15, 1776, from *Journals of the Continental Congress, vol. IV*, pp. 342, 357-358, as quoted in Greene, *Colonies to Nation*, 283.

5. Ibid., 283.

6. "Between 1776 and 1798 the first sixteen states wrote a total of twenty-nine constitutions, two of which were rejected. The two national constitutions bring the total for the era to thirty-one. The willingness to experiment with new institutions in the service of old, well-established political goals and principles was impressive. Thousands of pamphlets and newspaper articles commented upon the constitutions." Donald Lutz, *The Origins of American Constitutionalism* (Baton Rouge: Louisiana State University Press, 1998), 97.

7. For further exploration of this theme, see Lutz, *Origins.*

8. Lutz, *Origins*, 1.

9. Ibid.

10. Lutz, *Origins*, 5-7. For a good analysis of the origins of the American Constitutional tradition see Lutz. Lutz goes into some detail on how the early colonial documents, compact, and charters impacted the development of the state constitutions and eventually the U.S. Constitution of 1787.

11. Ibid., 5-7, 141.

12. Ibid., 14.

13. Ibid., 11.

14. For a more full explanation of the legal status of colonial governments see, Michael Les Benedict, *The Blessings of Liberty: A Concise History of the Constitution of the United States* (Lexington, MA: D. C. Heath and Company, 1996) 19-21; I refer here to liberty in terms of both positive

liberty referring to the inclusion of the colonists in self government; and negative liberty referring to the protection of specific individual rights.

15. "The American Revolution was the culmination of a bitter argument over the nature of the British constitution. At home and in the colonies, Britons argued over whether Parliament was sovereign in the modern meaning of the word—that is, whether Parliament had final, complete, unappealable authority over the British Empire." see Benedict, *The Blessings of Liberty*, 50; This point is further buttressed here, ". . . modern revolutions are usually thought of as social and economic rather than constitutional in nature, their purpose being to overthrow an oppressive ruling class and create a new order of society. The American Revolution differed from the stereotype of modern revolution. It produced significant constitutional change—the creation of thirteen republican state governments organized in a continental union—and the issues that provoked it were preeminently constitutional." in Alfred Kelly, Winfred A. Harbison, and Herman Belz, *The American Constitution Its Origins and Development: Vol I* (New York: W.W. Norton & Company, 1991), 43.

16. Kelly, Harbison, and Belz, *The American Constitution*, 61.

17. For a brief discussion of such issues see Benedict, *The Blessings of Liberty*, 1-18.

18. These theories are briefly outlined in Marc W. Kruman, *Between Authority and Liberty: State Constitution making in Revolutionary America* (Chapel Hill: The University of North Carolina Press, 1997), 8; for a fuller treatment, see John Phillip Reid, *Constitutional History of the American Revolution: The Authority of Law* (Madison, Wisconsin, University of Wisconsin Press, 1993), 3-8.

19. Kruman, *Between Authority and Liberty*, 8.

20. Ibid., 8-9.

21. James Otis, "The Rights of the British Colonies Asserted and Proved" from The Rights of the British Colonies Asserted and Proved, 1764, in Green, *Colonies to Nation*, 28.

22. Ibid., 28.

23. Ibid.

24. Ibid., 33.

25. Ibid.

26. Ibid.

27. Ibid., 28.

28. Ibid., 32.

29. Kruman, *Between Authority and Liberty*, 9; in addition, Otis argues that writs "violated fundamental principles of law which guaranteed a man security in his own home." Also "In 1768 the Circular Letter of the Massachusetts General Court to the assemblies of the other colonies argue that the constitution consisted in fundamental rules which neither the legislature nor the executive could alter." Furthermore, the Massachusetts deputies declared, "In all free states . . . the constitution is fixed, and the supreme legislative power of the nation, from thence derives it authority." Also in the Circular Letter it is argued that the constitution ascertains and limits sovereignty, and that the legislature could not "overleap the bounds of the constitution without subverting its own foundation." in Kelly, Harbison, and Belz, *The American Constitution*, 63.

30. James Otis, "The Rights of the British Colonies Asserted and Proved" from The Rights of the British Colonies Asserted and Proved, 1764, in Green, *Colonies to Nation*, 32.

31. Ibid.

32. Kruman, *Between Authority and Liberty*, 9.

33. Kelly, Harbison, and Belz, *The American Constitution*, 49.

34. Sir William Blackstone, "The Omnipotence of Parliament," from Commentaries on the Laws of England, 1765, Green, *Colonies to Nation*, 86-88.

35. Ibid., 86-88.

36. Ibid.

37. Kelly, Harbison, and Belz, *The American Constitution*, 62.

38. John Phillip Reid argues that the view of Parliamentary command was not fully dominant until the next century, but he concedes that it did seem to characterize British policy towards the colonies, see Reid, *The Authority of Law*, 3-8; also see Kruman's summary of Reid in Kruman, *Between Authority and Liberty*, 10.

39. Kruman, *Between Authority and Liberty*, 10.
40. Ibid., 10.
41. Ibid.
42. Ibid.
43. Interestingly, in protesting the Coercive Acts some Americans referred back to the language of the Declaratory Act in targeting the ill-conceived views of parliamentary authority; see Ibid., 12-14
44. For a good summary and primary sources on these acts, see Greene, *Colonies to Nation*, 202.
45. The Coercive Acts convinced many that the British Government meant to enslave the colonies, see Green, *Colonies to Nation*, 211.
46. Kruman, *Between Authority and Liberty*, 11.
47. Ibid., 11. As Kruman writes, "The Coercive Acts signaled to them the death knell of two constitutions: the colonial constitutions, composed of customary political practices and of charters for each colony that delineated the rights and obligations of the Crown and the colonists, and the customary English constitution that restrained Parliament."
48. Philodemus, "Conciliatory Hints, Attempting, by a fair State of Matters to Remove party Prejudice," from Charles Hyneman and Donald Lutz, *American Political Writing during the Founding Era 1760-1805 Vol. I* (Indianapolis: Liberty Fund, 1983), 614. *Philodemus* was Thomas Tudor Tucker of South Carolina who served in both the Continental Congress and the first two terms under the new Constitution in the House of Representatives.
49. Philodemus, "Conciliatory Hints," Hyneman and Lutz, *American Political Writing, Vol. I*, 611.
50. Ibid.
51. Ibid.
52. Ibid., 611-12.
53. Kelly, Harbison, and Belz, *The American Constitution*, 62.
54. Hyneman and Lutz, *American Political Writing, Vol. I*, 611.
55. Ibid., 620.
56. Kelly, Harbison, and Belz, *The American Constitution*, 63.
57. Clearly a natural rights philosophy drawn from Enlightenment and Classical political philosophy provided the foundation for such "fixed" constitutions to draw their authority from sources antecedent to normal government.
58. Kelly, Harbison, and Belz, *The American Constitution, Vol. I*, 63.
59. Ibid.
60. Ibid.; One could view a contemporary move towards accepting Constitutional adaptation, in place of formal amendment, is in effect a step back towards the English constitutionalism of custom, and tradition. For example, to the extent that the Constitution is "what the Supreme Court says it is" this seems quite similar to the amorphous customary Constitution of the British that was essentially dependent on "traditions" being internalized by governing officials.
61. Demophilus, The Genuine Principles of the Ancient Saxon, or English, Constitution, Philadelphia, 1776, from Hyneman and Lutz, *American Political Writing Vol. I*, 361. It is postulated that the author of this piece is George Bryan, Pennsylvania Whig, co-author of Pennsylvania's first state constitution, and prominent state legislator.
62. Philodemus, from Hyneman and Lutz, *American Political Writing, Vol. I*, 627.
63. Demophilus, from Hyneman and Lutz, *American Political Writing, Vol. I*, 341.
64. Lutz points out that the Declaration makes clear the dual nature of a compact in American political thought. The compact for government entailed two parts. First, the people agreed to form a society and agreed to be bound by the majority. Second they formed a government. In this way the people could throw off government, yet not risk anarchy—as Blackstone feared—but reconstitute government in an orderly manner as bound by the majority. See Lutz, *Origins*, 111.
65. Kyvig, *Explicit & Authentic Acts*, 17.

66. Samuel Adams, Mass. House of Representatives to the Speakers of Other Hoses of Representatives, February 11, 1768, Cushing, ed., Writings of Samuel Adams, I, 185; as quoted in Gordon Wood. *The Creation of the American Republic: 1776-1787* (New York: W.W. Norton & Company, 1969), 266.

67. Lutz puts it this way "[the U.S. Constitution's] form and content derived largely from the early state constitution, as borrowings and as reactions. These often-overlooked documents occupy a critical position in the development of American constitutionalism. They are the culmination of a long process, and the foundation upon which the United States Constitution rests. That is, the Constitution is an incomplete foundation document until and unless the state constitutions are also read." See, Lutz, *Origins*, 96.

68. Kelly, Harbison, and Belz, *The American Constitution, Vol. I*, 65.

69. For an example of this thinking see Thomas Tudor Tucker writing as *Philodemus*, from Hyneman and Lutz, *American Political Writing, Vol. I*, 606-630.

70. Kruman, *Between Authority and Liberty*, 157.

71. Samuel Adams; quoted in Wood, *The Creation of the American*, 266.

72. Anonymous, Four Letters on Interesting Subjects, Philadelphia, 1776, from Hyneman and Lutz, *American Political Writing, Vol. I*, 384-385.

73. Ibid., 387.

74. Ibid., 387-88.

75. Ibid., 389.

76. Ibid.

77. Anonymous, The Interest of America 1776, from Green, *Colonies to Nation* , 315-16.

78. Ibid.

79. Ibid.

80. Lutz, *Origins*, 10. For example Lutz points out that the percentage of the population that could vote in the least liberal state (Georgia) was four or five times greater than the percentage of the population that could vote in England.

81. Jefferson remarked on this point of a written text and its accessibility to the people, [America was] "the first of the nations of the earth, which assembled its wise men peaceable together to form a fundamental constitution, to commit it to writing, and place it among their archives, where everyone should be free to appeal to its text." Thomas Jefferson letter to Major John Cartwright, Monticello, June 5, 1824; from Merrill D. Peterson, *The Portable Thomas Jefferson* (New York: Penguin Books, 1975) 579.

82. Francis Newton Thorpe. *The Federal and State Constitutions Colonial Charters, and Other Organic Laws of the States, Territories, and Colonies Now or Heretofore Forming the United States of America* (Washington, DC: Government Printing Office, 1909).

Constitution of North Carolina- December 18, 1776; ". . . all political power is vested in and derived from the people only."

Constitution of Georgia- February 5, 1777, "We, therefore, the representatives of the people, from whom all power originates, and for whose benefit all government is intended. . ."

Constitution of Maryland- November 11, 1776, "That all government of right originates from the people, is founded in compact only, and instituted solely for the good of the whole."

Constitution of New Hampshire- 1776, "WE, the members of the Congress of New Hampshire, chosen and appointed by the free suffrages of the people of said colony, and authorized and empowered by them to meet together, and use such means and pursue such measures as we should judge best for the public good; and in particular to establish some form of government, provided that measure should be recommended by the Continental Congress. . . "

Constitution of New Jersey- 1776, "WHEREAS all the constitutional authority ever possessed by the kings of Great Britain over these colonies, or their other dominions, was, by compact, derived from the people, and held of them, for the common interest of the whole society."

The Constitution of New York- April 20, 1777, "This convention, therefore, in the name and by the authority of the good people of this State, cloth ordain, determine, and declare that no authority shall, on any presence whatever, be exercised over the people or members of this State but such as shall be derived from and granted by them."

Constitution of Pennsylvania- September 28, 1776, "WHEREAS all government ought to be instituted and supported for the security and protection of the community as such, and to enable the individuals who compose it to enjoy their natural rights, and the other blessings which the Author of existence has bestowed upon man; and whenever these great ends of government are not obtained, the people have a right, by common consent to change it, and take such measures as to them may appear necessary to promote their safety and happiness."

Constitution of South Carolina- March 26, 1776, "That this congress being a full and free representation of the people of this colony, shall henceforth be deemed and called the general assembly of South Carolina."

Constitution of Vermont- July 8, 1777, "WHEREAS, all government ought to be instituted and supported, for the security and protection of the community, as such, and to enable the individuals who compose it, to enjoy their natural rights, and the other blessings which the Author of existence has bestowed upon man; and whenever those great ends of government are not obtained, the people have a right, by common consent, to change it, and take such measures as to them may appear necessary to promote their safety and happiness."

The Constitution of Virginia- June 29, 1776, "All power is vested in, and consequently derived from, the people; that magistrates are their trustees and servants."

83. Kruman, *Between Authority and Liberty*, 54.

84. This is in part what Hamilton is referring to when he remarks that the American people have a chance to create a government from "reflection and choice" rather than "accident and force" in *The Federalist*, No. 1.

85. Anonymous, "The Interest of America 1776"; from Green, *Colonies to Nation*, 315-16.

86. Thomas Jefferson, in a letter to Major John Cartwright, Monticello, June 5, 1824; from Peterson, *The Portable Thomas Jefferson*, 577-582.

87. Ibid.

88. Kyvig, *Explicit & Authentic Acts*, 30. "As state after state wrestled with constitution making, methods emerged for turning popular sovereignty from a vague abstraction into a workable system for setting forth the terms of government. As a result, legislatures lost their status as absolute and therefore unrestrainable representatives of the people. Instead, the distinctively American notion of legislatures as finite powers operating within a defined framework emerged. If the ultimate authority of the people could be effectively expressed, then the power of government would always be limited."

89. By constitutive power I mean the power to constitute government. This is the power to create and define governments, which is different from the power to create law within the parameters of a given governmental structure. According to the Republican theory of the day the people were sovereign and as such the people wield this constitutive power.

90. Kruman, *Between Authority and Liberty*, 20.

91. Ibid., 20.

92. Ibid., 21-22. Kruman disputes the conclusions of Wood, Lutz, Adams, and others in their belief that the new constitutions were created merely by normal legislatures with procedures more similar to statutory law than fundamental law. For his convincing arguments see Ibid., 15-34.

93. Thomas Jefferson, Notes on the State of Virginia; from Peterson, *The Portable Thomas Jefferson*, 170.

94. Kruman, *Between Authority and Liberty*, 24.

95. Ibid., 22.

96. Ibid., 20; Only Virginia and South Carolina did not hold such special elections.

97. Ibid.

98. For a fuller account of the development of constitutional conventions see Wood, *The Creation of the American Republic*, 306-343.

99. Kruman, *Between Authority and Liberty*, 22-23; Virginia, South Carolina, and New Hamphsire.

100. Ibid., 22-23; Virginia, South Carolina, and New Hamphsire.

101. "How was a constitution to be established, especially during wartime? The answer differed according to the kind of government in place during the revolutionary crisis. Those colonies—like Massachusetts, Delaware, and Pennsylvania—that maintained legislative authority before the writing of the constitutions turned to the constitutional convention, an extralegal mode for creating a form of government. In those provinces with such temporary, extralegal political bodies already in place and governing, political leaders used provincial congresses to devise constitutions." Kruman, *Between Authority and Liberty*, 33.

102. Thomas Jefferson was critical of the Virginia Convention's creation of a permanent constitution. He had no problem with their creation of a temporary government given the limitations of the times, but he later contended that a new convention should be elected with the express will of the people to create a permanent constitution that was unalterable by the legislature; see Thomas Jefferson, "Notes on the State of Virginia" from Peterson, *The Portable Thomas Jefferson*, 166-176.

103. Kyvig, *Explicit & Authentic Acts*, 30; "In the course of devising their constitution, the newly independent American states wrestled with myriad problems. One was fundamental to the very notion of written constitutions. Given a dedication to concepts of higher law embodied in specific instruments endorsed by supermajorities, what was a sovereign people to do if it felt the need to change some or all of the basic terms of its government? Only by providing for a means of amending it, the Lexington, Massachusetts, town meeting declared in 1778, could a constitution 'give satisfaction to the people; and be a happy means, under providence, of preventing popular commotion, mobs, bloodshed and civil war.' A constitution, if it was to survive, must make provisions . . ."

104. Whether or not certain legislatures had the authority to amend or change certain constitutions became a matter of dispute in some states; for example see Thomas Jefferson, "Notes on the State of Virginia" from Peterson, *The Portable Thomas Jefferson*,166-176.

105. See Kyvig, *Explicit & Authentic Acts*, 19. This is further evidenced by the general trajectory of adding amending mechanisms to the state constitutions, the inclusion of an amending mechanism in the Articles of Confederation, and the United States Constitution of 1787.

106. For an example of this perspective see Thomas Jefferson, "Notes on the State of Virginia" from Peterson, *The Portable Thomas Jefferson*, 170.

107. Not everyone agreed that the Virginia Legislature could amend the constitution. Jefferson was vehement however in his contention that the Virginia constitution amounted to nothing more than a regular ordinance that could likewise be altered at will by the legislature. To see his full argument see Ibid., 170.

108. Kyvig, *Explicit & Authentic Acts*, 33

109. Benjamin Gale, "Brief, Decent, but Free Remarks and Observations, on Several Laws Passed by the Honorable Legislature of the State of Connecticut, since the Year 1775, Hartford, 1782," 24-28; quoted in Wood, *The Creation of the American Republic*, 277.

110. Hartford Connecticut Courant, June 4, 1787; quoted in Wood, *The Creation of the American Republic*, 277.

111. Hartford Connecticut Courant, November 13, 1786; quoted in Wood, *The Creation of the American Republic*, 277.

112. Demophilus, "The Genuine Principles of the Ancient Saxon, or English, Constitution, Philadelphia, 1776," in Hyneman and Lutz, *American Political Writing Vol. I*, 361.

113. Kruman, *Between Authority and Liberty*, 55.

114. Kyvig, *Explicit & Authentic Acts*, 30.

115. Ibid.

116. Ibid.

117. Bailyn points out that these two charters were designed to be instruments of government; see Bernard Bailyn, *The Ideological Origins of the American Revolution* (Cambridge, Massachusetts: Belknap Press, 1967) 191.

118. For a more detailed account see Willi Paul Adams, *The First American Constitutions Republican Ideology and the Making of the State Constitutions in the Revolutionary Era* (Chapel Hill, University of North Carolina Press, 1980) 66-68. From Rhode Island, "Two towns instructed their

representatives in 1779 to work toward drafting a real constitution. They argued that in accepting the charter of 1663 the settlers had recognized the king's 'power of government.' When the king violated this contract, he in effect annulled the charter, and governmental power reverted to the people." Because no new contract had established a new form of government, the current government of Rhode Island had no legal basis.

119. Kyvig, *Explicit & Authentic Acts*, 31.

120. Kruman, *Between Authority and Liberty*, 56.

121. Alan G. Tarr, *Understanding State Constitutions* (Princeton, New Jersey: Princeton University Press, 1988) 63.

122. Delaware Constitution in Thorpe, *The Federal and State Constitutions.*

123. Kyvig, *Explicit & Authentic Acts*, 41.

124. Pennyslvania Constitution, Thorpe, *The Federal and State Constitutions.*

125. Ibid.

126. Ibid.

127. Kruman, *Between Authority and Liberty*, 58.

128. See Kyvig, *Explicit & Authentic Acts*, 40. According to Kyvig, some called the council, "A jubilee of tyranny . . . when the foundation of government shall be torn up."

129. Ibid., 40.

130. Maryland Constitution of 1776, in Thorpe, *The Federal and State Constitutions.*

131. Dodd characterized the Maryland model, "The people did not vote directly on a proposed amendment, but it was considered sufficient to have an amendment passed by two successive legislatures, by a vote greater than that required for ordinary legislation. The people were presumed to have passed upon the amendment in the election of a new house of representatives, and if a proposed amendment were one of great popular interest, it would naturally have been made an issue in this election. This arrangement represented a decided step in advance in popular control over amendments, as compared with that first adopted in Delaware (1776) and South Carolina (1776), and for a time was considered to give a sufficient popular participation in the adoption of constitutional amendments." See Walter Fairleigh Dodd, *The Revision and Amendment of State Constitutions*, (Baltimore, The Johns Hopkins Press, 1910) 122-123.

132. The Maryland provision was for some time copied, but those of Delaware and South Carolina were not imitated. In fact both South Carolina in 1790 and Delaware 1792 copied the Maryland plan. See Dodd, *The Revision and Amendment of State Constitutions*, 122.

133. While Delaware and Pennsylvania did use supermajorities their purpose was not specifically stated. By implication I surmise that such supermajority requirements were used to ensure a broad consensus of the people rather than protect specific minorities. In this way the Maryland example is notable.

134. North Carolina Constitution of 1776, in Thorpe, *The Federal and State Constitutions.*

135. The Georgia Constitution of 1777, in Thorpe, *The Federal and State Constitutions.*

136. In fact, the legislature appointed three persons from each county to draft a new constitution in 1788, and then two conventions modified and ratified the new constitution which went into effect in 1789; see Dodd, *The Revision and Amendment of State Constitutions*, 42.

137. See Tarr, *Understanding State Constitutions*, 63, and Adams, *The First American Constitutions*, 85-86.

138. Governor John Rutledge resigned in protest over the process of creating the new constitution. For an account of this controversy, see Kruman, *Between Authority and Liberty*, 55-56.

139. The Constitution of South Carolina of 1778, in Thorpe, *The Federal and State Constitutions.*

140. Dodd saw a southern tendency to rely on legislatures for amendment early on, "The method of constitutional amendment through the regular legislative organs of the state had its origin in the South. The constitutions of Maryland (1776), Delaware (1776), and South Carolina (1778) made provision for partial amendment through legislative action," see Dodd, *The Revision and Amendment of State Constitutions*, 120.

141. Kyvig, *Explicit & Authentic Acts*, 33.

142. Adams adeptly chronicles the ups and downs of the ratification of the Massachusetts Constitution, see Adams, *The First American Constitutions*, 86-98. In March of 1778, people of Massachusetts rejected the first proposed constitution and it was not until 1780, with more than a little political maneuvering that the state was able to finally ratify a document.

143. Kyvig, *Explicit & Authentic Acts*, 33.

144. Kruman, *Between Authority and Liberty*, 59.

145. Thomas Jefferson for one openly criticized this deficiency in his state's constitution, see Thomas Jefferson, "Notes on the State of Virginia" in Peterson, *The Portable Thomas Jefferson*, 166-176.

146. Dodd had this to say, "The absence of provision for alteration in the constitutions of 1776-77, should not be taken as an indication that their framers thought the regular legislatures competent to alter or establish constitutions, but rather that they did not consider the matter at all," Dodd, *The Revision and Amendment of State Constitutions*, 27. Alan Tarr has a slightly different take on the absence of amending mechanisms, "Seven states at one time or another had a constitution that did not specify a procedure for constitutional change, and five of those constitutions remained in effect in 1800. But their failure to specify a mechanism for constitutional change was not meant to preclude such change. Rather, it reflected either inadvertence or, more interestingly, the view that such provisions were unnecessary." see Tarr, *Understanding State Constitutions*, 74.

147. I would argue that the English had idealized notions of popular sovereignty in the sense that they were mostly theoretical, but they were hardly "actual" as Blackstone's analysis illustrated. The Americans embraced similar notions of popular sovereignty, but they desired to "actualize" these abstract notions and make them a political reality. Thus, institutional mechanisms such as conventions and amending mechanisms can be seen as attempts to *actualize* the sovereignty of the people

148. William Blackston, *Blackstone's Commentaries on the Laws of England*, Yale Law School, The Avalon Project, http://avalon.law.yale.edu/subject_menus/blackstone.asp (accessed September 1, 2012)

149. Kyvig, *Explicit & Authentic Acts*, 35-36.

150. Ibid., 36.

Chapter 3
An Ultimate Remedy: Creating and Ratifying Article V

> The only real security of liberty, in any country, is the jealousy and circumspection of the people themselves. Let them be watchful over their rulers. Should they find a combination against their liberties, and all other methods appear insufficient to preserve them, they have, thank God, an ultimate remedy. That power which created the government can destroy it. Should the government, on trial, be found to want amendments, those amendments can be made in a regular method, in a mode prescribed by the Constitution itself.
>
> James Iredell, N.C. Ratifying Convention[1]

As is well documented elsewhere, the "critical period" between the end of the Revolution in 1783 and the adoption of the new Constitution in 1789 exposed the weaknesses of the Articles of Confederation and likewise the weaknesses of an unfettered shift to popular government in the states.[2] The new state governments exhibited the strains and excesses of democracy as witnessed by examples of legislative tyranny in Pennsylvania and Rhode Island and other popular crises such as Shay's rebellion.[3] In response to the weaknesses of the Articles and the excess of the states, the Federal Convention of 1787 sought to balance the need for democracy and stability. It was in Philadelphia that the framers sought to design governing institutions that would give practical voice to the political principles that had inspired the American Revolution. Just as the new Constitution reflected core political principles tempered by prudence and compromise, the design of Article V would reflect what *Publius* would describe in the *Federalist Papers* as the "new science of politics" that characterized much of the new constitution. Article V reflected the new federal relationship between the states and national government, relied upon deliberative bodies, allowed for popular convention, provided for an explicit formal means of amendment, drew upon the constituent power of the people, and ultimately sought to strike the delicate balance between flexibility and stability, progress and preservation. As such it was seen as a means of perfecting the Constitution as improvements became aware through experience. Since contemporary critics of Article V seek to undue the careful calibration of the Article V mechanism, it is especially important to take a deeper look at Article V's design and the governing principles that shaped its creation in order to understand Article V's importance to preserving the larger constitutional system.

Federal Convention of 1787

At the Federal Convention in Philadelphia in the summer of 1787 the delegates from the Commonwealth of Virginia led by their governor Edmund Randolph would take the initiative by proposing the bold nationalistic Virginia Plan. The Virginia Plan would basically scrap the state dominated Articles of Confederation for a true national government not totally beholden to state power. Fissures in the convention would emerge between the small and large states as well as the slave and non-slave states. Some delegates favored the security of a more state centered government while others were more comfortable with empowering the national government.

In the midst of these larger issues the delegates confronted several key questions related to constitutional amendment. The first question they confronted was the range of authority that the convention had to alter the Articles of Confederation. The second question was whether changes proposed by the Convention should be authorized by the people via their state legislatures or the people in special ratifying conventions. Third, by addressing issues of popular sovereignty and constitutional form, the answers to these questions would impact the design of Article V and its unique mode of tapping into the constituent power of the people to alter the Constitution once it was in operation.

Plans for both ratification and amendment of the Constitution were included in the initial Virginia Plan which was proposed by Edmund Randolph as the basis for consideration at the Federal Convention which opened on May 29 1787. The Virginia Plan represented a clear break from the Articles of Confederation by proposing the creation of a national government rather than the existing confederation of autonomous states. The 13 article of the Virginia Plan proposed "that provision ought to be made for the amendment of the Articles of Union whensoever it shall seem necessary, and that the assent of the national legislature ought not to be required thereto."[4] This rudimentary proposal represented the desire to provide for a means of amendment outside the normal arms of government. This proposal was the fetal origin of what would eventually become Article V of the new United States Constitution. Article V's final form would not be fully hammered out until the waning days of the convention, but here on the first day the intent was signaled that some mechanism for formal change was needed.

Convention Authority and Ratification

One of the first issues for the delegates to address was the extent of their authority which forced them to explore the basis of sovereignty in the new nation and the means by which that sovereignty might be exercised. The question that arose was whether or not the convention had the authority to replace the Articles or merely amend them, which in turn was tied to how the work of the convention should be ratified—via state legislatures or the people. As for ratification of the Virginia Plan the fifteenth article proposed that its work "be submitted to an assembly or assemblies of Representatives, recommended by the several legislatures to be expressly chosen by the people, to consider & decide thereon."[5]

The debate surrounding such matters generally reveals the delegates' expressed thoughts regarding constitutional change and the importance of formal ratification as a means of demarcating the lines of authority in the new republic. Were the people themselves the source of authority for the national government or did the state legislatures represent the people with regards to national issues? Was the Federal Convention bound by the state legislatures via the Articles of Confederation or could the Convention submit their proposals directly to the people in ratifying conventions? The various positions on these matters by many delegates were not debated along purely theoretical lines as their varying positions were often bound up in an amalgam of political principle and practical political concerns. For example, some who sought ratification by popular convention already favored a strong national government; likewise those who feared a strong national government sought ratification via the state legislatures. The debates surrounding these issues are helpful windows into the Framers' ideas regarding how best to draw upon the sovereignty of the people and do so in clear and regular ways.

In presenting the Virginia Plan, Randolph's assessment of the Articles found them deficient in their ability to prevent foreign invasion, maintain internal order and harmony among the states, produce national public goods, or to defend themselves against encroachments from the states.[6] He located the source of such weaknesses in the nature and timing of the creation of the Articles of Confederation. First, "*State constitutions* formed at an early period of the war, and by persons *elected by the people* for that purpose"; second, "The *confederation* was formed long after this, and had its ratification not by any *special appointment* from the people, but from the several assemblies"; finally "No judge will say that the *confederation* is paramount to a State constitution."[7]

The Articles of Confederation were created *after* the state governments and created *by* the state governments and thus lacked direct popular ratification. The newly proposed government must have a more firm popular footing; therefore the new constitution must reach back down to the original source of power located in the people in order to supersede the power of the states.[8] This proposition, as we shall see, was far from a given in the minds of some delegates, but would ultimately prove to be the final course of action.

In summing up his analysis of the situation, Randolph reiterated the inherent danger in the overly democratic state governments, "Our chief danger arises from the democratic parts of our constitutions. It is a maxim which I hold incontrovertible, that the powers of government exercised by the people swallows up the other branches. None of the constitutions have provided sufficient checks against the democracy."[9] Thus in introducing the Virginia Plan, Randolph argued that one weakness of the Articles were that they were not rooted directly in the authority of the people, while at the same time he laments the excessively popular nature of the state constitutions. This apparent contradiction was actually a vitally important attempt to balance popular authority against popular excess. This balance between popular authority as a foundation of government and popular excess in the exercise of government is a critical principle that shaped the design of the new constitution. As described in chapter 1, here we can see the challenge of Odysseus, to experience the sweetness and justness of democracy without succumbing to its dangers. What is important to note here is the importance of grounding the new government in the sovereign authority of the people directly rather than in a derivative form via the state governments. This theme would re-emerge during the debate on how to ratify the work of the Convention.

The delegates began their debate of the Virginia Plan on May 31 and by June 5 the convention was considering the fifteenth proposition which Madison noted as, *"recommending conventions under appointment* [of the people] *to ratify the new Constitution* &c."[10] In a brief objection, Roger Sherman first voiced that such a measure was unnecessary as the Articles of Confederation already provided for change via the state legislatures.[11] James Madison responded that proposition 15 was essential since the Articles were defective with respect to amendment. He argued that by relying on the formal agreement of state governments, the Articles set the foundation for supreme state authority where conflicts between the Congress and the states arose. Madison then compared the Articles to a treaty amongst sovereign states, where a breach of any one article by any party might absolve the other parties of the total obligation. For these reasons Madison thought it "indispensable" that the new Constitution be ratified by the "supreme authority of the people themselves."[12]

The most extended debate on the issue of ratification would take place on July 23 as the convention began to consider a proposal that advocated, "referring the new Constitution to Assemblies to be chosen by the people for the express purpose of ratifying it." Immediately upon consideration of the above proposal, Oliver Ellsworth of Connecticut moved that the new Constitution be referred to the Legislatures of the states for ratification.[13]

In an extended response to Elsworth's motion, George Mason, from Virginia, countered that the popular assembly proposal was "most important and essential of the Resolutions." First, he argued that the state legislatures had no power to ratify the new Constitution for they were "mere creatures of the State Constitutions, and cannot be greater than their creators."[14] Secondly, as a result he argued that they must resort to the "people with whom all power remains that has not been given up in the [state] Constitutions derived from them."[15] Mason continued saying that "this doctrine should be cherished as the basis of free Government." Third, legislatures do not have a competent authority to ratify because "succeeding Legislatures having equal authority could undo the acts of their predecessors; and the National Government would stand in each State on the weak and tottering foundation of an act of Assembly." Lastly, Mason argued that in some states—most notably his native Virginia—the ratification of the state constitutions by the people was in dispute. To further erect a national government on this shaky popular foundation would be unwise for, "A National Constitution derived from such a source would be exposed to the severest criticisms."[16] Edmund Randolph followed Mason's volley by reiterating that it would simply be imprudent to subject ratification of the new constitution to those bodies—the state legislatures—who would likely be most opposed to it.

Elbridge Gerry, of Massachusetts, stood with his fellow New Englander Elsworth against the two Virginians, arguing that Mason and Randolph should not disparage the authority of the current national government or the state governments as they, "have been too long acquiesced in, to be now shaken." He remained resolute in his opposition to popular conventions for, "Great confusion he was confident would result from a recurrence to the people. They would never agree on any thing."[17]

Nathanial Ghorum, also of Massachusetts, broke ranks with his regional colleagues when he rose to point out that legislatures would be the more likely to thwart or delay the new constitution where in contrast popular conventions would be better equipped to deliberate the matter. Namely conventions would allow many of the ablest men who are excluded from the legislatures—such as clergy—to contribute to the deliberations. Also conventions would, "discuss the subject more candidly than members of the Legislature who are to lose the power which is to be given up to the General Government."[18] Hugh Williamson of North Carolina seconded Gorhum's point arguing that popular conventions were, "to be preferred as more likely to be composed of the ablest men in the States."[19] Likewise, Rufus King also rose to argue that he preferred reference to the authority of the people expressly delegated to the conventions, "as the most certain means of obviating all disputes & doubts concerning the means of drawing forth the best men in the Sates to decide on it."[20] King also noted that some state officials might derive "scruples" from their oaths to support their state constitutions as a justification for opposing the new Constitution on means other than its efficacy.

Gouverneur Morris was the first to make the link between ratification and future amendments when he asserted that, "in case of an appeal to the people of the U.S., the supreme authority, the federal compact may be altered by a *majority of them*; in like manner as the Constitution of a particular State may be altered by a majority of the people of the State."[21]

After an extended period of debate, a young James Madison rose. He ultimately sided against the legislatures as he believed they were incompetent to make the proposed changes for it would be, "a novel & dangerous doctrine that a Legislature could change the constitution under which it held its existence." Madison reiterated his position that the "difference between a system founded on the Legislatures only, and one founded on the people, to be the true difference between a *league* or *treaty*, and a *Constitution*."[22] He again argued that a constitution is legally much more solid than a league or treaty—which could be undone by any one of the parties. Secondly, a judge would be obliged to rule laws in violation of the constitution as null and void, but would not be so obliged regarding laws that violate treaties. Lastly, Madison pointed out that all of the arguments for utilizing the Federal Convention as a means of proposing the new constitution—rather than the Continental Congress—also apply as valid reasons for using popular conventions—rather than state legislatures—for ratification.[23] Madison's statement ended the debate and Ellsworth's motion—to refer the plan to the legislatures—came to a vote and it lost while a vote to ratify via popular conventions was passed by a vote of nine to one, with only Delaware dissenting.[24]

While practical politics did factor in the decision for popular conventions, one cannot disregard the concern for ensuring that the new Constitution be erected on nothing but the proper foundation of authority. The debate displayed the delegates' deep concern for popular sovereignty and their belief that popular conventions were the most prudent and pure example of popular authority possible. If the written document were to have the proper authority over the states it must be fixed on the sovereign authority of the people and not on the state governments. There was also concern over the quality of decision-making and deliberation in the conventions as opposed to the legislatures, as a number of delegates noted that the "ablest men" were more likely to inhabit the popular conventions. Furthermore, the convention would have a singular focus and purpose and therefore might avoid some of the divided interests and loyalties that some state officials might bring to the table. In the end, the key issue centered on the best means of tapping the constitutive power of the people in a manner that respected the moral principle of democracy without unleashing its worst tendencies. For these reasons the Convention ultimately voted to endorse the convention route. As Kyvig notes,

> It did not hurt that this approach also appeared the most likely path to success in the upcoming contest over ratification. Nevertheless, a convention that had already accepted indirect selection of senators and would soon authorize indirect presidential elections stood steadfastly for popular endorsement of the basic frame of government.[25]

While ratification and amendment are certainly different things they are inherently related as they both seek to tap into the deep wells of sovereign authority that rest in the people. A brief examination of how this debate over ratification would be helpful here. First, and most obvious, there was a solid recurrence to the authority of the people as the only firm basis for the new government. As Madison clearly stated, "The people were in fact, the fountain of all power, and by resorting to them, all difficulties were got over. They could alter constitutions as they pleased. It was a principle in the Bills of Rights, that first principles might be resorted to."[26] Second, the delegates recognized that the creation of a written constitution required formal publicly recognized procedures. Now they greatly disagreed over the best and most politically feasible process, but there was clearly tacit agreement that a formal process was required. Third, a key principle was the importance of establishing clear lines of authority. More specifically, drawing on the first two principles, they were careful to establish a formal process that gave practical effect to their beliefs in popular sovereignty and a written constitution. Most notably they were concerned that if normal state governments had ratified the new Constitution then the new government would still be subservient to state authority, whereas a foundation directly on the people would establish the authority of the national government over and above the states in the realms delegated to the national government. Deciding how to ratify the new government would set important precedents over who had the power to alter or change that fundamental law in the future.

Fourth, care was taken in the design of the ratification process to avoid the democratic excess that had been witnessed in the states. For example, the delegates only considered the legislatures or representative conventions as the best means of tapping the constituent authority of the people they did not consider popular referendums or the like. Conventions were seen as the more popular form of the two, for they would allow the people to act directly through representatives chosen specifically for the purpose of ratification yet it would promote the ablest men to engage in serious deliberation. Last, there seemed to be some concern over the relative deliberative capacities of conventions versus legislatures. Several delegates commented that the conventions would most likely possess more able men and would not be divided in their loyalties and thus in a better position to deliberate on the matter before them.

As we shall see such concerns over popular authority, formal processes, lines of authority, the avoidance of democratic excess, and deliberation would also influence the convention's eventual plan for constitutional amendment.

Creation of Article V

The debate over the scope of the Convention's authority and the mode of ratification are clearly related to the issue of amendment in that they all seek to define the manner in which the sovereign authority of the people should be exercised for the purposes of founding a constitution. While altering an existing government and founding a new government are certainly different tasks, a recurrence to the sovereign power in society make them similar. Furthermore, all these issues try to grapple with how the sweeping and seemingly unlimited authority of the people should or could mesh with fixed written constitutions that sought to limit power and direct authority.

As noted earlier, the original Virginia Plan submitted by Edmund Randolph included a provision for formal constitutional amendment. Again, Randolph's rudimentary proposal simply stated, "that provision ought to be made for the amendment of the Articles of Union whensoever it shall seem necessary, and that the assent of the national Legislature ought not to be required thereto."[27] By proposing a formal means of constitutional amendment, the Virginia plan was sought to ensure that constitutional alterations would not be left to chance—this, as noted in the last chapter, is compatible with the trajectory of political thinking in the post-imperial period of state constitution-making. In addition Randolph clearly did not want to involve the National Legislature in the process, which would leave the entire process to the states or the people directly. Perhaps this was a bit of sugar to sweeten the nationalistic Virginia Plan or perhaps it was simply Randolph's belief that constitutional alterations should not be the province of the National Legislature.[28]

Debate on the Need for an Amending Procedure

The amending process debate begin with a very brief exchange. On the fifth of June, the delegates began discussing Randolph's vague proposal for an amendment process. When the proposal was offered before the chamber, Pinckney immediately rose in opposition. Unfortunately, we don't know what his specific objections to this proposal were since all Madison noted in his convention notes was, "Mr. Pinckney doubted the propriety and necessity of it."[29]

After Pinkney's objection, Elbridge Gerry rose to say that he favored the amendment proposal. Gerry argued that amendment provision was wise since the "novelty & difficulty of the experiment requires periodical revision." In addition he noted that just the prospect of such a revision would give "intermediate stability" to the Government and that "nothing had yet happened in the States where this provision existed to proves [sic] its impropriety." There was no further discussion on the matter at this time and after Pinkney's and Gerry's short remarks the motion was postponed for further consideration.[30]

The matter was taken up again six days later on June 11 and Madison's notes point out that several unidentified delegates failed to see the necessity of the provision, nor the need to exclude the National Legislature.[31] Without knowing the identity or the thoughts of those objecting to the proposal, one can only speculate about why some did not see the need for such a provision. Perhaps the objections reflected the lack of unanimity in the states on the need for a formal amending process, for while most states had adopted such measures, a number still had not. Regardless of their identity or rationale for opposing the measure, George Mason rose to defend the Virginia proposal,

> The plan now to be formed will certainly be defective, as the Confederation has been found on trial to be. Amendments therefore will be necessary, and it will be better to provide for them in an easy, regular, and Constitutional way than to

> trust to chance and violence. It would be improper to require the consent of the Natl. Legislature, because they may abuse their power, and refuse their consent on that very account. The opportunity for such an abuse may be the fault of the Constitution calling for amendment.[32]

It seems clear that Mason was seeking to educate those opposed to the proposal about the necessities of regular constitutional government and the need to tame all governing authority even the authority to alter the whole plan of government. If governing institutions and functions were not provided for in an "easy, regular, and Constitutional way" then matters would be left to "chance and violence." This had been the lesson and history of the English constitution where chance and violence had been the foundation of the ever-evolving British government. Centuries of thinking on the nature and origins of government seemed to die hard amongst some of the delegates at the convention. It was the job of those who understood the new nature of American Constitutionalism that they were attempting to bring as much of government under the constitution as was practicable. In this regard, Mason's remarks were emphasizing the importance of a formal process for amendment and the importance of formalities to written constitutionalism. In another vein, his comments regarding the national legislature were reflective of the hesitancy—by Mason and others—to cede too much control to a centralized authority. Randolph rose to agree with Mason's arguments and then the convention decided to split the clause into two parts. They voted in favor of a formal amending process, but deferred their discussion of the national legislature's role until a latter date.[33]

Much would happen between June 11 and July 23 when the issue of amendment would next be taken up. Patterson would submit the New Jersey plan and the Convention would come close to failure before securing the Great Compromise and slowly moving forward piecing together the new Constitution.

On July 23, when the issue arose again during a meeting of the full convention the delegates voted in favor of the following language, "That provision ought to be made for the amendment of the articles of union, whensoever it shall seem necessary." This language passed unanimously indicating that apparent agreement had been achieved regarding the necessity for a formal procedure, but the details of the process had yet to be worked out.[34]

Debating the Mode of Amendment

After accepting the need for a formal process, there was no more said on the issue until the Committee on Detail issued its report and August 30 the convention came to the amending article which at this point now read, "On the application of the Legislatures of two thirds of the States in the Union, for an amendment of this Constitution, the Legislature of the United States shall call a Convention for that purpose."[35] There was no debate on the matter at this time and only Gouverneur Morris suggested that "the Legislature should be left at liberty to call a Convention, whenever they please." No response or reaction was recorded, and the clause was voted unanimously in the affirmative. Thus heading into the very last weeks of the convention the delegates had so far agreed to rely solely on a convention called by the states for the purposes of amending the new Constitution. This provision would not undergo significant change again until the waning days of the convention.

On September 10, Elbridge Gerry asked the convention for a reconsideration of the proposed amending article. Elaborating on his motion to reopen the issue he said he was concerned about how the provision might be used against a minority of the states, "This Constitution . . . is to be paramount to the State Constitutions. It follows, hence, from this article that two thirds of the States may obtain a Convention, a majority of which can bind the Union to innovations that may subvert the State-Constitutions altogether."[36]

While Gerry sought to protect states, Alexander Hamilton, ever the nationalist, supported Gerry's motion but for a very different reason. Hamilton's concern was over the difficulty of the proposed amending mechanism. He pointed out that many had wished for an easier mode in the Articles of Confederation and likewise, "It was equally desirable now that an easy mode should be established for supplying defects which will probably appear in the new System." The proposed mode "was not adequate" as the state legislatures "will not apply for alterations but with a view to increase their own powers." An easier and more balanced way to introduce amendments would utilize the National Legislature, for it, "will be the first to perceive and will be most sensible to the necessity of amendments, and ought also to be empowered, whenever two thirds of each branch should concur to call a Convention" He added that there would be no danger in equipping the national government in this way since the people would finally decide the matter in conventions.[37]

Not only did Gerry and Hamilton see a need to reconsider, but so did Madison as he pointed out the "vagueness" of the terms calling for a Convention, "How was a Convention to be formed? [b]y what rule decide? [w]hat the force of its acts?" These alone were adequate reasons to reconsider. Thus at the behest of Gerry, Hamilton, and Madison the delegates voted to reopen the issue by a vote of nine to one.[38]

Once the matter was reopened Roger Sherman made a proposal that—seemingly aimed at addressing Hamilton's and Gerry's concerns simultaneously—sought to allow the National Legislature to propose amendments so long as no amendment was binding until consented to by "the several states." Wilson, ever concerned about the dangers of requiring unanimous consent for changes—as in the Articles of Confederation—proposed the insertion of "two thirds of" before the words "several states" in Sherman's proposal. When the "two thirds" language was voted down 5 to 6, Wilson proposed three-fourths as a compromise and that level of consensus was accepted in a unanimous vote.[39]

At this point Madison sought to combine all of the concerns raised that day in a comprehensive set of language that incorporated empowering two-thirds of the National Legislature to propose amendments and requiring three-fourths of the states for ratification. Madison's language also allowed either the legislatures or conventions to be used as the mode of ratification; the decision of which mode being left up to Congress.[40] After Madison's proposal was seconded by Hamilton, John Rutledge of South Carolina protested saying that he, "never could agree to give a power by which the articles relating to slaves might be altered by the States not interested in that property and prejudiced against it." To address his concern a provision was added that stipulated no changes to the constitutional provisions on slavery could be made until 1808. This alteration was agreed to and Madison's proposed language was then adopted as amended by a vote of 9-1-1, with New Hampshire divided and Delaware opposed.[41]

Final Debate on Article V

On September 10, the new Constitution was referred to a Committee of Revision and Style for alterations; the committee finished its revisions by the 12 and the convention started working through the revised document. On September 15, the convention got around to addressing the newly dubbed "Article V" proposal.[42]

The first salvo of the debate was fired by Roger Sherman who "expressed his fears" that even three-fourths of the states might use the amending power to harm individual states by either "abolishing them altogether" or "depriving them of their equality in the Senate." He argued that it was reasonable to extend the slave protections in Article V to also include protections "extended so as to provide that no State should be affected in its internal police, or deprived of its equality in the Senate."[43]

George Mason raised another objection altogether. He thought the plan of amending the Constitution was "exceptionable & dangerous," since both modes of alteration depended—the first mode initially and the second ultimately—on Congress. He argued that as such no "amendments of the proper kind" would be able to be obtained by the people if the government became oppressive, "as he verily believed would be the case."[44]

To address Mason's concerns, Gouverneur Morris and Eldbridge Gerry moved to alter Article V to "require a Convention on the application of 2/3 of the states." Madison responded saying he didn't see why Congress wouldn't be as obliged to submit proposals to the states as much as it would to call a convention, but he had no objections to the convention proposal. His only concern—which he was raising for the second time—was that "difficulties might arise as to the form, the quorum" etc. of such a convention. Despite Madison's objections the convention proposal passed without objection.[45]

In addition Sherman and Gerry made consecutive proposals to strike the three-fourths requirement for ratification by convention, but both motions were soundly defeated. At this point Sherman reiterated his concern over the safety of a minority of states against a three-fourths majority, by proposing, "that no State shall without its consent be affected in its internal police, or deprived of its equal suffrage in the Senate."[46] Madison opposed his suggestion commenting that once the delegates set the precedent of such "special provisos," then "every State will insist on them, for their boundaries, exports etc." Again Sherman's proposed changes were voted down. Not to be defeated Sherman then moved to strike out Article V altogether, which David Brearly of New Jersey seconded. Yet again Sherman was defeated. At this point Gouverneur Morris suggested dropping the language about internal police and settling for the following, "that no State, without its consent shall be deprived of its equal suffrage in the Senate." Regarding this compromise Madison's notes read, "This motion being dictated by the circulating murmurs of the small States was agreed to without debate, no one opposing it, or on the question, saying no."

At long last on September 17, the Convention voted to recommend the final document for ratification. Though some prominent members of the convention decided not to sign—for instance, Edmond Randolph who started the whole convention off with the Virginia Plan being one who withheld his signature—the document was forwarded to Congress and ratification. In the final document, Article V read as follows,

> The Congress, whenever two thirds of both Houses shall deem it necessary, shall propose amendments to this Constitution, or, on the Application of the Legislatures of two thirds of the several States, shall call a Convention for proposing Amendments, which, in either Case, shall be valid to all Intents and Purposes, as Part of this Constitution, when ratified by the Legislatures of three fourths of the several States, or by Conventions in three fourths thereof, as the one or the other Mode of Ratification may be proposed by the Congress; Provided that no Amendment which may be made prior to the Year One thousand with hundred and eight shall in any Manner affect the first and fourth Clauses in the Ninth Section of the first Article; and that no State, without its Consent, shall be deprived of it's equal Suffrage in the Senate.[47]

Article V had been born. Agreement on the need for a formal amending procedure seemed to be reached easily enough. The only the details required a bit of debate. Those details were the role of the Congress and the level of consent needed to ratify proposed amendments. Of course the issues of slavery and state equality rose their heads as well, but compromises on those issues were proposed and agreed upon in relatively short order. The most important point of the deliberations came from George Mason and his forceful argument that there will be a need to alter the Constitution and it would best be done in a "easy, regular, and Constitutional way" rather than leave such matters to "chance and violence." Mason's point, which was quickly and easily acceded to, expressed the implicit beliefs of the delegates that Article V would be a perfecting mechanism of the Constitution and a means of maintaining the legal higher law authority of the Constitution all the while empowering the people to maintain control over their form of government. All the seeds of the Imperial Crisis and the lessons of the state constitutional experience seem to be embedded in Mason's argument and ultimately in the design of Article V.

As the Framers of the Constitution completed their work in Philadelphia the real test of their work would be found in the state ratifying conventions. There was stiff opposition to this bold new powerful national government within many of the key states. The Anti-Federalists—as opponents of the Constitution would come to be known—would prove to be formidable adversaries in the ratification conventions. As the Federalists arrived at the conventions—often outnumbered—to do rhetorical battle with the Anti-Federalists they would soon find Article V to be a very helpful element in the newly proposed Constitution. While Article V was meant to be a perfecting mechanism of the new Constitution, it is likely that few Federalists could have anticipated how soon it would be utilized or how useful it would be in the debates over ratification. Article V would provide a very helpful tool for Federalists in absorbing the very potent criticisms of the Anti-Federalists.

The State Ratifying Conventions

During the various ratifying conventions Article V was not the focus of much direct debate, yet when it was brought up it often enjoyed earnest praise and only on rare occasions, criticism. While Article V did not take center stage, its role in perfecting the Constitution immediately became apparent. Not only was Article V an important and essential part of new written Constitution but it would instantly prove to be a vital means of securing ratification of the Constitution.

The opposition to the new Constitution by prominent revolutionary leaders such as Patrick Henry, Samuel Adams, and George Mason foreshadowed the coming struggle for ratification in the state conventions. The new Constitution created in the hot summer heat of Philadelphia, which in effect had created a new national government, was not going to be an easy sell to all of the states. Soon after the Federal Convention adjourned Congress forwarded the new document to the states for ratification by late September, after which the Federalists quickly mobilized and by January 9 five states had already signed on. Delaware, Pennsylvania, New Jersey, Georgia, and Connecticut all ratified early providing a solid foundation upon which the Federalists would attempt to build a national majority and secure the positive ratification of the other states.[48] Yet as more time passed the Anti-Federalist forces grew more organized and stronger and the Federalists faced a long vigorous battle to secure the required nine states.[49]

In their attempt to stem the tide of Federalist momentum and address their fears of an overbearing national government the Anti-Federalists desperately searched for, and found, a compelling argument against the new Constitution. The new document lacked a bill of rights that would secure the rights of individual citizens against a large powerful national state. To address such issues the Anti-Federalists called for a second convention, a convention that would derail not improve the new Constitution.[50] With open talk of altering the new document and perhaps even another convention, the desire for constitutional amendment suddenly became a key issue in several of the important state ratification conventions. In this regard, Article V's provision for amendment proved to be vitally important in the newly proposed Constitution. The existence of a formal, constitutional mode of amending the new document effectively enabled Federalists to parry the powerful thrust of Anti-Federalist appeals for a second convention. While certainly the eventual success of the Federalists, in securing the ratification of the new Constitution, was the result of myriad factors and vital efforts on the part of many, one cannot ignore the crucial role of Article V as a real political alternative to a second convention.[51]

A brief look at discussion and debate over Article V in the state ratifying conventions will further shed light on the immediate usefulness of Article V as well as the strong consensus that Article V was a sound and desirable part of the newly proposed Constitution.

Connecticut: Lauds from Law

While the ratifying conventions spent relatively little time discussing constitutional amendment, Article V did get some attention in Connecticut. In Connecticut, the fifth state to ratify, the new Constitution passed muster over light opposition with a vote of 128 to 40. In the waning moments of the convention as Federalists were summing up their arguments in support of the new Constitution at least one delegate, Richard Law, expressed the importance of Article V in the newly proposed government,

> Mr. President, the important subject before us has been examined so particularly, that I do not expect to add any thing new. As we have been a long time poring upon the defective parts of the Constitution, I think it will not be amiss to pay some attention to its excellences. There is one clause in it which provides a remedy for whatever defects it may have. The clause to which I refer is that which provides that, whenever two thirds of Congress, or a convention to be called at the instance of two thirds of the states, shall propose amendment, and they be agreed to by three fourths of the states, such amendments shall be valid, as part of the Constitution. This is an easy and peaceable way of amending any parts of the Constitution which may be found inconvenient in practice.[52]

Here we see the notion of Article V as a perfecting mechanism or a remedy for the Constitution's potential defects and it would be a recurring theme in the state ratification debates. Beyond this praise for Article V it seemed to play no serious role in the Connecticut debates; this was not the case however in Massachusetts.

Massachusetts: Barrell's Dilemma

Massachusetts, the next state to ratify would prove to be a far more difficult field of battle for the Federalist forces than Connecticut. Massachusetts was an important state economically and politically to the new union and its ratification could prove pivotal to the success of the new Constitution. The Massachusetts ratifying convention convened in the first part of 1788 and lasted for nearly a month from January 9, 1788 to February 6. The convention's length was largely due to Federalist insistence on reviewing the new Constitution clause by clause. As the delegates moved through the document those like James Bowdoin tried to bolster the Federalist cause with a dose of realism, a belief in representative democracy, and the assurance that any defects in the new government would be corrected,

> Like all other human productions, it may be imperfect; but most of the imperfections imputed to it are ideal and unfounded, and the rest are of such a nature that they cannot be certainly known but by the operations of the Constitution; and if, in its operation, it should in any respect be essentially bad, it will be amended in one of the modes prescribed by it. I say, will be amended, because the Constitution is constructed on such principles, that its bad effects, if any such should arise from it, will injure the members of Congress equally with their constituents; and, therefore, both of them must be equally induced to seek for, and effectuate, if possible, the requisite amendments.[53]

When the 5 Article of the document was read to the delegates and opened for discussion, it elicited a couple of responses from Rufus King and Dr. Charles Jarvis. Rufus King rose to give his support for the measure and to chastise critics for not fully realizing the utility of Article V for, "He believed gentlemen had not, in their objections to the Constitution, recollected that this article was a part of it: for many of the arguments of gentlemen were founded on the idea of future amendments being impracticable."[54]

Like Bowdoin, King was trying to communicate the rather simple message that any defects of the new document could be easily remedied using Article V once the new government was running thus undercutting any criticism of the new Constitution as a legitimate reason for not ratifying it. Furthermore, King tried to inspire pride in the new document by pointing out the unique and progressive nature of Article V and its security against abuse by the future government for he had, "Observed on the superior excellence of the proposed Constitution in this particular, and called upon gentlemen to produce an instance, in any other national constitution, where the people has so fair an opportunity to correct any abuse which might take place in the future administration of the government under it."[55] In these ways Article V was a valuable tool in constructing a formidable reply not only to calls for a second convention but also as a response to the rhetorical barrage from Anti-Federalists calling for amendments prior to ratifying the new Constitution.

More extended praise for Article V came from Jarvis who rose immediately after King in order to sing the praises of the proposed amending process:

> I cannot suffer the present article to be passed, without rising to express my entire and perfect approbation of it. Whatever may have been my private opinion of any other part, or whatever faults or imperfections I have remarked, or fancied I have seen in any other instance, here, sir, I have found complete satisfac-

> tion: this has been a resting place, on which I have reposed myself in the fullest security, whenever a doubt has occurred, in considering any other passage in the proposed Constitution.[56]

Like other delegates Jarvis found comfort in Article V for he saw it as the panacea for whatever ills may now, or in the future ail the new nation. Furthermore, he also, like King, emphasized the uniqueness of the amending mechanism as compared to other nations,

> Allow me to say, sir, as far as the narrow limits of my own information extend, I know of no such example. In other countries, sir,—unhappily for mankind,—the history of their respective revolutions has been written in blood; and it is in this only that any great or important change in our political situation has been effected, without public commotions. When we shall have adopted the Constitution before us, we shall have in this article an adequate provision for all the purposes of political reformation.[57]

Jarvis was trying to drive home the reality that, while other nations must rely on violent revolution to alter or replace their government, Article V would allow political reforms to be undertaken in a peaceful manner. Such comments hearken back to arguments by Americans during the Imperial Crisis and the drafting of the state constitutions that consistently compared the chance and violence of regime change and alteration in England and throughout human history. This theme of a reasoned, formal, constitutional means of altering the new regime as juxtaposed against the violent and bloody means of altering past governments is important in understanding the vital role Article V plays in the American constitutional system. Jarvis was not finished with his remarks however,

> I shall not sit down, sir, without repeating, that, as it is clearly more difficult for twelve states to agree to another convention, than for nine to unite in favor of amendments, so it is certainly better to receive the present Constitution, in the hope of its being amended, than it would be to reject it altogether, with perhaps, the vain expectation of obtaining another more agreeable than the present.[58]

In the end, Jarvis tied Article V to what would become a very familiar Federalist argument; that it would be easier to ratify and amend the new Constitution than to obtain amendments via the Articles of Confederation or to attempt a second constitutional convention.

How much of an impact such arguments made on the Anti-Federalists it is hard to surmise, however it seems plausible if not likely that one can see their effects on delegates such as Nathaniel Barrell. Barrell had many concerns about the new document yet voted against the wishes of those who sent him. It seems he largely voted against the instructions of those who sent him because in his judgment there was a desperate need for union and because of the availability of a means to amend the new Constitution. On February 5, the day before Massachusetts ratified, Barrell addressed the convention. After a lengthy list of criticisms of the new Constitution Barrell then tempered his dislike for the document with the following remarks,

> But, sir, although you may perceive, by what I have said, that this is not, in my view, the most perfect system I could wish, yet, as I am possessed with an assurance that the proposed amendments will take place; as I dread the fatal effects of anarchy, as I am convinced the Confederation is essentially deficient, and that it will be more difficult to amend that than to reform this; and as I think *this Constitution*, with all its imperfections, is *excellent*, compared with that, and that it is the best constitution we can now obtain; . . . I am almost tempted to risk their [his constituents] displeasure, and adopt it without their consent.[59]

The internal tension in Barrell is clearly apparent as he finds himself caught between the instructions of his constituents, and the persuasive arguments of his colleagues. His desire for union is clear, but his reservations regarding the new Constitution are strong. Nevertheless, the clear option to amend the constitution combined with Barrell's intense desire for union fostered a powerful argument for him to support the Federalists. Barrell ended up being only one in seventeen delegates from York County to support the Constitution. His example illustrates powerfully the ability of the Federalists to persuade Anti-Federalists to the genius of the new Constitution and it shows how helpful it was to have the prudent amending options found in Article V.

Finally, on February 6, the last day of the Massachusetts convention, delegates were making their last ditch efforts and summing up their arguments. The Rev. Samuel Stillman in a lengthy recap of his position stated the following,

> Having thus considered several of the checks to the powers of Congress, which are interwoven with the Constitution, we will now suppose the worst that can take place in consequence of its adoption: I mean, that it shall be found in some of its parts oppressive to the people; still we have this *dernier ressort*—it may be amended. It is not, like the laws of the Mede and Persians, immutable. The fifth article provides for amendments.[60]

Thus, in such a key state as Massachusetts a minor if important recurring theme was the excellence of the new Constitution with regards to future alterations. Federalist delegates sought to make it clear that any and all criticisms could be dealt with in a regular, peaceful, and effective manner by formal process laid out in Article V. The real impact of such arguments may never be reliably assessed, but it is quite clear that Article V gave Federalist delegates the rhetorical ammunition to silence the guns of Anti-Federalist discontent that sought to tear the new document apart with volley after volley of criticism. In the end Massachusetts would narrowly ratify by a vote of 187 to 168; there was only a small contingent 10 swing votes separating success and disaster. Such a victory was notable given some pre-convention predictions estimated that there would initially be 192 votes against and 144 for the new Constitution.[61]

The Massachusetts ratification was a great victory for the Federalist forces, and Maryland and South Carolina would follow that spring with a ratification of their own. This brought the ratification count up to eight states, one state shy of the number needed for ratification. However the ninth and final state would be difficult to come by.[62]

Virginia: The Clash of Titans

While the loss of Massachusetts was a big blow to the Anti-Federalist cause they were prepared to make their last stand in New York and Virginia. These two large states were vital to the new union for many political and commercial reasons, not the least of which was that their exclusion would prevent the new government from enjoying a geographically contiguous territory. Anti-Federalist forces were strong in both states and the political weight of New York and Virginia could perhaps prevent official ratification and precipitate the need for a second convention.[63]

The critical Virginia convention set the stage for a clash of political titans. Patrick Henry, George Mason, James Monroe, and Richard Henry Lee opposed the new Constitution on one side while Edmund Randolph, George Wythe, John Marshall, and James Madison favored the Constitution on the Federalists side.[64]

Patrick Henry v. James Madison

Despite the wealth of talent arrayed on both sides of the battle for ratification, Patrick Henry reportedly dominated the affair with lengthy speeches, rhetorical flair, and political acumen. As one historian put it,

> Like a legendary swordsman of the people, single-handedly fending off an entire royal guard, Henry held the field for twenty-three days against future presidents, chief justices, cabinet officers, senators, diplomats.[65]

Patrick Henry drew on every ounce of political wisdom to prevent ratification, and one part of his strategy was to attack the viability of Article V in order to thwart the Federalist strategy of postponing amendments until after ratification, as was done in Massachusetts. Thus, early on in the convention (June 5) Henry sought to deal a deadly blow to the notion that Article V was a viable alternative to conditional ratification or a second convention. In a lengthy speech, Henry attacked Article V as a difficult and undemocratic procedure (themes that contemporary critics often rely upon in attacking Article V). Henry argued that, "To encourage us to adopt it, they tell us that there is a plain, easy way of getting amendments. When I come to contemplate this part, I suppose that I am mad, or that my countrymen are so. The way to amendment is, in my conception, shut."[66] Amendment after ratification was not viable according to Henry because it requires supermajorities and it would rely on the character of those in power, and Henry was not optimistic about the possibility of men of sound character being in federal or state office. To Henry the new national government, once in power, will not allow any amendments that threaten its status; "However uncharitable it may appear, yet I must tell my opinion—that the most unworthy characters may get into power, and prevent the introduction of amendments . . .

but what is destructive and mischievous, is, that three fourths of the state legislatures, or of the state conventions, must concur in the amendments when proposed!"[67] Thus, in his initial volley Henry revealed his basic distrust of those who will inhabit the state legislatures and Congress. Building on this assumption he painted a bleak prospect for reaching the supermajority targets required by Article V for amendment. Continuing his valiant assault Henry elaborated upon these themes, "In such numerous bodies, there must necessarily be some designing, bad men. To suppose that so large a number as three fourths of the states will concur, is to suppose that they will possess genius, intelligence, and integrity, approaching to miraculous."[68]

Even more than his fear of "designing, bad men," Henry feared a tyranny of a minority due to the three-fourths requirement since four of the smallest states, "that do not collectively contain one tenth part of the population of the United States, may obstruct the most salutary and necessary amendments."[69] Another concern for Henry was that there would be competing amendments and not enough states could agree on the same amendments.[70] In essence Henry views the supermajority requirement as undemocratic, "A bare majority in these four small states may hinder the adoption of amendments; so that we may fairly and justly conclude that one twentieth part of the American people may prevent the removal of the most grievous inconveniences and oppression, by refusing, to accede to amendments."[71]

Building to a crescendo of rhetorical flourish Henry drove home his distrust of the individual members of Congress and the legislature as he elaborated on his argument that supermajorities are undemocratic. For Henry Article V will allow a small minority of the population to hold reasonable alterations hostage.

> A trifling minority may reject the most salutary amendments. Is this an easy mode of securing the public liberty? It is, sir, a most fearful situation, when the most contemptible minority can prevent the alteration of the most oppressive government; for it may, in many respects, prove to be such. Is this the spirit of republicanism?
>
> What, sir, is the genius of democracy? Let me read that clause of the bill of rights of Virginia which relates to this[72] . . . This, sir, is the language of democracy—that a majority of the community have a right to alter government when found to be oppressive. But how different is the genius of your new Constitution from this! How different from the sentiments of freemen, that a contemptible minority can prevent the good of the majority![73]

Again this recurring theme of the tension between the limits of constitutionalism and the sweeping nature of popular sovereignty arises. Henry seems to prefer no constitutional limits on the ability of a simple majority to alter their system of government. For Henry it is dangerous for the majority to grant extensive powers to the few and then bind itself to a process that allows the few to block the wishes of the many. Nearing the end of his address Henry drew deeply on his rhetorical talents to paint a stark picture of government oppression, for if the Federalists are allowed to succeed liberty will be the ultimate victim,

> If, then, gentlemen, standing on this ground, are come to that point, that they are willing to bind themselves and their posterity to be oppressed, I am amazed and inexpressibly astonished. If this be the opinion of the majority, I must submit; but to me, sir, it appears perilous and destructive. I cannot help thinking so. Perhaps it may be the result of my age. These may be feelings natural to a man of my years, when the American spirit has left him, and his mental powers, like the members of the body, are decayed. If, sir, amendments are left to the twentieth, or tenth part of the people of America, your liberty is gone forever. . . . The honorable gentleman who presides told us that, to prevent abuses in our government, we will assemble in Convention, recall our delegated powers, and punish our servants for abusing the trust reposed in them. O sir, we should have fine times, indeed, if, to punish tyrants, it were only sufficient to assemble the people! . . . Will the oppressor let go the oppressed? Was there ever an instance? Can the annals of mankind exhibit one single example where rulers overcharged with power willingly let go the oppressed, though solicited and requested most earnestly? The application for amendments will therefore be fruitless. Sometimes, the oppressed have got loose by one of those bloody struggles that desolate a country; but a willing relinquishment of power is one of those things which human nature never was, nor ever will be, capable of.[74]

One can imagine Henry pacing the floor, pounding the table, emphasizing every point, altering the pitch of his voice, mustering every oratory skill to quickly and efficiently knock out Article V as an effective tool of the Federalists. He knew that as in Massachusetts, Article V would be employed in the field against Anti-Federalist calls for a second convention and he was taking pains to remove Article V from the Federalist arsenal. He took careful aim at its reliance on super majorities as undemocratic, the inevitable corruption of the legislative bodies tasked with executing the plan for amendment, and the natural tendencies of national governments to use any and all means of extinguishing liberty at the expense of the people. One historian has described Henry's performance this way,

> Spectators and delegates alike sat frozen, hypnotized, as Henry ranged on and on, now thundering, now whispering, now threatening, now pleading. With masterful skill he found everyone's most vulnerable spot—his fears, principles, passions, prejudices—and pierced him there. . . . He portrayed the coming destruction of liberties so vividly that one spectator 'involuntarily felt his wrists to assure himself that the fetters were not already pressing his flesh. Even so worldly a pair of observers as Robert and Gouverneur Morris . . . sat awed by this man as if by one demonically inspired. Glumly, Madison wrote Hamilton that though the Federalists had a majority of three or four delegates, he feared that Henry would carry the day.[75]

Due to the efforts of Anti-Federalists such as Henry, the Federalists certainly had their work ahead of them. While many Federalists responded to Henry's efforts, none other than James Madison rose to confront the attack on Article V levied by Henry's formidable verbal batteries the day prior. On June 6, the day after Henry's display, James Madison, no doubt in his calm cool analytical manner, returned fire in defense of Article V and the ratification of the new Constitution. First, Madison chastised Henry for his rather vague references to tyranny and unscrupulous legislative bodies. Furthermore, Madison demanded hat Henry answer with specifics when making such accusations,

> He [responding to Henry] told us that this Constitution ought to be rejected because it endangered the public liberty, in his opinion, in many instances. Give me leave to make one answer to that observation: Let the dangers which this system is supposed to be replete with be clearly pointed out: if any dangerous and unnecessary powers he given to the general legislature, let them be plainly demonstrated, and let us not rest satisfied with general assertions of danger, without examination. If powers be necessary, apparent danger is not a sufficient reason against conceding them.[76]

Second, Madison attacked Henry's notions that tyranny will emerge in a quick and forceful manner,

> He has suggested that licentiousness has seldom produced the loss of liberty; but that the tyranny of rulers has almost always effected it. Since the general civilization of mankind, I believe there are more instances of the abridgment of the freedom of the people by gradual and silent encroachments of those in power, than by violent and sudden usurpations; but, on a candid examination of history, we shall find that turbulence, violence, and abuse of power, by the majority trampling on the rights of the minority, have produced factions and commotions, which, in republics, have, more frequently than any other cause, produced despotism. If we go over the whole history of ancient and modern republics, we shall find their destruction to have generally resulted from those causes.[77]

Madison noted that the United States was in danger of majority tyranny as was apparent in Rhode Island and in Massachusetts with Shays' Rebellion, but, "Perhaps, in the progress of this discussion, it will appear that the only possible remedy for those evils, and means of preserving and protecting the principles of republicanism, will be found in that very system which is now exclaimed against as the parent of oppression."[78] Here is Madison's articulation of the problem that faces all democracies. In chapter 1, it was compared to the dilemma of Odysseus as he passed the island of the sirens. The sweetness of the principles of republicanism—like the sweetness of the Sirens' song—can only be purchased at the price of binding majority will in certain respects in order to prevent the majority tyranny that so often destroys republics. What was needed was a constitution that bound rulers and the people alike.

Madison then criticized Henry for ignoring the real problems and crisis facing the young nation, for Henry seemed to gloss over the current real crises in the states and instead invented a series of hypothetical crises,

> I must confess I have not been able to find his usual consistency in the gentleman's argument on this occasion. He informs us that the people of the country are at perfect repose,—that is, every man enjoys the fruits of his labor peaceably and securely, and that every thing is in perfect tranquillity and safety. I wish sincerely, sir, this were true. If this be their happy situation, why has every state acknowledged the contrary? Why were deputies from all the states sent to the general Convention? Why have complaints of national and individual distresses been echoed and reechoed throughout the continent? Why has our general government been so shamefully disgraced, and our Constitution violated? Wherefore have laws been made to authorize a change, and wherefore are we now assembled here? A federal government is formed for the protection of its individual members. Ours has attacked itself with impunity. Its authority has been disobeyed and despised.[79]

Here Madison made clear that indeed it was democratic excess that precipitated the very need for the Philadelphia Convention, not the oligarchy of the few. Madison's subtle attack on Henry's demagoguery was the perfectly cool analytical counterpoise to the heated ferocity of Henry's display. Once Madison had repelled Henry's main assault on the Constitution, he immediately counterattacked to repel Henry's attempt to outflank the Federalists on the issue of constitutional amendment,

> I think I perceive a glaring inconsistency in another of his arguments. He complains of this Constitution, because it requires the consent of at least three fourths of the states to introduce amendments which shall be necessary for the happiness of the people. The assent of so many he urges as too great an obstacle to the admission of salutary amendments, which, he strongly insists, ought to be at the will of a bare majority. We hear this argument, at the very moment we are called upon to assign reasons for proposing a constitution which puts it in the power of nine states to abolish the present inadequate, unsafe, and pernicious Confederation! In the first case, he asserts that a majority ought to have the power of altering the government, when found to be inadequate to the security of public happiness. In the last case, he affirms that even three fourths of the community have not a right to alter a government which experience has proved to be subversive of national felicity! nay, that the most necessary and urgent alterations cannot be made without the absolute unanimity of all the states! Does not the thirteenth article of the Confederation expressly require that no alteration shall be made without the unanimous consent of all the states?[80]

Here Madison turns the tables on Henry for if Henry had his way the Articles of Confederation would remain intact and would require unanimous consent. This line of argument strikes at Patrick Henry's very credibility on this issue. Sensing that Henry's position was in full retreat Madison pursued with zeal, and he did not hesitate to leave the reputation of Rhode Island "that little member" in his wake as he attacked the unanimity requirement of the Articles which Henry implicitly defended:

> Could any thing in theory be more perniciously improvident and injudicious than this submission of the will of the majority to the most trifling minority?

> Have not experience and practice actually manifested this theoretical inconvenience to be extremely impolitic? Let me mention one fact, which I conceive must carry conviction to the mind of any one: the smallest state in the Union has obstructed every attempt to reform the government; that little member has repeatedly disobeyed and counteracted the general authority; nay, has even supplied the enemies of its country with provisions. Twelve states had agreed to certain improvements which were proposed, being thought absolutely necessary to preserve the existence of the general government; but as these improvements, though really indispensable, could not, by the Confederation, be introduced into it without the consent of every state, the refractory dissent of that little state prevented their adoption. The inconveniences resulting from this requisition, of unanimous concurrence in alterations in the Confederation, must be known to every member in this Convention; it is therefore needless to remind them of them. Is it not self-evident that a trifling minority ought not to bind the majority? Would not foreign influence be exerted with facility over a small minority? Would the honorable gentleman agree to continue the most radical defects in the old system, because the petty state of Rhode Island would not agree to remove them?[81]

Here Madison took away Henry's argument concerning the undemocratic nature of Article V by pointing out that Henry's opposition to the new Constitution in favor of the Articles of Confederation violated the very principle he was trying to uphold. As Madison pointed out, the required unanimity of the Articles left the union victim to the whims of that "petty state of Rhode Island."

Madison further addressed Henry's objection to the three quarters supermajority by pointing out that the new government is not a pure national government, but a mix of confederal and national governments. As such it would be inappropriate to empower a pure national majority, but rather a collection of state majorities is in order, unless one wants to diminish the role of the states *as states* in the new government,

> Who are the parties to it? The people—but not the people as composing one great body; but the people as composing thirteen sovereignties. Were it, as the gentleman asserts, a consolidated government, the assent of a majority of the people would be sufficient for its establishment; and, as a majority have adopted it already, the remaining states would be bound by the act of the majority, even if they unanimously reprobated it. Were it such a government as is suggested, it would be now binding on the people of this state, without having had the privilege of deliberating upon it.[82]

Madison makes clear that the people are indeed sovereign and that is the basis of the Constitution, but their will is expressed separately through the thirteen states. It seems that for Madison there is wisdom in maintaining these local attachments even as they move to create truly national institutions.

To address the criticism that Congress will have too large of a role in the amendment process Madison sought to bolster the convention method as a viable option.

> The Committee will see that there is another mode provided [for amendment], besides that which originates with Congress. . . . [convention method]. . . . The conventions which shall be so called will have their deliberations confined to a few points; no local interest to divert their attention; nothing but the necessary alterations. They will have many advantages over the last Convention. No experiments to devise; the general and fundamental regulations being already laid down.[83]

Thus, Madison expressed great confidence in the convention provision in Article V, which is interesting considering it had never been used. Madison was quite clear than any convention that would be called would have a very limited mandate and fears of a runaway convention are unfounded. Plus, while Madison did not address it here, any proposed amendments from a convention would still have to pass the muster of three-fourths of the states for ratification.

In the end, Madison in his understated methodical manner effectively rebutted Henry's energetic attacks on Article V. After this battle between Henry and Madison, Henry said little more concerning Article V for the duration of the convention. On June 9 Patrick Henry again briefly questioned the feasibility of the people's ability to actually amend their constitution, citing England and Ireland as examples and again citing the corruption of elected officials in preventing serious amendments.[84] Henry argued that power becomes so entrenched that "nothing but bloody war can alter them."[85] Henry seemed to fear the consolidation of power so much that he believed altering power relationships short of the use of force was impossible. In the end, Henry seemed to lack a basic faith in the very concept of amendment and the power of the people to use regular procedures to alter their government.

In a direct response to one of Henry's lengthy addresses Edmund Randolph—who opposed the new Constitution at the Philadelphia Convention, but now supported its ratification—rose to address many of the concerns raised by Henry. In his reply, Randolph briefly took care to dispute Henry's calls for amendments *prior* to ratification rather than after. Henry argued that amendments *after* ratification would be impossible and therefore must be demanded before ratification. Randolph, in response, pointed out that the states which had previously ratified would no doubt take offense at Virginia's demands for amendments prior to ratification and Virginia would be left out of the union. Besides, he argued there is a means provided for to amend the constitution *by the states themselves* so there is no need to press for something so disruptive before the new government is in operation,

> As there is a mode in the Constitution itself to procure amendments, not by reference to the people, but by the interposition of the state legislatures, will the people of Virginia bind themselves not to enter into the Union till amendments shall have been obtained? I refer it to any gentleman here, whether this may not entirely exclude us from the Union.[86]

John Marshall also saw fit to point out that Henry's arguments contradicted themselves, for if Henry felt that it was impossible for three-fourths of the states to agree after ratification how could he argue it was possible for *all* the states to agree before ratification.[87] Furthermore, Marshall saw great flexibility in the proposed amendment process and did not see why it shouldn't alleviate any fears Henry and other Anti-Federalists had about the new government,

> If you adopt it, what shall restrain you from amending it, if, in trying it, amendments shall be found necessary? The government is not supported by force, but depending on our free will. When experience shall show us any inconveniences, we can then correct it. But until we have experience on the subject, amendments, as well as the Constitution itself, are to try. Let us try it, and keep our hands free to change it when necessary. If it be necessary to change government, let us change that government which has been found to be defective. The difficulty we find in amending the Confederation will not be found in amending this Constitution. Any amendments, in the system before you, will not go to a radical change; a plain way is pointed out for the purpose.[88]

The common sense of Marshall's remarks showed Article V to be a prudent insurance against in "inconveniences" that might appear once the Constitution was in force.

Difficulty of Article V Revisited

On June 12, Mr. William Grayson rose to echo the sentiments of Patrick Henry with a brief note that, "The consent of so many states is necessary to introduce amendment, that I fear they will with great difficulty be obtained."[89] Also on June 12, Mr. Pendleton gave a measured response that pointed to Article V as an aspect of the new Constitution that gave him comfort despite certain misgivings about the proposed government,

> When I sat down to read that paper, I did not read it with an expectation that it was perfect, and that no man would object to it. I had learned, sir, that an expectation of such perfection in any institute devised by man, was as vain as the search for the philosopher's stone. I discovered objections—I thought I saw there some sown seeds of disunion—not in the immediate operation of the government, but which might happen in some future time. I wish amendments to remove these.[90]

Pendleton had serious reservations about the new document, and he desired that changes be made to the new government but he did not see these problems as fatal to the cause of ratification of the new Constitution, for it wisely provided for its own alteration,

> But these remote possible errors may be eradicated by the amendatory clause in the Constitution. I see no danger in making the experiment, since the system itself points out an easy mode of removing any errors which shall have been experienced . . . The Constitution points out a plain and ordinary method of reform, without any disturbance or convulsions whatever. I therefore think that we ought to ratify it, in order to secure the Union, and trust to this method for removing those inconveniences which experience shall point out.[91]

Ultimately, the notion that Article V was a perfecting mechanism for the Constitution became increasingly clear. Pendleton implored the convention to trust Article V as a solution for whatever problems the delegates saw lurking in the new Constitution. Contrary to Henry's warnings of "force" and violence as the only means of altering the new government Pendleton found Article V able to achieve change "without any disturbance or convulsions whatever" and an aspect of the Constitution that seems to enjoy his full confidence.

On June 17, Edmond Randolph also relayed that while he had some misgivings about the new Constitution, he believed that amendments after ratification were quite possible and securing the Union immediately was more important than risking separation while searching for perfection now,

> I would depend on the present actual feeling of the people of America, to introduce any amendment which may be necessary. I repeat it again, though I do not reverence the Constitution, that its adoption is necessary to avoid the storm which is hanging over America, and that no greater curse can befall her than the dissolution of the political connection between the states . . . I ask gentlemen whether, as eight states have adopted it, it be not safer to adopt it, and rely on the probability of obtaining amendments, than, by a rejection, to hazard a breach of the Union?[92]

Randolph who had opposed the new Constitution as the Philadelphia Convention wound down, had come to support the new document if even for prudential reasons. Clearly Article V had been a factor in Randolph's new found support for the Constitution.

In the end, Virginia ratified the Constitution by narrow margins. No doubt the ratification of the ninth state, New Hampshire, prior to the close of the Virginia convention eased the decision of some delegates as they did not want to be left out of the union. While certainly many factors contributed to the decision to ratify, the existence of an amending provision in the new Constitution definitely provided solace to those who had reservations. In addition, the Federalists were adept at using the Article V option to blunt the arguments for a new convention or for amendments prior to the new Constitution. In light of contemporary criticisms regarding Article V's difficulty it is interesting to note the very same debate was engaged in at the Virginia convention with numerous delegates defending the prudence and the ease of Article V.

Virginia's ratification was a great victory for the Federalists and its ratification had ripple effects in New York. To be sure, Virginia's decision to ratify did not ensure New York doing likewise but nevertheless the decisions of the politically powerful neighbor to the south couldn't help but impact the proceedings in New York.

New York: Hamilton's Stage, Smith's Prudence

In New York the Anti-Federalist forces were well organized as they had been mobilizing since the middle of the Federal Convention.[93] Anti-Federalists composed around two-thirds of the state convention, but they did not reject the Constitution outright for fear of "bringing matters to a crisis" between New York and the other states that had ratified.[94] Anti-Federalists were also concerned that outright rejection could lead the counties in southern New York to break away from the northern part of the state and join the union.[95] Thus, there were political incentives for the Anti-Federalists to at least give a hearing to the Constitution. Due to Anti-Federalist strength, there was no impetus for them to move quickly on ratifying the Constitution, but rather they were content to wait and see what New Hampshire or Virginia were going to do. Many were confident that Virginia would only ratify upon condition of a second Federal Convention.[96]

The New York convention convened on June 17 in Poughkeepsie and it began with a clause-by-clause debate through the Constitution. The Anti-Federalists led by Melancton Smith, Samuel Jones, John Lansing, Thomas Tredwell, and George Clinton, were content to force the Federalists, led by Alexander Hamilton, John Jay, and Robert Livingston, to futilely debate each clause secure in the knowledge that they had the votes to defeat ratification.[97] On June 24, the convention received news of New Hampshire's ratification. Even though this was the ninth state to ratify, thus triggering the official ratification of the Constitution, it made little impact on the deliberations in New York, for the Anti-Federalists were still confident in their belief that Virginia would not unconditionally ratify.[98] Without Virginia and New York, the stability and security of the union would be jeopardized and the other states would have to compromise given the importance of the two states.

A week later, the deliberations would take a turn that the Anti-Federalists were not prepared for. On July 2, the New York Convention received news of Virginia's unconditional ratification and the gravity and implications of this act threw the Anti-Federalists into a chaotic and confused state that would inevitably result in New York's unconditional ratification.[99] New York was now isolated and Anti-Federalists were now without any substantial ally in their fight against ratification. New York scrambled to assess the new realities of its position and quickly moved to act. In short, news of the Virginia ratification triggered a scramble of hurried debates in New York with the deliberations moving quickly towards a decision. Likely due to the haste, little record of these last debates was preserved.[100]

The fear of isolation from the rest of the states both politically and militarily seemed to play a large role in the deliberations and the convention's ultimate decision to ratify. For instance, Federalist delegate, Robert Livingston aptly expressed concerns over how New York would defend itself if left out of the union. First, New York's ports were on islands near Connecticut and New Jersey and would be hard to defend. Second, to the northeast was Vermont which had a "brave and hardy body of men" and New York had found itself with war with this state in the past and could be again.[101] Third, to the northwest were British posts with strong forces, and hostile Indians. Furthermore, the Hudson River cut the state in half and made it very difficult to move troops and defend the entire state. He ended by expressing the need for a strong central government that was supreme over central affairs mixed with local governments supreme over local affairs.[102]

Melancton Smith was considered to be the most well spoken and active of the Anti-Federalist camp at the convention and he acquitted himself well during the deliberations. However, according to one observer Alexander Hamilton still bested Smith on nearly every issue.[103] Hamilton was prepared and knowledgeable and seemed to have thought through every implication of any question raised by the opposition.[104] In the end Hamilton was able to win Melanction Smith over to ratification and the New York convention seemed to be more of a personal triumph for Hamilton than any other convention was for any single man.[105]

In the end, New York narrowly ratified on July 26 with a vote of 30 to 27 together with a list of recommended amendments to the new Constitution. The ratification also included language that they were ratifying with "full confidence" (not upon condition) that until a second Federal Convention should be called proposing amendments certain specified state rights claimed by New York should not be interfered with.[106]

While the record of New York's ratification debates is sparse, it does seem that the possibility of achieving amendment to the new Constitution contributed at least in part to building a consensus in favor of ratification. Certainly the "snowball" effect of ten states having already ratified and legitimate concerns about the dangerous isolation of the state should New York not ratify were powerful forces in that convention's decision to accept the new document. However, the existence of a reasonable amending mechanism seemed to play a part in the minds of key delegates, such as Smith, by allowing them to vote for ratification while maintaining the hope of still achieving key alterations to the new government.

For instance, there is an interesting exchange of letters between Melancton Smith and a Nathan Dane, a Hancock supporter from Massachusetts, regarding whether or not the New York convention should ratify with or without conditions.[107] In these letters Smith revealed that he thought that Virginia's ratification made it impossible for New York to put conditions on its ratification.

Eight days later on July 23, Smith rose to address the New York convention. He reiterated that he still had grave concerns about the newly proposed Constitution and he had sincerely hoped to achieve amendments to the defective Constitution prior to its ratification, but since Virginia's ratification he knew this was unattainable.[108] However, he had now decided that ratification was a necessity and that,

> He should herafter pursue his important and favorite object of ammendments, with equal zeal as before, but in a practicable way; which was only in the mode prescribed by the Constitution.[109]

Smith feared that a conditional ratification may result in New York not even being seated by the first Congress and he made it clear that he would vote against any proposition which would not be received as a ratification of the Constitution by the new government. Here again was a prominent Anti-Federalist leader who was now arguing for his state to ratify and he is taking some comfort in the fact that the new Constitution does have a regular means altering the document after its acceptance. The existence of Article V allowed him in good conscience to support the new Constitution and still press for the amendments he felt were of critical importance.

North Carolina: Iredell's Praise

Unlike the extended focus on Article V that the deliberations in Virginia inspired, North Carolina spent little time discussing the measure. North Carolina voters had overwhelmingly sent Anti-Federalist delegates to the convention where they more than doubled the number of pro-Constitution delegates.[110] Not surprisingly North Carolina rejected the Constitution and would not ratify until a full year later, long after the new government was in operation and George Washington had been elected President of the United States. Nevertheless despite the outcome of the North Carolina convention there was some discussion on Article V and the process of amendment that is worth examining.

On June 28, in defense of the proposed Constitution, Mr. James Iredell spoke eloquently to the issue of maintaining liberty and the necessity of both fostering the vigilance of the people as well as equipping them with a means of correcting the government,

> The only real security of liberty, in any country, is the jealousy and circumspection of the people themselves. Let them be watchful over their rulers. Should they find a combination against their liberties, and all other methods appear insufficient to preserve them, they have, thank God, an ultimate remedy. That power which created the government can destroy it. Should the government, on trial, be found to want amendments, those amendments can be made in a regular method, in a mode prescribed by the Constitution itself.[111]

A vigilant people and a means of correction is essential according to Iredell, and as the new government provides for such alterations thus Americans should not fear trusting themselves to the new government. He points out that other states have seen fit to trust their futures to the new government while also recommending alterations that can be easily adopted through Article V, "A constitutional mode of altering the Constitution itself is, perhaps, what has never been known among mankind before. We have this security, in addition to the natural watchfulness of the people, which I hope will never be found wanting."[112]

Although Iredell seemed to be the only delegate concerned with the unique ability and opportunity that Article V afforded Americans in their pursuit of good government, his comments are an eloquent defense of the measure and the importance that he seemed to place upon it are worth noting. In fact later in the convention, as the delegates were specifically examining Article V, Iredell addressed the unique and important nature of the proposed amending process,

> Mr. Chairman, this is a very important clause. In every other constitution of government that I have ever heard or read of, no provision is made for necessary amendments. The misfortune attending most constitutions which have been deliberately formed, has been, that those who formed them thought their wisdom equal to all possible contingencies, and that there could be no error in what they did. The gentlemen who framed this Constitution thought with much more diffidence of their capacities; and, undoubtedly, without a provision for amendment it would have been more justly liable to objection, and the characters of its framers would have appeared much less meritorious. [113]

On one level, Article V testifies to the wisdom of the Philadelphia Convention in their acknowledgement that their proposed Constitution was not perfect and as such they had the foresight to provide for an orderly means of alteration. He continues,

> This, indeed, is one of the greatest beauties of the system, and should strongly recommend it to every candid mind. The Constitution of any government which cannot be regularly amended when its defects are experienced, reduces the people to this dilemma—they must either submit to its oppressions, or bring about amendments, more or less, by a civil war. Happy this, the country we live in![114]

Iredell recognized that Article V represents an advance in the science of government. As he reformulated the undesirable dilemma between oppression and civil war that Blackstone had laid out under the English constitution, he also recognized the invaluable contribution of Article V that provides the people with a prudent emancipation from this political quandary. Furthermore, Iredell pointed out that not only does Article V provide a critical means of altering the new government, but it does so in a prudent manner that balances the need for ease of change while maintaining stability and drawing on the "general sense of the people."

> The Constitution before us, if it be adopted, can be altered with as much regularity, and as little confusion, as any act of Assembly; not, indeed, quite so easily, which would be extremely impolitic; but it is a most happy circumstance, that there is a remedy in the system itself for its own fallibility, so that alterations can without difficulty be made, agreeable to the general sense of the people.[115]

Iredell also found its use of the legislatures adequate to the needs of the young country. One can't help but remark at the difference between Patrick

Henry's distrust of the legislatures and Congress as opposed to Iredell's faith in the legislature's ability to reflect the opinions of the people,

> By referring this business to the legislatures, expense would be saved; and in general, it may be presumed, they would speak the genuine sense of the people. It may, however, on some occasions, be better to consult an immediate delegation for that special purpose. This is therefore left discretionary. It is highly probable that amendments agreed to in either of these methods would be conducive to the public welfare, when so large a majority of the states consented to them. And in one of these modes, amendments that are now wished for may, in a short time, be made to this Constitution by the states adopting it.[116]

Iredell also places a degree of faith in the convention method of amendment and argued that both methods provide a flexibility that should be admired and embraced.

Later in his address, Iredell also remarked on the compromise clauses of Article V were prudent concessions, that were made to certain states in order to achieve the greater goal of union.[117] The only other direct mention of the amendment provision was an exchange on whether or not the states' call for a constitutional convention was optional or mandatory on the part of Congress. Iredell assured his colleagues that,

> it was very evident that it did not depend on the will of Congress; for that the legislatures of two thirds of the states were authorized to make application for calling a convention to propose amendments, and, on such application, it is provided that Congress shall call such convention, so that they will have no option.[118]

While Iredell's efforts were in vain with respect to North Carolina's initial attempt at ratification, his arguments in defense of Article V illustrate the degree to which some delegates saw the new amending mechanism as a highly beneficial aspect of the new document. Furthermore, men like Iredell appreciated its novelty in the history of human governments and as such sought to highlight this prudent and advantageous addition to the new Constitution.

Conclusion

Clearly, Article V played an understated yet vital role in the state ratification debates. It was a vital tool in the Federalists' efforts to blunt the strong push by the Anti-Federalists to insist on another convention, or that amendments be made prior to ratification. One can merely speculate on the success of the ratification effort if the Federalists were unable to channel the Anti-Federalists' popular and forceful arguments, in favor of perfecting amendments, into the arms of Article V and its promise of orderly, peaceful, and popularly sanctioned alterations to the proposed Constitution. Given the very close votes in the Massachusetts, Virginia, and New York conventions, one would certainly not like the odds of immediate ratification if the Federalists did not have a ready and effective means of absorbing the push of the Anti-Federalists on the issue of amendments.

During the state convention debates the Federalist defense of the new Constitution in general, and Article V in particular, hinged on several prevailing arguments. First, they continually pointed out the advantages of a regular, formal, agreed upon mode for altering the new Constitution as opposed to the chaos and uncertainty of trying to alter a government that does not formally provide for such alterations. Once again, this was an important point: the former colonies had experienced the constricting nature of an English constitution that did not allow for orderly or formal alterations to the basic power relationships of the government structure. In addition, most delegates were learned enough to realize that the promise of government alteration without the prospect of bloodshed was a unique opportunity in human history. Related to this point is the fact that several of the delegates that expressed concerns with the new Constitution took comfort in the existence of a peaceable way to make alterations. A formal Constitutional means of tapping the constituent power of the people without requiring great convulsions or the use of force was very reassuring to those who had serious reservations about the newly proposed government.

Second, the Federalists seemed to believe that the supermajority requirements were a judicious balance between the extreme constrictions of the unanimity requirement embodied in the Articles of Confederation and the prospect of simple majorities abusing such a fundamental power within the context of a Constitutional system.[119] While there was some protest over the three-quarters requirement by some, the general sentiment seemed to lean towards accepting the supermajority requirement as a means of ensuring a national consensus without binding the whole union to the whims of one or a few imprudent states. In fact despite the supermajority requirements, many of the delegates that addressed the issue referred to the means of amendment as an "easy" mode of amendment and seemingly foresaw little problems with obtaining amendments that were truly found to be reasonable and necessary by the general public.

Third, several delegates expressed faith in state legislatures' ability to represent the views of the people. They either specifically mentioned the legislatures as able to fulfill this role, or more implicitly expressed confidence in that the general *will of the people,* would result in amendments when needed. Fourth, and related, a couple of delegates (one of which was James Madison) expressed a specific confidence in the convention method of amendment. They seemed to view this as a promising means of mobilizing the people more directly without the possible distorting effects that legislative bodies may produce from time to time.

Fifth, the delegates' confidence in the legislatures, or the conventions, was simply reflective of their deeper philosophical commitment to the sovereignty of the people and the importance of empowering them to alter the new government in a sufficiently deliberative setting. It is important to reiterate the degree to which Article V and the amending procedure were seen as a unique expression of the people's constitutive powers. It was essential for the founding generation that Article V would reflect this philosophical commitment in real political terms by using political institutions designed to foster the requisite amount of deliberation. The debates in the state ratifying conventions give evidence that the delegates had full confidence in the ability of Article V to reflect the constitutive will of the people and provide a democratically legitimate means of improving the Constitution.

Sixth, Madison alone pointed out that the mode of amendment reflected the mixed nature of the new system and its unique blend of state and national power. Utilizing the states as states and allowing Congress a role were critical supports to the new federal government that had been created. As such the mode of amendment is a crucial Constitutional support for the American brand of federalism that has developed in the years since.

Lastly, it was important to note the level of deliberation that did take place at the conventions. Principled arguments based on reason were exchanged and minds were changed. The ratification debates in the states modeled the manner in which the people could assemble and debate matters of the utmost importance and then exercise reflection and choice in their governing forms. In the end, the historical record shows Article V to be a vital part of American Constitutionalism and it was repeatedly stated to be a remedy for the imperfections of the new Constitution.

Notes

1. Jonathan Elliot, ed. *The Debates In the Several State Conventions On the Adoption of the Federal Constitution, as Recommended by the General Convention at Philadelphia, in 1787*, vol. 4, (Philadelphia: J. B. Lipincott Company, 1901) 176. Cited in the American Reference Library [CD-ROM]. Orem, Utah: Western Standard Publishing Company, 1998. Herafter cited as *Debates.*

2. For a good treatment on the critical period see Wood, *The Creation of the American*, 393-429.

3. For a good account of the tyranny in Rhode Island see Joseph Bessette, *The Mild Voice of Reason: Deliberative Democracy and American National Government* (Chicago: The University of Chicago Press, 1994), 11-12.

4. Max Farrand ed., *The Records of the Federal Convention of 1787*, 4 vols (New Haven: Yale University Press, 1937), I: 22. At least in Madison's note the plan was listed in fifteen separate proposals. Hereafter cited as *Records*

5. Ibid., I: 22.

6. Ibid., I: 25-26.

7. Ibid., I: 26.

8. It is interesting to note that far from the direct democracy we see today, a direct appeal to the people in this instance still involved representative assemblies, but assemblies that were selected directly by the people for an expressed purpose.

9. Farrand, *Records*, I: 26-27. Randolph goes on, "The feeble Senate of Virginia is a phantom. Maryland has a more powerful senate, but the late distractions in that State, have discovered that it is not powerful enough. The check established in the constitution of New York and Massachusetts is yet a stronger barrier against democracy, but they all seem insufficient."

10. Ibid., I: 122; as quoted in Madison's notes.

11. Ibid.

12. Ibid., I: 122-123.

13. His motion was seconded by Paterson, Farrand, *Records*, II:88.

14. Ibid., II:88.

15. Ibid.

16. Ibid., II:89.

17. Ibid., II:88; Remember Gerry had brought up a fear of referring the plan to peoples in the east back on June 5 of the Convention. Gerry's hesitance to recur to popular convention could be due to the extended delays experienced in Massachusetts in their efforts to erect a constitution utilizing a form of popular ratification in the town meetings. For a description of the delays in Massachusetts see Adams, *The First American Constitutions*.

18. Farrand, *Records*, II:90.

19. Ibid., II:91; it is interesting to note that such a number of delegates believed that the "ablest men" were to be found in a popular convention and not in a state legislature.

20. Ibid., II:92.

21. Ibid.

22. Ibid., II:93.

23. Ibid., II:93; Here Madison's point seems to be that the delegates realized that Congress was too politically entrenched to be competent to suggest the radical changes that were needed, likewise state legislatures suffered from the same malady in terms of ratifying such far reaching changes.

24. Ibid.

25. Kyvig, *Explicit & Authentic Acts*, 51.

26. Ibid., II:476.

27. Ibid., I: 22; At least in Madison's note the plan was listed in fifteen separate proposals.

28. To be sure the involvement of Congress in the Article V process was one concern of George Mason who did not support the new Constitution, see Ibid., II:629, S:270.

29. Ibid., I: 121.; It is not entirely clear from Madison's notes what the "it" Pinckney is referring to. As Kyvig points out in his study, it is unclear whether Pinckney was referring to the "it" being the plan for amendment or the exclusion of the national legislature. Pinckney had included a provision for constitutional change in his plan but simply put such matters in "the assent of the Legislature of [blank] states shall be sufficient to invest future additional Powers in U.S." See Farand, *Records*, II:136. It seems most likely that Pinckney was referring to the formal process for amendment itself, especially given Gerry's response to Pinckney's statement.

30. Ibid., I: 122; In the end Gerry would not sign the Constitution but at this point he clearly favored a formal amending process.

31. Ibid., I: 202.

32. Ibil., I: 202-203.

33. Richard B. Bernstein and Jerome Agel, *Amending America* (New York: Times Books-Random House, 1993), 17; Bernstein and Agel give a nice clear account of this portion of the Convention's proceedings.

34. Farrand, Records, II: 84.

35. Ibid., II: 188; Bernstien and Agel believe that Wilson greatly influenced this clause in the Committee of Detail's work, also see Bernstein and Agel, *Amending America*, 17-18.

36. Farrand, *Records*, 557-8.

37. Ibid., II: 558.

38. Ibid.

39. Ibid., II: 558; Remember it was Wilson who argued for less than a consensus in the ratification process back on June 5th so it makes sense that he would still be pressing this issue with regards to amendment as well, also see Ibid., I:123

40. Ibid., II: 559; Madison's language would provide a template for the final set of language, "The Legislature of the U.S. whenever two thirds of both Houses shall deem necessary, or on the application of two thirds of the Legislatures of the several states, shall propose amendments to this Constitution, which shall be valid to all intents and purposes as part thereof, when the same shall have been ratified by three fourths at least of the Legislatures of the several States, or by Conventions in three fourths thereof, as on or the other mode of ratification may be proposed by the Legislature of the U.S." Hamilton seconded Madison's motion.

41. Ibid., II: 559.

42. Ibid., II: 581, 629; in the version that went to the Committee of Style the amending provision was Article XIX but after their changes it became Article V as we know it today. (See Farrand, *Records*, II:578 as compared with Farrand, *Records*, II:602.)

43. Ibid., II: 629.

44. Ibid.

45. Ibid., II: 630.

46. Ibid.

47. Ibid., II: 662.

48. Delaware, December, 7; Pennsylvania, December 12; New Jersey, December 18; Georgia, January 2; Connecticut, January 9.

49. Forrest McDonald, *E Pluribus Unum: The Formation of the American Republic 1776-1790* (Indianapolis, Liberty Fund, Inc. 1979), 340-341.

50. Ibid., 351.

51. For a compelling account of the ratification amongst all the states and a blow by blow portrayal of the great battle between the Federalists and Anti-Federalists see Ibid., 333-371.

52. Elliot, *Debates*, II: 200.

53. Ibid., 84.

54. Ibid., 116.

55. Ibid.

56. Ibid., 116-117.

57. Ibid., 118.

58. Ibid.

59. Ibid.,161; Barrell was one of only six out of the seventeen delegates from the county of York to vote in favor of ratification.

60. Ibid., 169; Stillman added, "It has been said, it will be difficult, after its ratification, to procure any alterations. By no means, sir, for this weighty reason—it is a general government, and, as such, will have a general influence; all states in the Union will feel the difficulty, and, feeling it, will readily concur in adopting the method provided by the Constitution. And having once made the trial, experience will teach us what amendments are necessary. Viewing the Constitution in this light, I stand ready to give my vote for it, without any amendments at all."

61. McDonald, *E Pluribus Unum*, 342. Certainly the eventual support of titans such as Samuel Adams and John Hancock—who initially opposed the new document—provided strong political cover for many delegates. However, a full explanation must also look to the ability of the Federalists to blunt Anti-Federalist assaults with the promise of future amendments. Article V made such promises more credible and seemed to help the sides reach a compromise of submitting suggested bill of rights along with the ratification notice. Massachusetts was the first state to submit suggested amendments in the form of a bill of rights along with the ratification notice.

62. Ibid., 346-348; New Hampshire would adjourn without ratification until June, Rhode Island rejected the Constitution, and North Carolina looked as if it would not ratify either. The spring of 1788 was not an encouraging time for the Federalist cause.

63. New York, Virginia, and New Hampshire conventions took place during the same month and overlapped. NY June 17-July 26; VA June 2-25; NH June 18-21.

64. McDonald, *E Pluribus Unum*, 356.

65. Ibid.

66. Elliot, *Debates*, III: 49-52.

67. Ibid.
68. Ibid.
69. Ibid.
70. Ibid.
71. Ibid.
72. 3d clause: "—that government is, or ought to be, instituted for the common benefit, protection, and security of the people, nation, or community. Of all the various modes and forms of government, that is best, which is capable of producing the greatest degree of happiness and safety, and is most effectually secured against the danger of mal-administration; and that whenever any government shall be found inadequate, or contrary to those purposes, a majority of the community hath an indubitable, unalienable, and indefeasible right to reform, alter, or abolish it, in such manner as shall be judged most conducive to the public weal."
73. Elliot, *Debates*, III:49-52.
74. Ibid.
75. McDonald, *E Pluribus Unum*, 357.
76. Elliot, *Debates*, III: 87.
77. Ibid.
78. Ibid., III: 88.
79. Ibid.
80. Ibid.
81. Ibid., III: 89.
82. Ibid., III: 95.
83. Ibid.; June 6th
84. Ibid., III: 175; June 9th: "Mr. HENRY-Look at Britain: see there the bolts and bars of power: see bribery and corruption defiling the fairest fabric that ever human nature reared! Can a gentleman who is an Englishman, or who is acquainted with the English history, desire to prove these evils? See the efforts of a man descended from a friend of America—see the efforts of that man, assisted even by the king, to make reforms. But you find the faults too strong to be amended. Nothing but bloody war can alter them. Look at Ireland. . . . (me: Ireland struggled to get amendments). But, I ask you again, where is the example that a government was amended by those who instituted it? Where is the instance of the errors of a government rectified by those who adopted them?"
85. Ibid., III: 175.
86. Ibid., III: 195; June 10th
87. Ibid., III: 224; June 10th Marshall in reply to Henry: "He then stated the necessity and probability of obtaining amendments. This we ought to postpone until we come to that clause, and make up our minds whether there be any thing unsafe in this system. He conceived it impossible to obtain amendments after adopting it. If he was right, does not his own argument prove that, in his own conception, previous amendments cannot be had? for, sir, if subsequent amendments cannot be obtained, shall we get amendments before we ratify? The reasons against the latter do not apply against the former.
88. Ibid., III: 233-234; June 10th.
89. Ibid., III: 290; June 12th, Grayson.
90. Ibid., III: 303-304; June 12th, Pendleton.
91. Ibid., III: 303-305; June 12th, Pendleton.
92. Ibid., III:.471; June 17th.
93. Van Doren, Carl, *The Great Rehearsal: The Story of the Making and Ratifying of the Constitution of the United States* (New York: Viking Press, 1948), 231.
94. Ibid., 232.
95. Ibid.
96. Mc Donald, *E Pluribus Unum*, 361.
97. Ibid., 362.
98. Ibid.
99. Ibid.
100. Van Doren, *The Great Rehearsal*, 232.
101. Ibid., 232-233.

102. Ibid.
103. Ibid., 234.
104. Ibid.
105. Ibid.
106. Most of the above account was drawn from, Ibid., 234-235.
107. McDonlad identifies Dane as a Hancock supporter; see McDonald, *E Pluribus Unum*, 334.
108. Ibid., 852.
109. Ibid.
110. McDonald, *E Pluribus Unum*, 350.
111. Elliot, *Debates*, IV: 130-131; June 28th, N.C. Iredell.
112. Ibid., 130-131; June 28th, N.C. Iredell.
113. Ibid., 176-177; June 28th, N.C. Iredell
114. Ibid.; June 28th, N.C. Iredell
115. Ibid.
116. Ibid.
117. Ibid.; June 28, N.C. It is interesting to note Iredell's treatment of the Slavery clause in Article V for he argues that S.C. and Georgia are largely responsible for its inclusion. Iredell: "A compromise likewise took place in regard to the importation of slaves. It is probable that all the members reprobated this inhuman traffic; but those of South Carolina and Georgia would not consent to an immediate prohibition of it one reason of which was, that, during the last war, they lost a vast number of negroes, which loss they wish to supply. In the mean time, it is left to the states to admit or prohibit the importation, and Congress may impose a limited duty upon it."
118. Ibid., 177-178; June 28, N.C. Iredell
119. It is important to make the distinction between the operation of majorities in principal and the operation of majorities within a Constitutional system. The requirement of supermajorities is not a rebuff of the Delcaration of Independence and its statement of the "Right of the People to alter or to abolish it, and to institute new Government, laying its foundation on such principles and organizing its powers in such form, as to them shall seem most likely to effect their safety and happiness." While some certainly hold that Democratic theory based on a principle of equality will require a mere simple majority as all that is necessary to alter a government, the founders seemed to believe that mere majorities could and should be restrained to a certain extent within the confines of a given Constitutional system, but not rejected as a general ruling principle.

Chapter 4
The Founders' Article V Consensus

> It has been the misfortune, if not the reproach, of other nations, that their Governments have not been freely and deliberately established by themselves. It is the boast of ours that such has been its source and that it can be altered by the same authority only which established it. It is a further boast that a regular mode of making proper alterations has been providently inserted in the Constitution itself. It is anxiously to be wished therefore, that no innovations may take place in other modes, one of which would be a constructive assumption of powers never meant to be granted. If the powers be deficient, the legitimate source of additional ones is always open, and ought to be resorted to.
>
> James Madison[1]

Constitutional Ideas and Amending Institutions

So did the Founders view Article V as one option among many? Did they envision constitutional adaptations that altered or conflicted with a plain reading of the constitutional text? Did they see Article V as an ancillary expendable part of the constitutional tradition? Was Article V seen as an undemocratic, difficult process? What exactly was the Founding consensus regarding Article V? After examining the role of constitutional amendment in the Imperial Crisis, the development of the state constitutions, the Constitutional Convention, and the ratifying debates it is now possible to construct a set of amendment principles that guided the Founders in their design of Article V. These principles naturally flowed out of the American Constitutionalism of the founding generation.

The Article V amending process outlined in the Constitution reflected a coherent set of ideas that emerged in American constitutional thought during the founding era. These principles regarding constitutional amendment were ultimately rooted in the very nature of the American political system. For this first generation of patriots and statesmen, American democracy was firmly rooted in the natural rights of mankind out of which logically followed the core beliefs in limited government and the sovereignty of the people.[2] In the founding generation's view the best practical political means of securing limited government and establishing popular sovereignty was to create a fixed written constitution. Such a constitution would enable the people to exercise their sovereign power in a clear and decisive manner and simultaneously create a fundamental law limiting the role of government. Finally, if a fixed written constitution were to retain both its form and its accountability to the people, any changes or alterations of that document must be made formally, publicly, and in a manner that clearly draws upon the sovereign power of the people. Thus, as a direct response to the ideas of natural rights, limited government, popular sovereignty, and written constitutionalism, Article V was a direct reflection of the most fundamental principles of American Constitutionalism.

Not only was Article V deeply rooted in the very core of American political thought its efficacy was demonstrated by its role in the ratification debates and subsequently the successful adoption of the first ten amendments. Thus Article V played a critical role in serving to further solidify public confidence in the new untested Constitution and government. Thus, for this first generation of American leaders, and thinkers, Article V played an integral role in the thought and practice of American Constitutionalism. It was indeed seen as a perfecting mechanism of the new Constitution that allowed for change, flexibility, accountability, and yet maintained the stability and the binding form of the fundamental law.

There are no lengthy treatises from the founding era extrapolating these core principles with regard to Article V, yet they are clearly articulated in the writings and public documents of the founding generation. Key founders did not spend much time elaborating the fundamental principles of amendment largely because it was so tightly engrained in the logic and nature of American constitutionalism. Often these principles appear in writings as a "given," ideas that so naturally flowed from the coherence of the larger constitutional structure that they needed little if any written elaboration. Accordingly, during the founding era, there were no serious challenges to the exclusivity of Article V and the procedure was largely seen as an effective and progressive development in the science of government. It was seen more as a logically necessary, a "matter of fact," addition to the new form of constitutionalism that had evolved, hence there seemed little need to produce a full-fledged defense of Article V and its principles.

The Founders' consensus on Article V and constitutional amendment can be expressed in a set of principles that reflect their philosophical and political commitments. These principles can also allow one to judge or measure any alternative amending mechanism that might be suggested by scholars and politicians alike. These principles clearly guided the deliberations that created Article V and established its place in the American constitutional order. Perhaps the most important single articulation of the founding principles regarding Article V and constitutional amendment was made by none other than George Washington on the occasion of his Farewell Address in 1796. The force and power of his remarks on this issue demand attention and will provide a sound point of embarkation for exploring the Founders' guiding principles for amending procedures.

Washington's Farewell Address

As part of his Farewell Address of September 1796, George Washington made a definitive statement regarding Article V and its fundamental importance to American Constitutionalism. In addressing the question of constitutional change and usurpation, Washington implicitly outlined the Founders' core principles for any constitutionally legitimate amending process. The importance of the address in American political history and his articulate affirmation of Article V and its vital importance to the new Constitution warrant an extensive analysis of his remarks. Here was a man retiring from public life, whose revered stature and sheer popularity were irreplaceable factors in the quest for union and the new Constitution.

Washington began his address with an explanation of his desire not to seek reelection after which he expressed a "deep acknowledgement of that debt of gratitude which I owe to my country, for the many honors it has conferred upon me."[3] Washington then gave the nation and its posterity the benefit of his experience and wisdom as he left public service. It is important to note that Washington's comments are the culmination of a lifetime of service to his country and much of his life's work and legacy were poured into forging a successful young nation where ordered liberty would reign. One must not take lightly Washington's sentiments that his comments are the result of "much reflection" and his belief that his advice was "important to the permanency of your felicity as a people." So what are Washington's words of wisdom, what parting advice does he leave to the young nation whose permanent success and stability are yet to be cemented in history? First he began by emphasizing the importance of union as the basis for American liberty, "The Unity of Government which constitutes you one people is also now dear to you. It is justly so, for it is a main Pillar in the Edifice of your real independence, the support of your tranquility at home, your peace abroad, of your safety, of your prosperity, of that very Liberty which you so highly prize."[4]

Washington forcefully reminds the American people that the union of the states is essential to the success of the young nation. Certainly a fledgling nation must be able to achieve a level of military and economic self-sufficiency in order to resist the influence and expansionist powers of much more established and mighty European nations. Just because the colonies were able to win their freedom from Britain did not mean they would be able to keep it. To ensure that the economic or military will of other world powers is not imposed on the young nation, the newly formed states must foster a strong and unbreakable union. A collection of states that are not able to pull together their economic and military might, behind a united national vision, would be easy prey for foreign influence or domination, or internal strife that would eat away at the young nation like a cancer.

Certainly it is important for Washington to so fully emphasize the importance of *union*, but certainly all patriots and statesmen agree on this point. Does Washington have advice on how the people are to maintain this union despite regional and economic differences? Here Washington immediately points to the Constitution as a key means of securing union into the future. The new Constitution fundamentally represents a rejection of the atomized Articles in favor of a stronger national government. Washington knows that the attachment of the people to the Constitution is essential if national unity is to be fostered and maintained. The Constitution has created a political union of the states, thus channeling their resources and cooperation into one national government. Such political cooperation, facilitated by the Constitution, will help secure the nation's liberty and prosperity. Thus, Washington seeks to reinforce the people's prejudices in favor of the new Constitution by making a reasoned appeal on its behalf. In doing so, Washington provides a list of constitutional features that the people should cherish as excellent principles of good governance essential to national unity and liberty:

> This Government, the offspring of our own choice, uninfluenced and unawed, adopted upon full investigation and mature deliberation, completely free in its principles, in the distribution of its powers, uniting security with energy, and containing within itself a provision for its own amendment, has a just claim to your confidence and your support. Respect for its authority, compliance with its laws, acquiescence in its measures, are duties enjoined by the fundamental maxims of true liberty.[5]

It is notable that here in a very short list of reasons why the new Constitution has a "just claim" on the "confidence" and "support" of the American people Washington highlights that the new document has a "provision for its own amendment." The people chose the new government, they deliberated over it, they established it on free principles, they established a prudent distribution of powers, it has security and energy, and they can alter it according to their will by its own provision. The ability to amend the new government via orderly Constitutional methods seems of fundamental importance for Washington here. It is important to Washington that the Constitution was created via the people's own "choice" with "full investigation" and "deliberation." This new and prudent innovation is not to be underestimated. Washington elaborates this point later in an eloquent statement of how Article V as the amending process is at the very core of American Constitutionalism:

> The basis of our political systems is the right of the people to make and to alter their constitutions of government. But the constitution which at any time exists till changed by an explicit and authentic act of the whole people is sacredly obligatory upon all. The very idea of the power and the right of the people to establish government presupposes the duty of every individual to obey the established government.[6]

These are perhaps the most important words spoken by a founder on the issue of constitutional amendment. The alteration of the "constitutions of government" is the very "basis of our political systems" according to Washington. If the union is key to the nation's success and survival and the Constitution is vital to maintaining union, then it is important to maintain the integrity of the Constitution. Thus, Washington must remind the people of the fundamental importance of not usurping the people's sovereign authority and the legal integrity of the Constitution by ignoring the properly appointed means of its amendment. In the end, the Constitution is "sacredly obligatory on all" unless changed by an "explicit" and "authentic" act.

Here Washington introduces the key nomenclature for a proper amending process. Having an "explicit" process known to all and agreed upon by all, as well as an "authentic" process that truly draws upon the constituent power of the people, is essential in maintaining constitutional integrity and popular sovereignty. Finally, Washington reminds the public that the very "right of the people to establish government," this "basis of our political systems," "presupposes the duty of every individual to obey the established government." This statement not only includes members of government seeking to act within their proper spheres of authority, but it extends to attempts to alter the Constitution in a manner that undercuts the nation's very basis of government. If individuals seek to alter the Constitution by means that are not explicit or authentic, they are violating the "right of the people to establish government." They are altering the Constitution in violation of the very political principles that gave them their office to begin with. They are violating the principles that justify the very basis of American government and that led to the creation of a Constitution that can secure the union and provide for American liberty and prosperity.

Certainly Washington's statement is brief, but its parsimony should not detract from its power or importance. One must remember that Washington could have addressed any myriad of issues in his final remarks and he must have wrestled much over what words he should leave the country that he had dedicated his life to. He chose to devote key passages to this theme and he did so in very strong and forceful language. It seems clear that Washington feared the human tendency for innovation and informal modes of exercising power and he wanted to put those who would, intentionally or unintentionally, subvert constitutional integrity on notice in a very decisive and public manner. Accordingly, Washington devotes several lengthy passages to exposing the dangers of ignoring constitutional forms and indulging the human tendency towards excessive innovation:

> Toward the preservation of your Government and the permanency of your present happy state, it is requisite not only that you steadily discountenance irregular oppositions to its acknowledged authority, but also that you resist with care the spirit of innovation upon its principles, however specious the pretexts. One method of assault may be to effect in the forms of the Constitution alterations which will impair the energy of the system, and thus to undermine what cannot be directly overthrown. In all the changes to which you may be invited remember that time and habit are at least as necessary to fix the true character of governments as of other human institutions; that experience is the surest standard by which to test the real tendency of the existing constitution of a country; that facility in changes upon the credit of mere hypothesis and opinion exposes to perpetual change, from the endless variety of hypothesis and opinion; and remember especially that for the efficient management of your common interests in a country so extensive as ours a government of as much vigor as is consistent with the perfect security of liberty is indispensable. Liberty itself will find in such a government, with powers properly distributed and adjusted, its surest guardian. It is, indeed, little else than a name where the government is too feeble to withstand the enterprises of faction, to confine each member of the society within the limits prescribed by the laws, and to maintain all in the secure and tranquil enjoyment of the rights of person and property.[7]

Washington is clear that government must be strong and vigorous but Americans must still guard against excessive innovation and the "facility in changes" upon mere credit of "hypothesis and opinion" that lead to "perpetual change." That is to say for the government to remain firm and strong Americans must resist the democratic urge to constantly innovate and change without proper deliberation and experience.

Continuing his caution against informal alterations of the Constitution and the need to develop good constitutional habits, Washington reminds the public of the need to reinforce and respect the separation of powers laid out in the Constitution:

> It is important, likewise, that the habits of thinking in a free country should inspire caution in those entrusted with its administration to confine themselves within their respective constitutional spheres, avoiding in the exercise of the powers of one department to encroach upon another. The spirit of encroachment tends to consolidate the powers of all the departments in one, and thus to create, whatever the form of government, a real despotism. A just estimate of that love of power and proneness to abuse it, which predominates in the human heart is sufficient to satisfy us of the truth of this position. The necessity of reciprocal checks in the exercise of political power, by dividing and distributing it into different depositories, and constituting each the guardian of the public weal against invasions by the others, has been evinced by experiments ancient

> and modern, some of them in our country and under our own eyes. To preserve them must be as necessary as to institute them.[8]

He fears a "spirit of encroachment" that will lead to administrators seeking to extend their power beyond their constitutionally prescribed limits. As Washington finishes his thoughts on the importance of the doctrine of separation of powers, he returns to the topic of constitutional amendment and its fundamental importance in the proper maintenance of American Constitutionalism:

> If in the opinion of the people the distribution or modification of the constitutional powers be in any particular wrong, let it be corrected by an amendment in the way which the Constitution designates. But let there be no change by usurpation; for though this in one instance may be the instrument of good, it is the customary weapon by which free governments are destroyed. The precedent must always greatly overbalance in permanent evil any partial or transient benefit which the use can at any time yield.[9]

This is the third time in the heart of his address that Washington refers to constitutional amendment and it is again a very clear and concise statement of principle based on the fundamental design of the American system of government. If the people wish to alter the Constitution they must utilize the Article V process provided by that very document. To do otherwise, even once, and even for a temporary good, is to indulge a precedent that "is the customary weapon by which free governments are destroyed." This prohibition against "usurpation" fits neatly within Washington's encouragement of developing good Constitutional habits. For he must realize, even if not directly stated, that if the people ultimately allow their leaders in normal government to alter the Constitution, outside of Article V, it will produce poor habits of governance and will undermine the Constitution. Such poor habits will lead to usurpation, and while initially done under the watchful eye, and even with the endorsement, of the people, will eventually result in usurpation beyond the gaze and outside the will of the people. If the people cede this power through neglect or expediency, it may prove fatal to the long-term survival of the Constitution as a viable document. Furthermore it doesn't matter that such deviations are for good causes or of noble motives for, "The precedent must always greatly overbalance in permanent evil any partial or transient benefit which the use can at any time yield." If reflected upon properly, the power of Washington's warnings should not be taken lightly. It is significant that he devotes a serious part of his address to this issue and that he mentions it more than once in direct conjunction with the Constitution's vital importance in maintaining the union that is in turn the "main pillar" of American security, prosperity, and liberty.

Thus, Washington's address concisely places Article V at the heart of American Constitutionalism and by inference at the heart of American liberty. Powerful in its brevity and directness, these passages of this timeless speech clearly articulate the importance of Article V and they implicitly outline the essential principles for any legitimate Constitutional amending process. Washington's remarks clearly and succinctly reflect the Founding consensus on constitutional amendment. By building on Washington's remarks it is now possible to clearly lay bare the principles that represent the Founders, consensus on Constitutional amendment and the ideas that shaped Article V's design and operation.

Amendment Principles

The Founders, amending principles can be broken down into three sets in descending order of importance, namely first order, second order, and third order principles. The first order principles reflect the American commitment to the rule of law; the second order reflects a commitment to wisdom or justice in the people's decisions; the third order reflects a commitment to prevent the consolidation of power that may lead to tyranny. First order principles are fundamental, essential, or constitutive to the constitutional system. Second order principles are vital, critical, or crucial to maintaining the constitutional system. Third order principles are meant to reinforce, buttress, fortify, or sustain key elements of the larger constitutional system. To meet the first order principles an amendment process must be *explicit, authentic,* and *exclusive.* To meet second order principles an amendment process must be *deliberative* and *prudent.* To meet third order principles an amendment process must respect the Constitution's commitments to *federalism* and *separation of powers.* Article V alone was designed to reflect all of these principles. This is why it naturally commanded the admiration and respect of the founding generation and why it was seen as a means of perfecting the Constitution. The founding principles for establishing an amending procedure are as follows:

First Order Principles: These principles are fundamental, essential, or constitutive to the constitutional system. Together they preserve the American commitment to the rule of law.

explicit
authentic
exclusive

Second Order Principles: These principles are vital, critical, or crucial to maintaining the constitutional system. They seek to promote wisdom and justice in the public voice.

deliberative
prudent

Third Order Principles: Principles that reinforce, buttress, fortify, or sustain key elements of the larger constitutional system. They seek to prevent the consolidation of power.

federalism
separation of powers

First Order Principles

First order principles are fundamental or essential to the constitutional system. In a sense, these principles reflect the deep American commitment to the rule of law and to the written Constitution as fundamental or higher law. An amending mechanism that fails to reflect these principles will undermine the very essence of the constitutional structure and fundamental ideas or principles that animate the entire regime. In the American system, government's primary purpose is to secure the natural rights of its citizens. In seeking to secure the natural rights of fellow citizens, Americans have made primary commitments to the ideas of the people's sovereign authority and a written constitution as the source of fundamental law created by that authority. To maintain the primacy of these ideas in the American system, any amending mechanism must conform to certain institutional principles, which in turn serve to translate these abstract commitments into concrete political reality. Accordingly, the principles in this category require that an amending mechanism must be: 1) Explicit, 2) Authentic, 3) Exclusive.

Explicit

First, the amending process must be *explicit* so as to preserve the integrity of written constitutionalism and its accountability to the sovereign people who created it. If a written constitution is to be the fixed fundamental law of the land, then the manner in which it is altered must be clearly defined in a formal process that is understood and accepted by all parties to the document. Without an explicit amending procedure the Constitution will likely become subject to battles by competing institutions of normal government, institutions which may or may not reflect the will of the people in their sovereign constitutive capacity. If normal institutions simply begin to disregard the constitutional text, the authority and legitimacy of the fixed written constitution is undeniably undermined over time, because the text has become irrelevant as a practical political matter.[10] In short, if the Constitution is a fixed written document, then it logically follows that the mode of amending it should be fixed and written as well. Not only does an explicit process help ensure the integrity of the constitutional text, but it helps preserve the practical ability of the people to continue to exercise their sovereign authority. With an explicit publicly stated means of amendment, the people know what political measures they must take to propose and ratify such amendments. By merely establishing a uniform set of rules, an explicit process empowers the people to act, to modify their fundamental law, and in the end rule themselves. Thus, simply by outlining an explicit mode of making changes to the Constitution, the founding generation believed they were establishing a sound practice that would both reinforce the integrity and authority of the written document, while institutionalizing the people's sovereign authority.

Furthermore, an explicitly stated process also ensures that constitutional change is not only public, but regular and orderly as well. Thomas Jefferson took occasion to boast about the American commitment to orderly constitutional change in a letter to a Frenchman Msgr. Dumas in 1787:

> Happily for us, that when we find our constitutions defective and insufficient to secure the happiness of our people, we can assemble with all the coolness of philosophers, and set it to rights, while every other nation on earth must have recourse to arms to amend or to restore their constitutions.[11]

Jefferson's comments illustrate that many Founders recognized orderly constitutional change as a significant progression in the science of government that set the American state constitutions apart from their counterparts in history or other quarters of the world. Jefferson was making these remarks to Msgr. Dumas while the Federal Convention of 1787 is still in session, thus his sentiments illustrate how the principle of formal amendment was already firmly established as a constitutional practice during the creation of the state constitutions and the Articles of Confederation. While most of human history has shown the alteration of the constitutions of government to be violent and bloody, the Americans sough to ensure that such changes were provided for in a regular and orderly manner.

Authentic

Second, the amending process must be *authentic*. It follows that if the people are to wield their sovereign authority via the amending process, then the procedures must ensure that it truly is the people's will that is reflected by the proposal and ratification process. Thus, "authenticity" is the requirement that any constitutional amendments must legitimately draw upon the constitutive power of the people. The constitutive power of the people is that fundamental authority to create governments based on popular consent as articulated in the Declaration of Independence. Thus, legitimate alterations to the fundamental law must seek to approximate same reservoir of popular authority that created the fundamental law. This can be done via special conventions or through popularly elected legislatures that conform to higher levels of consent than required via normal law. Conversely, alterations that do not draw sufficiently upon the people, or do not have the clear sanction of popular consent, violate the American commitment to popular sovereignty and the principle of equality. Furthermore, alterations that are not authentic undermine the status of the Constitution as fundamental or higher law, for if the fundamental law can be altered by actors or institutions that do not represent the constitutive power of the people then its creation by the people becomes meaningless over time. In other words if the fundamental law is first created by the people and then altered by normal government, the Constitution slowly loses its direct accountability to the people and hence the color of authority from the people. If the people are the fount of all political authority and they created the Constitution based upon that authority (derived from natural rights), then it logically follows that the people must also be involved in any legitimate changes to the Constitution. The Constitution is to stand above normal law and normal government. It is given the status of higher law and only by utilizing forms and institutions that exceed the requirements of normal law in amendment can the Constitution maintain this status as higher law.

In addition, "authenticity" is mutually dependent upon the precept of "explicitness." If the people are to collectively utilize their authority to alter the Constitution, there must be some "explicit" formal institutional arrangements, otherwise it is nearly impossible to marshal and channel popular authority. The absence of an "explicit" procedure at a minimum hampers, and at a maximum disables, the exercise of popular authority, for there is no clearly agreed upon means for the people to organize and act. Furthermore, if there is no explicit means of articulating popular will, then the necessary ambiguity that exists creates room for less popular or less responsible institutions and political actors to act as imposters, in place of, or on behalf of the people. Many different institutions could claim to be the legitimate or "authentic" means of articulating popular authority. This would result in an untenable form of constitutional anarchy with regard to which institutions and which powers in society have the authority to alter the fundamental law of the nation. In this manner authenticity and explicitness are inexorably related and vital aspects of founding thought on constitutional amendment specifically and the maintenance of a written constitution more generally.

Put another way, the authenticity criterion seeks to prevent "minority tyranny" or elite amendment and to ensure that the people meaningfully participate in the amending process either directly or through representative bodies such as legislatures or constitutional conventions. Three tests of *authenticity* are the: *democratic test, national consensus test,* and the *higher law test*. If a procedure is authentic it will utilize democratic forms such as legislatures or conventions. Furthermore, if it is authentic it will seek to provide a national consensus for a given proposal. In other words, the amending procedure will be designed to register the opinion of a broad geographic and numerical *national consensus*. Lastly, to be a reflection of *higher law* an amending procedure must seek to access the *constitutive* power of the people rather than their opinion as it is expressed through normal law. Article V does this by requiring a super majority in Congress and a super majority of state legislatures (put another way a super majority of state majorities). Article V also allows for conventions to be used at the state and federal level, but is also designed so that some legislative body is part of the process. For instance, state legislatures can petition Congress for a convention, or Congress can designate conventions in the states. Either way popularly elected legislatures are involved in the process. Since the days of early state constitution making, the American tradition has required that constitutional amendments utilize either supermajorities in legislatures or non-legislative bodies to differentiate a constitutional amendment as "higher law" from "normal law." If a procedure does not seek to reflect the higher law nature of a constitutional amendment, then it would fail to meet a critical aspect of the authenticity criterion.

Clearly, if the people are sovereign, the mode of accessing their sovereign power must be legitimate or "authentic," but what measure of popular opinion makes a given method of amendment "authentic" or not? What if the processes outlined in the Constitution do not produce a popular majority? Madison makes a clear distinction between *constitutional majorities* and *popular majorities*, and he clearly endorses the former over the latter. A *constitutional majority* is produced naturally when adhering to the forms prescribed in the Constitutional text. For example, the electoral college will produce a constitutional majority for the purposes of electing the president, Congressional elections may produce a constitutional majority for the purposes of passing legislation, and the Article V will produce a constitutional majority for the purposes of amendment. These *constitutional majorities* may very well not represent a *popular majority* of the whole population, due to many factors such as voter apathy, equal representation in the Senate, and different voting patterns in Congressional districts, or states electoral votes.[12] For James Madison this distinction between *constitutional* and *popular* majorities naturally flows out of constitutional representative government and is not something that can be avoided,

It may be objected to majority governments, that the majority, as formed by the Constitution, may be a minority when compared with the popular majority. This is likely to be the case more or less in all elective governments. It is so in many of the States.[13] While this is certainly a problem in Confederacies, who provide each state with an equal vote regardless of population, the republican system in the United States may also produce disparities between constitutional and popular majorities.[14] Madison admits that this disparity could be abused at times, but such risks are ultimately unavoidable in a constitutional system of government:

> That this departure from the rule of equality, creating a political and constitutional majority in contradistinction to a numerical majority of the people, may be abused in various degrees oppressive to the majority of the people, is certain; and in modes and degrees so oppressive as to justify ultra or anti-constitutional resorts to adequate relief is equally certain. Still the constitutional majority must be acquiesced in by the constitutional minority, while the Constitution exists. The moment that arrangement is successfully frustrated, the Constitution is at an end.[15]

Madison is quick to point out that there are natural political checks on constitutional majorities (that are in fact popular minorities) via public opinion as long as the numerical minority is not backed by force:

> It is a favourable consideration, in the impossibility of securing in all cases a coincidence of the constitutional and numerical majority, that when the former is the minority, the existence of a numerical majority with justice on its side, and its influence on public opinion, will be a salutary control on the abuse of power by a minority constitutionally possessing it: a control generally of adequate force, where a military force, the disturber of all the ordinary movements of free governments, is not on the side of the minority.[16]

For Madison, the expectation that Constitutional majorities will always coincide with numerical majorities is utopian at best. A commitment to republican government and constitutional government requires sober expectations and a perspective that gives the Constitutional observer a clear vista into the less desirable alternatives that have been offered up by history and experience:

> The result of the whole is, that we must refer to the monitory reflection that no government of human device and human administration can be perfect; that that which is the least imperfect is therefore the best government; that the abuses of all other governments have led to the preference of republican government as the best of all governments, because the least imperfect; that the vital principle of republican government is the lex majoris partis, the will of the majority; that if the will of a majority cannot be trusted where there are diversified and conflicting interests, it can be trusted nowhere, because such interests exist everywhere.[17]

The search for perfection in government leads to dangerous expectations. Madison is cautioning critics to realistically assess the tradeoff between constitutional republican government and its protections (which inherently includes the occasional disparity between constitutional and numerical majorities) or other governmental forms which history has shown to be much more of a threat to individual liberty.

The founding generation clearly rejected notions of direct democracy that seem to permeate modern politics. They feared the chaotic impact of subjecting government to the waves of popular passions that were so endemic to popular government. The founding generation preferred to insulate government from such instability while still making it ultimately accountable to the popular will. Representative institutions such as the state legislatures and the Congress served to channel popular sentiments and reflect them in their legislation. In addition, the deliberation of the legislatures would serve to "refine and enlarge" public opinion thus dispensing the popular will in a manner more consistent with good government than the raw democratic impulses that could often sweep a democratic society wreaking havoc on sound public policy and individual liberty. Thus, the requirement of *authenticity* in an amending process could quite logically and easily be met by utilizing representative institutions such as state legislatures and the national Congress. While state legislatures and the Congress are arms of normal government, they are utilized by Article V to tap the constituent power of the people by utilizing them in a non-normal manner. Article V takes the popular institutions that are familiar to the people and utilizes them in unusual ways, by "drafting" them into the service of constitutional amendment. The distinction between normal law and higher law is kept by the requirement of super majorities on the federal and state levels. Thus, the people can seek to alter their constitution through familiar institutions provided those institutions meet the heightened standards required by the amending process. Of course, in addition Article V always provides for the convention method if for some reason the state or federal legislatures are not desired as the proper venues for a given issue. It is to be noted however, that one cannot avoid both legislative bodies, for Article V channels the amending process through either the state legislatures or the Congress. One cannot avoid both of them.

In the end, any amending process must set up procedures that require the formation of an authentic voice of the people via the creation of a constitutional majority. In order for this authentic voice to form, the amending process must be explicitly stated and clearly understood to all in the political community.

Exclusive

Third, the need for an explicit and authentic mode of amendment argues powerfully for the *exclusivity* of any amending provision that meets these two principles. Only amending provisions that are explicitly provided for and that tap into the authentic voice of the people should be recognized as legitimate. Again in the words of Washington, "If in the opinion of the people the distribution or modification of the constitutional powers be in any particular wrong, let it be corrected by an amendment in the way which the Constitution designates."[18] Thus legitimate form of amendment is restricted *exclusively* to the "way which the Constitution designates," anything else is seen as *usurpation*. Most leading founders would see any non-Article V amendment efforts as either unconstitutional. Put another way, to allow for non-explicit or non-authentic amending mechanisms to function alongside explicit and authentic methods is to undermine the very nature of a written constitution that provides for such measures within its text.

In commenting on the *McCulluch v. Maryland* decision, Madison summarizes well the founding vision of amendment as embodied by this first set of first order principles:[19]

> It has been the misfortune, if not the reproach, of other nations, that their Governments have not been freely and deliberately established by themselves. It is the boast of ours that such has been its source and that it can be altered by the same authority only which established it. It is a further boast that a regular mode of making proper alterations has been providently inserted in the Constitution itself. It is anxiously to be wished therefore, that no innovations may take place in other modes, one of which would be a constructive assumption of powers never meant to be granted. If the powers be deficient, the legitimate source of additional ones is always open, and ought to be resorted to.[20]

Here Madison deftly weaves the three core elements of amending theory into a single coherent statement. Referring to the need for the Constitution to be "altered by the same authority only which established it," supports the notion of *authenticity* by requiring a similar exercise of the people's constitutive power to the one that created the Constitution. Furthermore, his use of the word "only" here also supports the notion of *exclusivity* by clearly implying that modes of alteration that do not tap into this popular constitutive authority are not legitimate. In addition, his reference to a "regular mode" clearly reinforces the need for an *explicit* means of amendment. Then Madison immediately ties this in with a more direct statement regarding the *exclusivity* of Article V when he states, "no innovations may take place in other modes" and ostensibly he is referring to modes other than the "regular" one provided in the Constitution. Thus, Madison is clear that additional powers should not be granted by "construction" by the branches of government, but, "if the powers be deficient, the legitimate source of additional ones is always open, and ought to be resorted to."

These first order principles are fundamental, essential, and constitutive to maintaining the constitutional system. Put conversely, an amending mechanism that abandons these principles will fundamentally undermine the American constitutional order. Embracing modes of amendment that are not explicitly recognized impair the American commitment to a written constitution as the fundamental law of the nation. Legitimizing methods of amendment that are not authentic severely weakens the American commitment to popular sovereignty by removing the most fundamental political choices from popular control. In this way, it is essential to American constitutionalism to maintain an *exclusive* means of amendment that is both *explicit* and *authentic.*

Second Order Principles

The second order principles are 1) Deliberation and 2) Prudent Consent Requirements. Second order principles are vital, critical, or crucial to maintaining the Constitutional system. They are not "first order" because they are not as directly tied to the very essence of constitutionalism in the sense that a constitutional system could be designed that was less deliberative or had lower consent requirements while still maintaining, at least in theory, a binding written constitution. However these principles make the Constitution more stable and they guard against the Constitution falling prey to the excesses of popular government. In general while they may not be essential to *constitutional* government but they are essential to *good* government that is stable and a product of wisdom rather than rash impulse. Put another way, while the first order principles seek to ensure that the amending process supports American commitments to *authentic* democracy and an *explicit* written Constitution, the second order principles seek to ensure that the government makes sound or just decisions, not just democratic and constitutional decisions.

Deliberation

The principle of deliberation requires the democratic impulse to be moderated by representative bodies designed to contemplate and debate what is best for the public good. This criterion recognizes the danger of majority faction in the use of directly or excessively democratic mechanisms and in doing so, seeks to "refine and enlarge" public opinion through deliberative bodies.[21] In *The Federalist No.10*, Publius addresses the concern among many of the founding generation for the severe problem of majority faction. Witnessing the excess and injustice in many of the early state governments,[22]

> Complaints are everywhere heard from our most considerate and virtuous citizens, equally the friends of public and private faith and of public and personal liberty, that our governments are too unstable, that the public good is disregarded in the conflicts of rival parties, and that measures are too often decided, not according to the rules of justice and the rights of the minor party, but by the superior force of an interested and overbearing majority.[23]

The shortcomings of democracy were on full display in the state governments after the colonial break from England. The frailty and danger of democracies were well known to the Framers and this too was articulated clearly in *Federalist No. 10*:

> Hence it is that such democracies have ever been spectacles of turbulence and contention; have ever been found incompatible with personal security or the rights of property; and have in general been as short in their lives as they have been violent in their deaths.[24]

Here Publius reminds the readers of *Federalist No. 10* of the frailties of democracies and the importance of the American commitment to "A republic, by which I mean a government in which the scheme of representation takes place, opens a different prospect and promises the cure for which we are seeking."[25]

Representation was a vital element in ensuring a government that did not recede into majority tyranny and injustice where individual rights and liberties are threatened. In describing the newly proposed Senate, Publius makes it clear that body is not to yield to the public passions:

> Such an institution may be sometimes necessary as a defense to the people against their own temporary errors and delusions. As the cool and deliberate sense of the community ought, in all governments, and actually will, in all free governments, ultimately prevail over the views of its rulers; so there are particular moments in public affairs when the people, stimulated by some irregular passion, or some illicit advantage, or misled by the artful misrepresentations of interested men, may call for measures which they themselves will afterwards be the most ready to lament and condemn. In these critical moments, how salutary will be the interference of some temperate and respectable body of citizens, in

> order to check the misguided career and to suspend the blow meditated by the people against themselves, until reason, justice, and truth can regain their authority over the public mind?[26]

This is a fine summary of the Founders' fear of institutions that merely reflected the immediate will of the people, rather than the "cool and deliberate sense of the community." In certain moments the people may not be equipped to choose well, and may enact laws or support measures that they would immediately repudiate. Thus, there was seen a need for some deliberative body that will give pause and make a more temperate decision. In buttressing his point, Publius points to Athens as a historical example of where democratic impulses were not properly restrained as the Athenian assembly rushed to execute Socrates only to later regret their hasty execution of their city's greatest citizen:

> What bitter anguish would not the people of Athens have often escaped if their government had contained so provident a safeguard against the tyranny of their own passions? Popular liberty might then have escaped the indelible reproach of decreeing to the same citizens the hemlock on one day and statues on the next.

Publius makes clear that the cool and deliberate sense of the community actually will prevail over time. No representative institution can resist the direct will of its constituents any longer than the next election (or in the case of the Senate, the next two). Thus, it is likely that only the truly just and reasoned views of the public will sustain itself over extended periods of time and as such they will eventually be enacted.

Thus, by trusting the amending process to legislative bodies at the state and national level or constitutional conventions, the Framers sought to ensure that alterations to the fundamental law would receive the requisite deliberation due such acts. They sought to ensure that not only would amendments to the Constitution be enacted by the authentic voice of the people but also their reasoned and deliberative voice. It was not enough that the people choose, but they must choose well.

Prudent Consent Requirements

The criterion of prudence seeks to ensure a balance between flexibility and stability in the amending process. If the amending mechanism requires too little or too much consent it can be harmful to good government and written constitutionalism. If consent requirements are too low then the Constitution can become burdened with excessive amounts of amendments and soon become as lengthy and unwieldy as normal legislation, thus jeopardizing the *higher law* nature of the Constitution. Accordingly, the authority of the Constitution will suffer as it gets longer and approximates normal legislation. If the consent requirements are too high then the popular will is unduly stifled and the written text becomes impervious to reasonable national consensus on important matters. A prudent balance of requiring a reasonable supermajority consensus rather than a simple majority, on one hand, or extremely high supermajorities or only elite opinion (for example, elites such as judges) on the other hand is desirable. Put another way, it should seek a balance between flexibility and stability.

Again Publius makes it clear that Article V was crafted with an eye towards prudent moderation. Such moderation was an important element in the formation of a sound amending procedure and the perpetuation of good government. The Founders did not want a Constitution that was too "mutable" as they had just shed the fluid British constitution and sought to avoid the dangers and inconveniences of that system. However, with a sense of humility about the perfection of their work, the convention also knew that changes would need to be made and some mode must be provided that avoids "extreme difficulty" in seeking those alterations.

> That useful alterations will be suggested by experience could not but be foreseen. It was requisite, therefore, that a mode for introducing them should be provided. The mode preferred by the convention seems to be stamped with every mark of propriety. It guards equally against that extreme facility, which would render the Constitution too mutable; and that extreme difficulty, which might perpetuate its discovered faults. It, moreover, equally enables the general and the State governments to originate the amendment of errors, as they may be pointed out by the experience on one side, or on the other.[27]

Thus, it was important for Publius to point out that the amending process sought a balance between "extreme facility" on one hand and "extreme difficulty" on the other hand, and was designed to find a balance between flexibility and stability. The Framers of the Constitutional Convention sought to avoid the overly restrictive requirements for unanimity in the Articles of Confederation and the dangers of irresponsible simple majorities violating liberties in the state governments. The use of representative institutions and supermajorities helped to ensure that the amending process was thoroughly democratic, but also tapped the democratic reservoir of authority in a prudent and responsible manner. Furthermore, the Framers sought to limit the number of amendments to those that were of such sound and just nature that they could command the consent of supermajorities in the national legislature and a supermajority of state legislatures. Amendment proposals that could not marshal these majorities were likely not worthy and just additions to the fundamental law.

Thus, these second order principles are vital, as they seek to secure the responsible use of popular authority in the alteration of the nation's fundamental law. They are crucial elements in ensuring that the *authentic* voice of the people is sound and measured in its pronouncements. Finally, such principles are critical to helping the amending process promote not just democratic government, but a stable, sound, and just government.

Third Order Principles

The third order principles are meant to reinforce, buttress, fortify, or sustain key elements of the larger constitutional system. The best amending procedure will respect or even utilize key forms that are important elements of the Constitution. In this way the amending process will be in harmony with the larger system, and reinforce the institutional commitment to other features of the Constitution. These principles help to ensure a "good fit" between the amending process and the Constitution. These principles are, 1) Federalism and 2) Separation of Powers.

Federalism

This principle seeks to ensure that the best amending procedure will reflect and reinforce the natural contours of the American federal system. American federalism is a natural outgrowth of the colonial heritage of the nation and state governments have provided an important balance to the potentially unwieldy nature of an immense national government. Accordingly, the Founders thought that an amending procedure should reinforce and reflect this key element of the American political system. In this way the amending procedure is a "good fit" with the larger constitutional structure and the unique characteristics of American political life.

Few statements better reflect the fullness of Article V's integration into the very structure and nature of the Constitution than Publius's description of federalism and Article V in *Federalist No. 39*. Here Publius is trying to explain the exact nature of the newly proposed government and whether or not it would be a national government or a federal government. Publius argues that it is both, a mix of federal and national traits, and thus it is a unique mix of the two never before seen in the history of governments. In explaining this mixed power structure Publius uses the Article V amending process as an example of this new distribution of power:

> If we try the Constitution by its last relation to the authority by which amendments are to be made, we find it neither wholly national nor wholly federal. Were it wholly national, the supreme and ultimate authority would reside in the majority of the people of the Union; and this authority would be competent at all times, like that of a majority of every national society to alter or abolish its established government. Were it wholly federal, on the other hand, the concurrence of each State in the Union would be essential to every alteration that would be binding on all. The mode provided by the plan of the convention is not founded on either of these principles. In requiring more than a majority, and particularly in computing the proportion by States, not by citizens, it departs from the national and advances towards the federal character; in rendering the concurrence of less than the whole number of States sufficient, it loses again the federal and partakes of the national character.[28]

The proposed Constitution, therefore, according to Madison is, in strictness, neither a national nor a federal Constitution, but a composition of both. In its foundation it is national in the sense that *the people* not the state governments created it, but it is federal in that *the people* ratified it acting in state conventions and simultaneously acting as citizens of their state and the national government.[29] Similarly, the amending process reflects this mixed national/federal nature of the Constitution.

Madison's use of the amending process as the model to describe how the American concept of federalism operates is worthy of note. While Madison clearly has other purposes here, his utilization of Article V in this instance illustrates just how fully Article V is ingrained in the very nature and structure of the Constitution. Such comments serve to highlight the degree to which the design and operation of Article V clearly supported such key institutions and principles of the new Constitution as federalism and separation of powers. It is worth considering then how the alteration of Article V or the abandonment of Article V might weaken these other fundamental principles of the American regime, much as the removal of a crucial joist or beam in a building might weaken the entire structure and its integrity as a viable edifice.

Separation of Powers

An amending mechanism should also respect the key role that *separation of powers* plays in the American constitutional system. Most fundamentally, an amending process should not require the various branches to step outside of their sphere of power. Ideally the judicial and executive branches should not exercise the *creative* or legislative power, nor should the legislature exercise executive or judicial power. While recognizing a certain sharing of powers as outlined by the Constitution (e.g. the President exercising legislative veto power) the different branches are generally charged with exercising only that power (legislative, executive, and judicial) which was vested in them by the Constitution. The creation of the fundamental law is essentially a legislative power and therefore it properly belongs to democratically accountable institutions such as legislatures, or constitutional conventions. At every stage in American constitutional development during the founding era, constitutions were created and altered only by institutions that were directly accountable to the people. This was done with an understanding that the creation of law is an essentially creative and potentially limitless function; therefore it should be properly restrained by popular accountability and shaped by popular representation. Article V respects this commitment to a sound understanding of separation of powers and firmly places the amendment of fundamental law in the hands of legislatures at both the national and state levels. Again, either the state legislatures can be avoided or the Congress can be avoided but not both. Article V does demand that any amendment travel through some legislative body, be it the state legislatures or the national Congress.

What about maintaining the proper distribution of powers between the branches? This is certainly an important concern as Madison makes clear in the following passage:

> As the people of the United States enjoy the great merit of having established a system of Government on the basis of human rights, and of giving to it a form without example, which, as they believe, unites the greatest national strength with the best security for public order and individual liberty, they owe to themselves, to their posterity, and to the world, a preservation of the system in its purity, its symmetry, and its authenticity. This can only be done by a steady attention and sacred regard to the chartered boundaries between the portion of power vested in the Government over the whole, and the portion undivested from the several Governments over the parts composing the whole; and by a like attention and regard to the boundaries between the several departments, Legislative, Executive, and Judiciary, into which the aggregate power is divided. Without a steady eye to the landmarks between these departments, the danger is always to be apprehended, either of mutual encroachments and alternate ascendancies incompatible with the tranquil enjoyment of private rights, or of a concentration of all the departments of power into a single one, universally acknowledged to be fatal to public liberty.[30]

According to Madison, the American people are charged with the task of preserving the essence of the system that was bequeathed to them, in fact, "they owe to themselves, to their posterity, and to the world, a preservation of the system in its purity, its symmetry, and its authenticity." How this is exactly to be done is not fully outlined. Madison does seem to make a distinction between maintaining the separation of powers among the branches and extending the power of branches into areas not clearly granted by the Constitution.

In *Federalist No. 49*, Madison argues against using popular conventions as a means of preventing encroachments by the branches upon one another's authority. His main argument against appealing to conventions rests mostly on the danger of recurring to the constitutive authority of the people too often, "Every appeal to the people would carry an implication of some defect in the government, frequent appeals would, in great measure, deprive the government of that veneration which time bestows on everything, and without which perhaps the wisest and freest governments would not possess the requisite stability."[31]

Rather than depending upon the people to maintain the proper balance of powers Madison argues in *Federalist No. 51* that the branches of government should be empowered to check each other and to maintain the proper balance of powers. Exterior provisions are found to be inadequate the defect must be supplied, by so contriving the interior structure of the government as that its several constituent parts may, by their mutual relations, be the means of keeping each other in their proper places.[32] As Madison put it "ambition must be made to counteract ambition," the different branches must be empowered and motivated to maintain the proper boundaries that separate them from each other.

However, regarding the *extension* of powers not clearly granted by the Constitution Madison does see a role for the amending process, although as viewed through the lens of *Federalist No. 49* such instances should be rare so as to maintain the "veneration that time bestows on everything." For instance, when discussing the power of Congress to make internal improvements, Madison believed that the national legislature did not possess such a power. However, he realized that there are differing opinions on the exact scope of this power. In this context, he makes the following remarks, "Between these adverse constructions [of legislative power] an intermediate course must be the true one; and it is hoped that it will finally, if not otherwise settled, be prescribed by an amendment of the Constitution."[33] In referring to the limits of the power of Congress to provided for the "common defense and general welfare" if the Constitution does not give to Congress the unqualified power to provide for the common defense and general welfare, the defect cannot be supplied by the consent of the States, unless given in the form prescribed by the Constitution itself for its own amendment.[34]

Thus, Article V was designed as a seamless element of the new constitutional structure that both reflected and supported core constitutional principles such as federalism and separation of powers. In reflecting and supporting federalism, Article V's process drew upon both state and national powers and institutions. In support of separation of powers, Article V properly utilizes the legislative power at both the state and federal level, thus avoiding an improper mixing of powers with the judicial and executive branches. While Article V is not meant as the primary means for maintaining the proper balance of power between the branches, on rare occasions it should be utilized to add to or modify the powers of a given branch when necessary.

Article V as Constitutional Remedy

As the new Constitution began to operate, there did arise certain disputes over the proper distribution of power between the states and national government and between the executive and legislative branches. In addressing these pressing issues, James Madison indirectly outlined his view of Article V's role as the ultimate constitutional remedy for constitutional disputes.[35] Furthermore, as he outlined Article V's role as a remedy for such disputes, he affirmed the triad of amending precepts such as the need for explicit, authentic, and exclusive means of amending the document. In his view, Article V provided a peaceful, constitutional, and republican remedy for constitutional disputes over power. His thoughts on these issues lay out a vision of the importance of having a formal constitutional mechanism for addressing constitutional disputes or protecting the document against usurpation of power.

Madison forcefully confronted the role of Article V as a remedy for constitutional disputes during the debates on nullification. Writing in 1835, Madison was clarifying the Virginia Resolutions of 1798, which he authored. He was defending the *resolutions* from being co-opted into the rhetorical arsenal of those arguing for the right of nullification. Madison clearly argues that the Virginia resolutions do not support the right of nullification. Instead Madison maintains that the resolutions advocate what he calls "interposition." While *nullification* held the right of a single state to nullify federal law, Madison argued that no single state had that right. Rather, *interposition* referred to the collective right of the states to seek to preserve the Constitution from usurpation. Thus, no state could unilaterally nullify federal law; only the states acting together could take action and even then Madison does not argue that they collectively have the right to simply ignore federal law. When interposing the states could "explain, amend, or remake the Constitution."[36]

In addition, Madison argued that the term "state" could mean, "the people composing those political societies, in their highest sovereign capacity."[37] Thus, he argued that the majority of the people, acting through the states in their sovereign capacity, were the source of the Constitution. As such, when the states take action collectively (not by themselves) they can act in "their authority as the *parties* to the Constitution, the authority which, in fact, made the Constitution."[38] Given that Madison desires the states to draw on the authority that made the Constitution, one can only assume that he is referring to *all*, or at least a supermajority, of the states acting together as the "parties to the Constitution" and not just a few or a majority of states. If all the states are acting together they would be surely representing a majority of the people and they could stand against the national government to seek to preserve the Constitution.

What form would interposition exactly take? Madison was not wholly specific but he did say that, "The mode of their interposition, in extraordinary cases, is left by the Resolution to the parties themselves; as the mode of interposition lies with the parties to other Constitutions."[39] Furthermore, the mode of interposition is to take place, "under the forms and by the means provided by the Constitution."[40] Several times Madison says that when interposing the states could, "apply a remedy by explaining, amending, or remaking it [the Constitution]."[41] Even later Madison explains that in the Virginia Resolutions and the Virginia report it was not necessary "that the mode should be pointed out," but that the authority to interpose should be established, "The authority being plenary, the mode was of its own choice, and it is obvious, that, if employed by the States as coparties to and creators of the Constitution it might either so explain the Constitution or so amend it as to provide a more satisfactory mode within the Constitution itself for guarding it against constructive or other violations."[42]

It seems that in an act of interposition, the states could collectively pass resolutions "explaining" the proper constitutional construction. Or, acting in concert they could certainly "amend" the Constitution, presumably by petitioning Congress for a convention as prescribed by Article V. Or the states can "remake" the Constitution; again Madison does not elaborate, but the term would suggest the States could try to implement an entirely new Constitution through a similar method that had created the U. S. Constitution of 1787. In the end, the states can act as a collective to interpose (or stand between) the federal government and the people, but their options in doing so seem to range from mere protest, to amendment, to creating a new Constitution.

In answering those advocating nullification, Madison clearly outlines the options available to those fearing the usurpation of power under the Constitution:

> It has been asked whether every right has not its remedy; and what other remedy exists, under the Government of the United States, against usurpations of power, but a right in the States individually to annul and resist them.
>
> The plain answer is that the remedy is the same under the Government of the United States as under all other governments, established and organized on free principles. The first remedy is in the checks provided among the constituted authorities; that failing, the next is in the influence of the ballot-boxes and hustings; that again failing, the appeal lies to the power that made the Constitution, and can explain, amend, or remake it. Should this resort also fail, and the power usurped be sustained in its oppressive exercise on a minority by a majority, the final course to be pursued by the minority must be a subject of calculation, in which the degree of oppression, the means of resistance, the consequences of its failure, and the consequences of its success, must be the elements . . .
>
> Should the constituted authority of the State unite in usurping oppressive powers; should the constituent body fail to arrest the progress of the evil through the elective process, according to the forms of the Constitution; and should the authority which is above that of the Constitution, the majority of the people, inflexibly support the oppression inflicted on the minority, nothing would remain for the minority but to rally to its reserved rights, (for every citizen has his reserved rights, as exemplified in declarations prefixed to most of the State constitutions,) and to decide between acquiescence and resistance, according to the calculation above stated.[43]

Madison clearly argues that failing internal checks, and electoral remedies, constitutional amendment is an important last Constitutional remedy left to those who believe they are oppressed by the normal arms of government. Furthermore, such formal amendment is the key to maintaining the Constitution, for beyond amendment lay either peaceful submission to an oppressive government or violent revolution. It is important to note that Madison clearly distinguishes between constitutional means of redressing injustice and non-constitutional means. Usurpation can be addressed constitutionally by institutional checks, elections, and finally amendment, but if all of these constitutional measures fail, then Madison makes it clear that the next step is one that lies beyond the Constitution. The next step is a calculation of prudence based upon whether or not it is better to suffer the injustice or whether there is a chance of successfully replacing the Constitution or government through other means either peaceful or violent. Once one proceeds beyond the Constitution one leaves the protections of the Constitution as well. Subverting the current government or constitutional arrangements, even in the pursuit of justice, risks the chaos or anarchy that can result from a return to the *state of nature*. Thus, the calculation of whether to move beyond constitutional remedies is a risky proposition dependent on a sober calculation of prudence. If Madison wasn't clear enough above, he is more so in the following comments made in a letter addressing the nature of majority governments:

> Still the constitutional majority must be acquiesced in by the constitutional minority, while the Constitution exists. The moment that arrangement is successfully frustrated, the Constitution is at an end. The only remedy, therefore, for the oppressed minority is in the amendment of the Constitution or a subversion of the Constitution. This inference is unavoidable. While the Constitution is in force, the power created by it, whether a popular minority or majority, must be the legitimate power, and obeyed as the only alternative to the dissolution of all government.[44]

Thus, the existence and legitimacy of the Constitution depend upon a commitment, even by an oppressed minority, to follow the prescribed method of constitutional amendment. If one is committed to the Constitution one must follow its forms. However if there are those who view the Constitution as generally undesirable, then they can seek to replace it at their own peril or risk, and they forgo the protections that it currently provides. Nevertheless, Madison is clear that within the bounds of the Constitution there is only one proper, final, remedy to constitutional disputes:

> However deficient a remedial right in a single State might be to preserve the Constitution against usurped power, an ultimate and adequate remedy would always exist in the rights of the parties to the Constitution, in whose hands the Constitution is at all times but clay in the hands of the potter, and who could apply a remedy by explaining, amending, or remaking it, as the one or the other mode might be the most proper remedy.[45]

Madison clearly articulates the total sovereignty of the people acting through their state governments which are the "parties to the Constitution" and as such the Constitution is "at all times but clay in the hands of the potter."

In the end, Article V was seen as a valuable institution that provided a regular constitutional remedy of last resort, to settle disputes that arise under the Constitution. While prudence would dictate it not be the first remedy sought by those seeking change, it should certainly precede any attempts to subvert or overthrow the Constitution. As Madison makes clear, to ignore the will of constitutional majorities by seeking a remedy outside constitutional forms is to risk bringing the Constitution to an "end."

Thus, the design of the amending process must not only reflect American commitments to federalism and separation of powers it must also serve as a potential means of preserving those commitments. An amending process must serve as a final constitutional means of policing the boundaries of national power. To do this properly, it must reflect the federal distribution of power and it must not improperly involve judicial or executive arms of government in such a characteristically legislative endeavor. In this way the third order principles reinforce, buttress, fortify, and sustain key elements of the constitutional system.

A Note on Thomas Jefferson

Thomas Jefferson expressed views regarding amendment that were divergent from the dominant view expressed in the Constitutional Convention and implicit in the design of Article V. Unlike Madison, Jefferson seemed more comfortable with frequent change initiated by more popular means. In terms of differences between Jefferson and Madison, one scholar put it this way:

> Jefferson usually expressed less caution than Madison about constitutional change, he emphasized express rather than implied consent, and he was more willing to experiment with the convention mechanism and was less wary of ongoing popular input into the Constitution.[46]

In his *Notes on the State of Virginia*, Jefferson proposed an amending mechanism whereby two out of the three branches of government could call a constitutional convention to correct flaws in, or repair breaches of, the Constitution. Madison critiqued this approach thoroughly in *Federalist No. 49* arguing that it would likely produce instances where the legislative branch could use its resources to ally with another branch for purposes not conducive to maintaining a sound Constitution. Furthermore, Madison argued that such an amending provision would likely produce too many recurrences to the people and "deprive the government of that veneration which time bestows on everything." Lastly, Madison argued that such an arrangement was more likely to allow the legislature to aggrandize its own power and even when the judicial and executive branches had an advantage it was more likely that the *passions* of the people, and not their *reason* would rule over the convention.[47]

While we do not know Jefferson's reaction to Madison's arguments in *Federalist No. 49*, we do know that Jefferson supported the proposed Constitution and when writing to Madison from France, on his impressions of the proposed document, he did not express any displeasure regarding the amending process. In fact, near the end of his letter he writes, "After all, it is my principle that the will of the Majority should always prevail. If they approve the proposed Convention in all its parts, I shall concur in it cheerfully, in hopes that they will amend it whenever they shall find it work wrong."[48] It may be that Jefferson still preferred his proposal in his *Notes*, but he certainly did not make the amending process a source of concern, and in fact to the contrary he expressed some confidence that it would allow the people to correct any defects.

In another famous letter, Jefferson outlined his views " '*that the earth belongs in usufruct to the living*'; that the dead have neither powers nor rights over it."[49] While Jefferson had much more to say about the ability of generations to pass on debts and property to future generations, he also extended his analysis to apply to laws and constitutions:

> On similar ground it may be proved that no society can make a perpetual constitution, or even a perpetual law. The earth belongs always to the living generation. They may manage it then, and what proceeds from it, as they please, during their usufruct. They are masters too of their own persons, and consequently may govern them as they please. But persons and property make the sum of the objects of government. The constitution and the laws of their predecessors [are] extinguished then in their natural course with those who gave them being. This could preserve that being till it ceased to be itself, and no longer. Every constitution then, and every law, naturally expires at the end of 19 years. If it be enforced longer, it is an act of force, and not of right.[50]

Jefferson then was working through this notion that no generation could bind another either by law or through the creation of a perpetual constitution. In his letter he asks Madison to, "Turn this subject in your mind, my dear Sir . . . and develop it with that perspicuity and cogent logic so peculiarly yours."[51]

In responding to Jefferson's thoughts and honoring his request to examine his theory closely, Madison responded with a clarity and depth that Jefferson likely desired and expected. Madison expressed deep concern over the instability that would result from perpetually renewing the constitutions of government every nineteen years. There would likely be periods between governments that would invite mischief and problems; furthermore, such "ever-changing" governments might become "too mutable and novel to retain that share of prejudice in its favor which is a salutary aid to the most rational Government."[52] In short, such periodic change would invite an instability and open room for "pernicious factions" to "agitate the public mind" unnecessarily.

Madison also addressed the issue of generations binding one another. Rather than viewing each generation as an island unto its own carefully trying not to bind generations, Madison saw generations as being more interwoven and interdependent for, "The improvements made by the dead form a debt against the living, who take the benefit of them . . . there seems, then, to be some foundation in the nature of things, in the relation which one generation bears to another, for the descent of obligations from one to another. Equity may require it. Mutual good may be promoted by it."[53] For Madison, separating out the accountability of each generation is not that simple nor does one want to encourage diminishing the mutual obligations that bind generations together in a mutual endeavor. The living are certainly indebted to the dead in most cases, "and all that seems indispensable in stating the account between the dead and the living is, to see that the debts against the latter do not exceed the advances made by the former."[54] Madison subtly complements Jefferson's philosophical rigor even as he points out the limitations of applying philosophical conclusions to real political matters. For one, the general politician is just not capable of such reasoning, "further light must be added to the Councils of our Country before many truths which are seen through the medium of Philosophy become visible to the naked eye of the ordinary politician."[55]

There seems to be no record of Jefferson's reaction to Madison's response. One wonders if he welcomed Madison's clear and cogent rejection of his ideas as a prudent check on Jefferson's propensity for grand sweeping visions. The characteristic qualities of each man's mind come through strongly here. Jefferson's intense optimism about the potential of political man, contrasted with Madison's grounded understanding of the limits of corruptible human nature yet each mind in pursuit of excellence and precision. While we do not know Jefferson's exact response, we can speculate that Jefferson perhaps held to the truth of his philosophical ruminations, while recognizing and appreciating Madison's careful and prudential analysis. One can certainly see the potential benefits in a division of intellectual labor between the two men that surely paid dividends in their political alliance that would emerge in a few years. In the end, Jefferson supported the Constitution and by extension the amending process, even if tacitly. Still years later in 1813, in a letter to John Epps, Jefferson would still refer to the need for constitutional change every nineteen or twenty years.[56]

In the end, given that Jefferson was in France during the framing and ratification of the new Constitution, it is unlikely that his views had any impact at all on the design of Article V or the dominant view of the amending process in general. It is worth noting Jefferson's thoughts on these matters if only to highlight the exception that proves the rule; meaning most of the framers and leaders of the founding generation found Article V to be a prudent and efficacious means of amendment that embodied the dominant thought regarding such matters.

Conclusion

The Founders firmly embraced Article V as a perfecting mechanism of the Constitution. Article V facilitated *explicit* and *authentic* amendments which reflected their primary commitments to a written Constitution that would have the force of law and their commitment to the sovereignty of the people. As the sole mode of amendment promulgated in the Constitution, the Founders clearly saw Article V as the *exclusive* means of amending the Constitution. Furthermore Article V's design sought to ensure that while amendments were sufficiently democratic they would also reflect sound *deliberation* and would prudently require *prudent levels of consent* that would balance flexibility against stability. In addition Article V reflected the political realities of American *federalism* as well as the philosophical commitment to *separation of powers*. In the end, these principles reflected the Founders firm commitments to rule of law, prudence, deliberation, federalism, and separation of powers.

The writings of key founders show that Article V was not merely an ancillary afterthought, but a vital aspect of the Constitution that was fully engrained in the very fabric of American politics and American Constitutionalism. Article V was an institution that reflected core ideas and elements of the American political system, both as it had evolved and had been designed by those present at its inception. They embraced a coherent set of principles, which grew out of foundational political tenets and the logic of a written constitution. These principles guided their creation of an amending process that would preserve the core political ideas of the nation and engrain them in the everyday functioning of the governing institutions. These principles seek to balance the inherent tension of the American system, a system devoted to both popular sovereignty and to constitutionalism. It is meant to be democratic yet also to bind popular majorities and channel their impulses into deliberative institutions as a matter of prudence and good government. It was an obvious point to the Founders that just as the people had bound themselves to the limits of the Constitution, that in turn they had also bound themselves to Article V as the sole "mode" of amendment.

How can the people as the source of all legitimate political authority be limited in their exercise of government? A written constitution seeks to achieve a prudent calibration of that tension and the amending process is a vital aspect of this balancing act. The amending process must also seek to balance the demands of popular authority with the necessary limitations on government power and authority. A keen attention to maintaining this critical balance and managing this inherent tension in the American system is surely evident in these principles for a sound amending mechanism.

Given the strength and clarity of the founding generation's commitment to a written constitution and the formal amending process of Article V, why then is there confusion among contemporary scholars as to the proper role of Article V in American politics? The answer to this question rests in the emergence of a competing constitutional ideology that challenged many of the core principles of the Founding Constitutionalism. The emergence of this new ideology and its impact on Article V and the notion of an amending process are examined next.

Notes

1. Marvin Meyers, ed. *The Mind of the Founder: Sources of the Political Thought of James Madison* (London: University Press of New England, 1981), 361.

2. If one believes that all men are "created equal" with certain "inalienable rights" then the concepts of limited government and popular sovereignty logically follow. If all men are equal then only governments that gain the consent of a majority of the equal citizens are legitimate. Similarly if all men have certain rights then the government must be designed to preserve such rights. In other words government must be limited (to preserve rights) and be grounded in the authority and consent of the people (based on the notion of equality).

3. George Washington, *Farewell Address*, 1796, Yale Law School Avalon Project, http://avalon.law.yale.edu/18th_century/washing.asp (accessed December 20, 2012).

4. Ibid.

5. Ibid.

6. Ibid.

7. Ibid.

8. Ibid.

9. Ibid.

10. This is similar to what happened to the English constitution (although it is not a written one). As the constitution changed along with the changes of normal government the fundamental customs and precepts that had guided the English constitution became irrelevant over time thus creating a rift between the Colonies and their home country.

11. Thomas Jefferson To Msgr. Dumas, Paris, 10 September 1787, *The Writings of Jefferson,* 294-295.

12. The distinction between popular majorities and constitutional majorities has certainly been a controversial issue in modern American politics. One has only to remember the rancor over the 2000 presidential election and the fact that Al Gore won a popular majority while Bush won a constitutional majority. It is to Gore's credit that he was able to clearly understand and accept this distinction. Gore eventually recognized and honored the modes prescribed in the Constitution for establishing a constitutional majority for the purposes of presidential election.

13. James Madison, *Letters and Other Writings of James Madison, Fourth President of the United States*, 4 vol. (Philadelphia: J.B. Lippincott & Co. Published by Order of Congress), IV: 333. Accessed in electronic form in the *American Reference Library*. Orem, Utah: Western Standard Publishing Company, 1998. Hereafter cited as *Writings of James Madison.*

14. *Writings of James Madison*, IV: 333.

15. Ibid.

16. Ibid.

17. Ibid., IV: 334.

18. George Washington, *Farewell Address.*

19. While Madison supported the decision in McCulloch v. Maryland and had no "clear objection" to Marshall's finding that Maryland did not have the right to tax the bank in Baltimore, Madison nonetheless he had some questions about the scope of the jurisprudence utilized by Marshall. He had serious questions about Marshall's reasoning that Congress could employ any means to address the "ends" that were granted as within Congressional power by the Constitution. See Meyers, *Mind of the Founder*, 358.

20. Ibid., 361.

21. For a good account of the Framers' design of deliberation in American political institutions, see Bessette, *Mild Voice of Reason*, 13-39.

22. Ibid., 6-12; see this section, for a good summary of the problems inherent in the state governments leading up to the Constitutional Convention.

23. *The Federalist, No.10.*

24. Ibid.

25. Ibid.

26. *The Federalist, No. 63.*

27. *The Federalist, No. 43*

28. *The Federalist No. 39.*

29. Ibid.

30. *Writings of James Madison*, IV: 138.

31. The *Federalist No. 49.*

32. *The Federalist No. 51.*

33. *Writings of James Madison*, IV: 147.
34. Ibid., IV: 138.
35. Which as we will see leaves open the option of non or un-constitutional remedies to such disputes.
36. *Writings of James Madison*, IV: 417.
37. Meyers, *The Mind of the Founder*, 233.
38. Ibid., 420.
39. Ibid.
40. Ibid.
41. Ibid., 426.
42. Ibid., 431.
43. *Writings of James Madison*, IV: 417.
44. Ibid., 333.
45. Ibid., 417; here Madison is referring to the collective states as the "parties to the Constitution" in their capacity to represent the majority of the people in their highest sovereign capacity.
46. Vile, *The Constitutional Amending Process in American Political Thought*, 59.
47. *Federalist No. 49*.
48. Merrill D. Peterson, *The Portable Thomas Jefferson* (New York, Penguin Books, 1975) 432.
49. Ibid., 445.
50. Peterson, *The Portable Thomas Jefferson*, 449.
51. Ibid., 450.
52. Meyers, *The Mind of the Founder*, 176.
53. Ibid., 177.
54. Ibid.
55. Ibid., 179.
56. Vile, *The Constitutional Amending Process in American Political Thought*, 66.

PART II
Criticism of Article V

Chapter 5
The Progressive Challenge to Article V

> Society is a living organism and must obey the laws of life, not of mechanics. . . All that Progressives ask or desire is permission—in an era when 'development,' 'evolution,' is the scientific word—to interpret the Constitution according to the Darwinian principle; all they ask is recognition of the fact that a nation is a living thing and not a machine.
>
> Woodrow Wilson[1]

As the nineteenth century unfolded the United States faced new challenges as a nation and a polity. The geographic size of the nation rapidly expanded along with the population, the country endured a devastating Civil War, cities were burgeoning, industry developed, and new forms of transportation emerged. Along with these changes new intellectual currents emerged that spawned new legal theories and political views. During this period, some among the scholarly and political elite began to challenge the "founding consensus" regarding American Constitutionalism. As new political ideas emerged and matured, so did the call for alterations to the institutional structure of American government and political life. Swept up in these new challenges to the traditional constitutional order was the issue of constitutional amendment. As such, Article V became the focus of examination and debate.

The rise of Progressive thought brought an emphasis on direct democracy and harnessing governmental power to address growing social concerns; in this context Article V became seen as an overly rigid and formalistic means of altering the nation's fundamental law. The scope and power of the Progressive critique made a lasting impression on the American political landscape and more specifically American Constitutionalism. Here again, new ideas beget new institutional proposals and suggested new political norms within existing institutions. Just as founding era ideas shaped their creation of new governing institutions, Progressive ideas shaped efforts to reform or alter governing institutions in America.

Cracks in the Article V Consensus

The last chapter outlined the firm consensus that existed regarding Article V and its place in the larger constitutional structure. This Article V consensus held intact until well into the nineteenth century before a trickle of criticism began to be raised; as the nineteenth century gave way to the twentieth, the trickle would become a torrent. In the 1860s, Sidney George Fisher was notable in his rejection of Article V and its place in the constitutional order, and most notably, he represented a distinctly uncommon voice at the time, "Most American commentators on the amending process to the time of Sidney George Fisher appear to have been favorably impressed with this mechanism, which they frequently praised as an adequate 'safety valve' or as an alternative to revolution."[2] It had indeed served as a means of perfecting the Constitution. Fisher, however, saw problems with Article V and argued for a more informal, more "democratic," means of amendment. Fisher's 1862 work was very critical of Article V, and perhaps his work was an early indication that serious scholarly reassessment of the Article V amending procedure was on the horizon.[3]

Fisher, a sometimes lawyer from Philadelphia, argued that Article V was too difficult to be useful, and like Progressive scholars to follow him, he pointed to England as an example of how constitutional change should take place.[4] In reference to amendments, Fisher had this to say,

> Why should they not be made by Congress if demanded by necessity, as they would be by an English Parliament? Should they be approved and ratified by the people, what is the difference, whether their consent be expressed by a Legislature or by a Convention which they have elected, or before or after the alteration is made? It would still be the wishes of the same people carried into effect. If the people should be dissatisfied, they can say so through another Congress. If they continue to be satisfied after the alteration is tried, it would be thus established as a precedent to be engrafted on the Constitution, as is the case in England.[5]

One is struck by Fisher's references to England as the model for constitutional amendment less than a century removed from the founding generation's explicit rejection of such constitutional forms. The contrast between Fisher's praise for the evolutionary and informal English constitution and the criticism of such practices by many of the founding generation is certainly worthy of note.

Furthermore, Fisher argued that judicial review, the normal check on Congressional overreach, and the power of the court to strike down legislation should be limited to just unintentional violations of the Constitution, criminal assumptions of power, and the dominance of federal courts over the states.[6] "The Constitution belongs to the people—the people of 1862, not those of 1787. It must and will be modified to suit the wishes of the former, by their representatives in Congress, just as the English Constitution has been modified by Parliament, or it will be destroyed."[7]

Fisher argued that radical action by Congress was actually "Constitutional" since the "necessary and proper" clause made government's powers without limits.[8] Fisher also compared the language in the Articles of Confederation—which specified only one means of amendment—with Article V noting that the latter does not contain a mention of its exclusivity.

Near the turn of the century as Progressive thought began to rise, more commentators began to find fault with Article V and the Founder's Constitutionalism. For example, in the 1880s and 1890s Christopher Teideman also argued against the efficacy of Article V. Teideman, a legal scholar and Dean of the University of Buffalo law school, took a realist approach to the law and argued for the place of laissez-faire economic theories in constitutional interpretation.[9] More to the point Teidemen characterized the United States Constitution in organic terms likening the Constitution and constitutional law to "the anatomy and physiology of the body politic."[10] Teideman recognized that such views were inherently similar to the British conceptions of constitutionalism and he maintained that the "flesh and blood of the Constitution," was "unwritten," and as such it was just as "flexible" as the British constitution.[11]

> For if by judicial interpretation, in obedience to the stress of public opinion or private interests, the express limitations of the written Constitution are made to mean one thing at one time, and at another time an altogether different thing, there is very little restraint imposed by these written limitations. The only obstacle in the way of an untrammelled popular will is the bald letter of the Constitution; and even that does not chain the popular will in times of great excitement and extreme necessity.[12]

Tiedeman argued that the written text of the Constitution could not withstand the onslaught of normal government when backed by strong expressions of popular will.[13] In his focus on power over law, one can also see in Tiedeman's work the early seeds of a fundamental challenge to the founding era's core philosophical beliefs in natural rights. In referring to the doctrine of natural rights, Tiedeman remarked that, "The doctrine reaches the extreme limits of absurdity."[14] Tiedeman scoffed at the further absurdity of a "social contract" and "in the claim that all governmental authority, and hence the binding force of law, is derived from the agreement or consent of the governed; and that all men are possessed of certain natural rights, rights enjoyed by them in a state of nature, and which no government can rightfully infringe or take away."[15]

In a Holmesian fashion, Teideman, held that the moral sentiment of the people determined the nature and extent of citizens' rights thus rights could not be inalienable or absolute.[16] As such the power of government is not derived from the consent of the governed but rather the exercise of political power by the few rests on the "possession by the few of the superior strength, both moral and material."[17] Teideman's realism is a stark departure from the views of the founding generation who sought to found government on "real" understandings of human nature while still believing that there were universal principles that governed humanity and hence the law. In contrast, Teideman clearly believed that all law is rooted in human institutions, and as such there can be no appeals to "unalienable" rights or universal principles that stand outside of human society. All rights are alienable if human societies wish to deprive individuals of these "rights." Ultimately Teideman argued that theories of the social contract and ideas of tacit consent that rooted the law in universal principles and the actions of past generations made it difficult for many to recognize the reality of "the present will of the people as the living source of law."[18]

One cannot minimize the impact of abandoning the notion of "unalienable" rights that are derived from a "creator" or some force outside of human society. For if human society really "creates" rights via governmental fiat and consensus, then it would make sense to streamline governmental powers and remove any obstacles to the popular will. However, if there are rights that exist outside of government then it would be in order to create a system that sought to check, or frustrate, the popular will. For such a system would seek to prevent the majority from trampling rights of the minority, rights that exist irrespective of the majority's wishes.

In sum, scholars such as Fisher and Teideman were the first to critique Article V and break with the founding generation's view of an American Constitutionalism; a view that had explicitly rejected the evolutionary unwritten constitution of England for the fixed written constitutions of the states and the new United States Constitution. Where the founding generation saw instability and an unacceptably malleable foundation for natural rights when looking at unwritten constitutions, scholars like Fisher and Teideman saw, in a legislatively dominated unwritten constitution, the immediate translation of popular will into constitutional change. Where the Founders generally feared the "impetuous vortex" of legislative power, Fisher and Teideman embraced legislative power as the ultimate manifestation of popular power. Fisher and Teideman's views reflect the beginning of major shifts in legal philosophy that saw law not as fixed and universal but as merely the result of contemporary social forces and popular will. Such views on Article V would be the precursor to an expanding number of scholars and politicians who would begin to challenge the fixed written nature of the Constitution and Article V's role within it.

Progressive Legal Thought: The Rise of the Living Constitution

Progressivism, as a movement, became a political force in the first third of the twentieth century and drew upon a growing optimism regarding the potential for human nature to perfect itself and its social conditions. Advances in science and changing social theories created an atmosphere where an unlimited human potential seemed capable of confronting America's growing social ills; ills which resulted largely from the country's rapid industrialization and urbanization. Politically, Progressivism sought to harness the tremendous potential of governmental power to address the growing political and economic inequalities in America.[19] Progressives were especially wary of the deleterious impact of entrenched financial interests and corporations, which had blossomed during the Gilded Age, and now seemed to hold preeminent positions of influence in American politics. If government was to be the engine of social change it must first be freed from the constraints and influence of these corrupt corporate or financial interests. Government must be returned to the people. Most often returning government to the people meant the creation of directly democratic institutions that gave popular majorities a means of circumventing legislatures and elected officials. Mechanisms such as the recall, referendum, and initiatives were established and flourished in many states during this era. In this sense Progressives did not share the founding generation's reliance on representative deliberative democracy, nor the founding era's fears of demagogues and the instability of direct democracy.

If government could be tethered more directly to popular majorities then it would be safe to grant government expansive new powers and authority, to regulate business, and to address the growing social inequalities. Given the intense focus on an active and powerful government devoted to the will of popular majorities, the deliberative democracy envisioned by the founders—institutionally supported by the Constitution, with designed separation of powers and checks and balance—was a natural source of frustration for Progressive activists. Progressive thought also encompassed new legal theories and approaches which in turn began to question the orthodox view of written constitutionalism and the utility of Article V as the best and only means of altering the Constitution.

American legal thought underwent radical changes during the late nineteenth century and early twentieth century, and one could generally classify this rising intellectual tide as *Progressive Legal Thought*.[20] A foundational aspect of this new mode of legal thinking was a commitment to the idea that law is essentially political. In other words, laws and legal orders cannot exist as neutral arbiters of political conflict, and law is often used as an instrument to achieve political or social ends. This major shift in legal thought began to impact the commitment of American scholars and jurists to the precepts of written constitutionalism and formal amendment, for the existing order and Constitution came to be viewed as bulwarks of more conservative or corporate interests in society.[21] Such ideas led to the emerging notion that the application of the law by judges was in fact based on considerations other than formal rules and precedents. In reality, argued legal realists, partisan concerns, social factors, or partisan agendas drove the decisions of judges in their application and interpretation of the law.

At its philosophical core, such legal thought rejected the notion that law has a foundation based in something larger and more enduring than human society.

Law is created by, and altered by, human society and thus is essentially a political question. As a political question law is subject to evolving moral and social concerns rather than fixed abstract principles rooted in nature or universal truth. Therefore, law cannot, and should not, be constrained by overly cumbersome forms or procedures, rather such obstructions should give way to more dominant social concerns. Law became an instrument to achieve certain policy goals and as such, the "rule of law" was no longer an end to be achieved and could no longer be separated from the "rule of politics." Law was a political means to achieve political ends.[22] Only by admitting and addressing such "realities" could the study of law be conducted in an objective scientific manner worthy of the emerging professions of political science and history.[23]

Within this larger legal context the Constitution was more than just a fixed written document produced by the people, in their sovereign capacity, to limit and define the role of government. The Constitution was a political instrument created to serve the agenda of those who created it, and it was often interpreted to serve partisan aims or achieve desired social outcomes. The Constitution was not a set of formal rules that established a clear and fair playing field, rather it was a set of stated rules that provided rhetorical and political cover for those who sought to use the Constitution to preserve or shape society according to their wishes. It became less important to study the formal legalistic aspects of the Constitution, for these failed to capture the dynamic political process that animated it and shaped it. More important were the informal practices of political actors, the political agendas of those who created it, or the social aims of those who interpreted it. Those who sought to understand the Constitution in an overly legalistic or formalistic manner were missing the real political impact of the document and failed to observe the institutional changes that had evolved over time which were the real driving force behind constitutional law. The Constitution was no longer a machine, it was an organism. In the end, this emerging Progressive legal thought provided the philosophical foundation for an array of ideas that logically flowed from its premises, such as a Darwinian view of the Constitution, sociological jurisprudence, legal realism, historicism, anti-formalism, and pragmatism. In turn these ideas began to shape how scholars, political actors, lawyers, and judges came to view the Constitution and in turn institutional arrangements such as Article V.[24]

The Progressive Constitution

Progressivism saw itself as a more modern scientific approach to politics and such self-awareness—combined with a legal realist framework—led Progressives to adopt a contagious and powerful organic metaphor for the Constitution. Progressives rejected a fixed mechanistic "Newtonian" view of the Constitution in favor of an organic biological "Darwinian" view of the Constitution. Rather than a formal machine with set rules and fixed institutions, the Constitution came to be viewed by many in the legal elite as a living organism whose rules and institutions would adapt and change over time in a more natural unpredictable manner.[25] Ever an eloquent spokesman for the Progressive movement, Woodrow Wilson articulated this shift in intellectual metaphors for the Constitution, "Society is a living organism and must obey the laws of life, not of mechanics. . . All that Progressives ask or desire is permission—in an era when 'development,' 'evolution,' is the scientific word—to interpret the Constitution according to the Darwinian principle; all they ask is recognition of the fact that a nation is a living thing and not a machine."[26]

Wilson's articulate message captures so much of the Progressive outlook as it wanted to be portrayed, an outlook that was modern, scientific, realistic, and able to adapt to the new facts of the industrial age. Progressives did not want to be bound by the mechanics of the past rather they wanted to be free to pursue new solutions to new problems unconstrained by the ideas of bygone eras. A Constitution with fixed rules and precedents that constrained the rapid pursuit of desired policy goals only hindered the dynamic evolution of the social organism known as the American polity.

One does not have to search long to find the possible impact of such thinking on the view of a fixed written constitution, for an unrestrained ever evolving live organism is in certain respects at odds with a mechanically operated fixed structure.[27] For instance, Wilson points out that constitutional government, "does not remain fixed in an unchanging form, but grows with the growth and is altered with the change of the nation's needs and purposes. . . [G]overnment is not a machine, but a living thing. . . It is accountable to Darwin, not to Newton."[28]

Contrast Wilson's depiction with that of George Bancroft, and one can clearly see the stark contrast in Constitutional metaphors and their impact on amendment theory. Bancroft writing in the 1880s argued,

> An interpretation of the constitution by the court, to be permanently valid, must not only be the opinion of the court at the moment, but must be in conformity to the constitution, and every time it is repeated must owe its validity to that conformity. . . Men believe in Sir Isaac Newton's law of gravity, not because it was pronounced by Sir Isaac Newton, though he was the highest judge of his day on the laws of the planetary motions; but because Sir Isaac Newton in laying down the law pronounced that which is true. It is with legal science as with every branch of science; truth alone has the right to endure, and truth alone does endure. Bury it, and it will spring from beneath the earth. The court that tried Galileo gave the decision that the earth does not move; "but it does move" said Galileo, adhering to the truth, while submitting to the judgment in the case.[29]

The contrast between the Darwinian metaphor embraced by Wilson and other leading Progressives, and Bancroft's Newtonian metaphor which was consistent with the founding era's constitutionalism, could not be more clear. For Wilson constitutional law was to be created by each generation as it grew and changed with the times. For Bancroft constitutional law was an act of discovering fixed principles. It was Newtonian, fixed, and permanent, not Darwinian, organic, and evolving.

Other Progressive legal scholars such as Oliver Wendell Holmes seconded Wilson's transition in metaphors, "the provisions of the Constitution are not mathematical formulas having their essence in their form; they are organic living institutions transplanted from English soil,"[30] Holmes aptly articulates the Progressive view that a fixed written constitution is a stale static "mathematical" formula which is clearly less desirable than an "organic living" institution. In addition, Holmes also supported a more legislative approach to constitutional change, which was much in keeping with the Progressive resurgence of a neo-British organic constitutionalism.[31]

This powerful Darwinian analogy animated much of Progressive thought during this period and its assumptions and premises produced a variety of intellectual offspring which manifested themselves in emerging schools of legal thought. As alluded to already, such an evolutionary approach to constitutionalism was partly rooted in *historicist* assumptions about the nature of law. Such *historicism* held that law draws its direction not from timeless, universal truths, but from the ever-evolving standards of each society in its own historical era. As such, constitutional alterations and interpretations were only accountable to contemporary historical standards, not standards that existed outside of time and society. Such *historicism* was well argued by Oliver Wendell Holmes,

> The life of the law has not been logic: it has been experience. The felt necessities of the time, the prevalent moral and political theories, intuitions of public policy, avowed or unconscious, even the prejudices which judges share with their fellow men, have a good deal more to do than the syllogism in determining the rules by which men should be governed. . . The substance of the law at any given time pretty nearly corresponds, so far as it goes, with what is then understood to be convenient; but its form and machinery, and the degree to which it is able to work out desired results, depend very much upon its past.[32]

For Holmes the law, and in this case fundamental law, must derive from "prevalent moral and political theories," not universal principles rooted in nature. This historicism that rejected any permanent mooring for rights was a radical departure from the universal moral claims articulated in the Declaration of Independence and had a profound effect on Progressive legal thought. Such historicism made rights subject to human social evolution not fixed principles of human nature. It subtly shifted government's role from a power built on natural rights with a core purpose of securing natural rights, to a power that ushered in an ever evolving historical sense, a power that never rested and was continually expanding to pick winners and losers as history dictated. Rights now came from government and were subject to its evolutionary path.

Another product of Progressive legal thought and the new Darwinian view of the Constitution was a form of *sociological jurisprudence*, championed by Roscoe Pound, who held that law would inevitably accommodate the changing needs of society and therefore legal concepts would continually be reinvented. If social changes would and should impact the direction of the law, then it followed that judges should rely on disciplines outside of the law such as the political and social sciences to aid them in their judicial rulings.[33] Also judges should eschew overly formalistic rulings or "mechanical jurisprudence" in favor of rulings that simply sought to create just and equitable decisions in individual cases. This of course assumed that judges knew what the most just and equitable thing to do was and it further assumed that commitment to the rule of law did not already largely embody justice and equity to the extent humanly possible. One corollary of sociological jurisprudence was that legislatures were much better at collecting social data and therefore courts should defer to legislative judgment in most cases.[34]

Progressives also embraced a form of legal *pragmatism,* which "purports to demonstrate how legal decisions have always been made with some reference to the acceptability of their social impact and not in accordance with purely formalist criteria."[35] Such a view rejected the legal tendency to give great weight to precedents and formal legal rules and practices if such practices prevented beneficial social ends. In the words of William James, arguably the father of pragmatism as a philosophy, "Pragmatism is willing to take anything, to follow either logic or the sense and to count the humblest and most personal experiences. . . Her only test of probable truth is what works best in the way of leading us . . . but you see already how democratic she is."[36] As Brad C. S. Watson comments, "It is indeed the very protean nature of pragmatism—its willingness to absorb *anything*—combined with its democratic ethos and faith in scientific intelligence, that has made it an enduringly popular doctrine for Americans."[37]

Progressive constitutionalism also embraced an *anti-formalism,* which rejected what Progressives might describe as overly legalistic conceptions of the Constitution. Progressives rejected the tendency by judges to assign legal disputes to formal legal categories and conceptions as a means of achieving a neutral application of the law. Nineteenth century jurists largely held that the Constitution's meaning did not change, therefore they should adapt to changing social conditions by applying emerging modern legal disputes to the already existing formal categories and concepts embedded in the Constitution.[38] Progressives on the other hand attacked such notions as artificial and limiting, instead preferring that judges engage in acts of "balancing" and the "weighing of social interests."[39] The emphases on historicism, sociological jurisprudence, and pragmatism, placed increasing pressure on the legal forms and formalities that had characterized American law from the beginning. An emphasis on the rule of law and legal forms was premised on the belief that immediate impulses in public opinion or fleeting opinions on what is just or fair by a judge in a given moment must yield to a larger social commitment to formal deliberation on such matters.

Allow of these modes of thought began to erode traditional American legal thought and by the 1920s conceptions of *legal realism,* reminiscent of Tiedeman, had gained strength and they embraced the common notion that formal law was out of touch with reality.[40] Legal realism became extremely skeptical about the utility of reason and morality as guides for the legal order.[41] Such thinking undermined the established legal and constitutional theories that embraced the ability of human actors to use reason as a guide for constructing efficacious political and constitutional orders. By contrast legal realists were governed by a moral skepticism; for legal realists reason certainly could not arrive at, nor utilize, considerations of morality or moral argument as reliable guides for legal and political thought. In the absence of moral certainty, the law became a tool for subjective uses of power. Law did not structure politics, law became a tool of politics. Such moral skepticism is obviously at direct odds with the language and philosophy of the Declaration of Independence and its heavy reliance on reason and moral considerations as foundations for the American political order.

In their ambitious attempts to create new legislative and governmental solutions to growing social needs, Progressives rejected the many prudence of constitutional constraints on government action represented in the founding orthodoxy. Political ideas and institutional realities such as separation of powers, federalism, checks and balances, enumerated powers, all frustrated the Progressive impulse for social change through governmental action. All of these intellectual trends in political and legal thought emerging under the general heading of "Progressivism" began to congeal into a notion of the "living constitution," that stood in contrast to the founding notions of fixed constitutions. In general it can be said that, "By the 1920s the traditional conception of a Constitution whose meaning was fixed and immutable was coming under siege by different versions of the living Constitution."[42] Sociological jurisprudence, pragmatism, historicism, anti-formalism combined with a potent Darwinian metaphor driven by commitments to legal realism all combined to form a daunting philosophical alternative to the founding era consensus. Progressive thought saw law as rooted in human society, a society that should be free to determine itself how to order the polity and address social concerns. In this vein the Constitution must be very malleable and responsive to direct democratic impulses. Any formal constraints on these efforts were essentially obstructionist. On the other hand, the constitutionalism of the founding generation was philosophically based on notions that law was rooted in nature and thus it could be universalized and rights were unalienable. As such their system was rooted in a fixed written constitution created by the people in their sovereign capacity that served as a fundamental law designed to limit government and preserve rights rooted in universal principles. The Constitution of the Founders was designed to initially resist unwise popular impulses and redirect them if necessary. In contrast, the Progressives sought to unleash the popular will from the constraints of the Constitution. Odysseus wanted to be unbound.

Since Article V was designed to fit well within the larger constitutional system it has come under scrutiny as the pragmatic strains of Progressive thought have sought to push for less formal constitutional change. To the extent that Progressives resisted the counter-majoritarian elements of the Constitution, they also resisted Article V's counter-majoritarian elements; likewise to the extent that they resisted the formalism of the Constitution they also resisted Article V's formalism. In short, in some ways Article V was caught up in the larger assault on the constitutionalism of the Founders and in other ways it was seen as the lynchpin of undoing the traditional American Constitutionalism and thus was singled out for reproach.

The purpose of this brief sketch of Progressive legal thought is to give a bit of context to the critiques of Article V. The critiques of Article V only make sense when based in premises that are at fundamental odds with American Constitutionalism as it existed since the founding period. The Progressive movement operated on philosophical and legal premises that were radical departures from the moral realism and natural rights philosophy of the Founders. Nevertheless this disjuncture between the constitutionalism of the Founders and the constitutionalism of the Progressives has framed, in one way or another, much of the contemporary debate and dialogue surrounding American Constitutionalism. For example, the basic premises of Progressive legal thought have come to characterize a powerful force in the legal academy and its strains can be easily seen influencing contemporary critics of Article V. Like Progressives, there are important contemporary legal scholars who argue that Article V is too difficult, undemocratic, and too formalistic. It is along these three broad and interlocking fronts that the assault on Article V has been advanced. These three prongs of attack will be examined and a defense of Article V will be given in response. We will now turn to examine the criticisms of Article V in turn.

Notes

1. Wilson as quoted in Howard Gillman, "The Collapse of Constitutional Originalism," *Studies in American Political Development* 11 (Fall 1997) 191-247.
2. John R. Vile, *The Constitutional Amending Process in American Political Thought*, (New York: Praeger, 1992), 137.
3. Sidney George Fisher, *The Trial of the Constitution* (New York: Da Capo Press, 1972; reprint of J. B. Lippincott & Co., 1862). Fisher was a precursor to the Progressives in his questioning of whether or not Article V was flexible enough to meet the needs of good government. For a good account of Fisher's work see Vile, *The Constitutional Amending Process*, 96-108.
4. Vile, *The Constitutional Amending Process*, 98.
5. Fisher, *The Trial of the Constitution*, 55; quoted in Vile, *The Constitutional Amending Process*, 99.
6. Vile, *The Constitutional Amending Process*, 99.
7. Fisher, *The Trial of the Constitution*, 96-97; quoted in Vile, *The Constitutional Amending Process*, 99.
8. Vile, *The Constitutional Amending Process*, 100.
9. Ibid., 116; for another analysis of Tiedeman also see Gillman, *Studies in American Political Development*, 191-247.
10. Ibid., 118.

11. Ibid.

12. Christopher Tiedeman, *The Unwritten Constitution of the United States* (New York: C. P. Putnam's Sons, 1890) 43-44; quoted in Vile, *The Constitutional Amending Process,* 119.

13. No one doubts this. If the people want to support and encourage normal government to ignore the written nature of the Constitution, then there is nothing that can be done for who is left to stop this from happening. However, just because one can argue that a thief can be very effective when a majority of the family invites him into their house to take their property, against the wishes of a minority of the family, does not mean that thievery has not taken place. The *de facto* argument that the text can be ignored when enough segments of government and society array against it, does not translate into a *de jure* argument that it is a proper functioning of our constitutional system and should be encouraged.

14. Tiedeman, *The Unwritten Constitution,*70-71; quoted Vile, *The Constitutional Amending Process,* 120.

15. Tiedeman, *The Unwritten Constitution,*70-71; quoted Vile, *The Constitutional Amending Process,* 120.

16. Vile, *The Constitutional Amending Process,* 120.

17. Ibid., 122.

18. Ibid., 123.

19. Kelly, Harbison, and Belz, *The American Constitution,* 408. "In general the object of Progressive reform was to redress the imbalances and inequalities of political and economic power caused by the new system of industrial capitalism." An expanded role for government would also necessitate an expanded view of federal power and the Constitution. See Ibid., 416: "The expansion of governmental authority for regulatory purposes required the formulation of new doctrines of constitutional power, especially at the federal level."

20. For a good account of this transformation, see Morton J. Horwitz, *The Transformation of American Law 1870-1960: The Crisis of Legal Orthodoxy* (New York: Oxford University Press, 1992), 3-7. Horwitz argues that there was a struggle between Classical legal thought and Progressive legal thought during the turn of the century culminating in the practical success of the New Deal which was predicated upon legal ideas and modes of thought championed by Progressives and legal realists earlier in the century.

21. Herman Belz, *Living Constitution or Fundamental Law?* (Lanham, Maryland: Rowman and Littlefield Publishers Inc., 1998), 58-59.

22. Gillman, *Studies in American Political Development,* 193. "Legal texts have always been vulnerable to partisan interpretation, and this makes it possible to argue that there is no reason to privilege the partisan interpretations of the past over the interpretations that are most convenient for our purposes."

23. See Belz, *A Living Constitution or Fundamenal Law?*, 57.

24. Gillman addresses many of these developments in his excellent article on the philosophical challenges to the orthodoxy of originalism. Gillman, *Studies in American Political Development,* 191-247.

25. Ibid., 194; Gilliam writes: "Perhaps the most obvious feature of this modernist assault on the concept of constitutional originalism was the shift from using Newtonian metaphors to describe the Constitution to using Darwinian metaphors, or more specifically, the shift away from viewing the Constitution as a reliable and durable mechanism toward viewing it as an organism."

26. Wilson as quoted in Gillman, *Studies in American Political Development,* 216.

27. Gillman, *Studies in American Political Development,* 215.

28. Wilson as quoted in Gillman, *Studies in American Political Development,* 216.

29. George Bancroft, *A Plea For the Constitution of the United States, Wounded in the House of its Guardians* (New York: Harper & Bros, 1886), 68-69.

30. Gillman, *Studies in American Political Development,* 219.

31. Ironically, Holmes also supported the "natural outcome of dominant opinion" should prevail in legislation and courts should not intervene except when absolutely necessary. Such minimalist views of constitutional interpretation are consistent with many current conservatives who argue for the Supreme Court to allow legislative supremacy to be the de facto status in constitutional matters. Holmes is quoted from Gillman, *Studies in American Political Development,* 218-219.

32. Oliver Wendell Holmes, *The Common Law* (Boston: Little, Brown, 1881), 1-2; quoted in Gillman, *Studies in American Political Development,* 218.

33. William Wiecek, "Sociological Jurisprudence," *Oxford Companion to the Supreme Court,* 1992. ed.

34. Gillman, *Studies in American Political Development,* 193; In Gillman: "Sociological Jurisprudence" "demonstrated the inevitability of the law's accommodation of change and development, and this can lead to fatalism about the need for periodic reconceptualizations of legal principles and categories." Also, the deference of this viewpoint to legislatures instead of courts is an argument trumpeted by current conservative critics of the liberal activist courts. This fact highlights the reality that issues of constitutional form are essentially non-partisan for they merely establish the rules of the game. Liberals and Conservatives will be tempted to favor the formal conditions that favor their policy preferences during the era in which they live. Secondly, it is worth noting that most of today's conservative critics would not do away with judicial review altogether, but would prefer that the courts defer to the legislatures on close or questionable cases, but not on all cases.

35. Gillman, *Studies in American Political Development,* 193. Also Gillman wrote "Holmes was the first of a number of legal pragmatists who wanted to accommodate change by having courts abandon their traditional 'preservationist function' and instead defer to the judgment of legislatures. In a nutshell they were proposing a transference of power from traditional popular sovereignty to contemporary popular majorities." Furthermore, "One argument in favor of this transference was that it was a *fait accompli*; given historicist and pragmatist assumptions it was inevitable that the law would reflect current power configurations, and it was futile (if not dangerous) for courts to think that they were in a position to prevent 'the natural outcome of dominant opinion' from working its way into law." Ibid., 220

36. William James, as quoted in Watson, *Living Constitution Dying Faith,* 79.

37. Watson, *Living Constitution Dying Faith,* 79.

38. Horwitz, *The Transformation of American Law,* 18.

39. Ibid., 18.

40. Ibid., 187-188.

41. Ibid., 170.

42. Gillman, *Studies in American Political Development,* 223.

Chapter 6
The Critics: Article V is Too Difficult

> The traditional system possessed one specific form which, just as a matter of political mechanics, did more than anything else to convert a constitutional democracy into semi-democratic constitutionalism. This form consisted in the amending clause of the Constitution, which made the process of amendment almost insuperably difficult.
>
> Herbert Croly[1]

The most common criticism of Article V is that its supermajority requirements are just too difficult to be of any practical use. Article V's difficulty became a contentious issue for Progressives who sought to remove barriers to the immediate expression of popular will in politics. Progressives saw Article V and its use of supermajorities as unduly difficult and a cumbersome relic from a bygone era. Such concerns eventually resulted in the New Deal era shift to judicial alterations of the Constitution. Even contemporary scholars refer to Article V's difficulty as a reason for such exercises in judicial power, "The difficulty of the constitutional amending process undoubtedly prods the judiciary to be more creative than it might be if the process were easier."[2] In fact, Article V's supermajority standards lead even supporters of Article V to occasionally mention its difficulty.[3]

Arguments about Article V being too difficult are often intertwined with complaints that it is undemocratic—largely because both arguments see the supermajority requirements of Article V as a major problem—but in the end they are distinct enough to be treated separately. For instance, one could still hold a position that the supermajority requirements are *not undemocratic* and yet one could logically still maintain that such supermajority requirements are simply too difficult to be of use. The *democracy* argument looks more to issues in democratic theory, while the *difficulty* argument looks more to issues of simple logistics and political efficacy. Put another way arguments of *difficulty* hinge on assessing Article V's utility, while arguments about *democracy* hinge on assessing its legitimacy. The critique of Article V being "undemocratic" will be dealt with more directly in the next chapter.

To be certain, compared to passing a normal piece of legislation in Congress or in a state legislature, the supermajority requirements of Article V do raise the bar regarding the level of political consensus needed to enact changes to the fundamental law. Thus, on some level, the critique is true that Article V is *more difficult* than the enactment of mere normal law. In one sense, this is of course perfectly consistent with the traditions of American Constitutionalism that view the Constitution as *higher law* or *fundamental law*: law that is logically antecedent, chronologically prior, and therefore superior to normal legislation. On the other hand, critics charge that these supermajority requirements are simply too high or too "rigid" for Article V to be a useful tool in amending the Constitution and facilitating the evolving needs of the American polity. Indeed it is often noted that the United States has the most difficult amending process in the world today.[4] Such criticisms began during the Progressive era and continue unabated. Charges that Article V is too difficult are rarely, if ever, followed by any analysis to illustrate its ineffectiveness. That is to say, critics of Article V often use the term *supermajority* as a trump-card to be played as self-evident proof of Article V's ineffectiveness; this trump card is rarely if ever followed by any semblance of analysis elaborating the charge. Unsubstantiated or not, critics do raise a valid question: "Is Article V simply too difficult to use effectively in making changes to the United States Constitution?"

Progressive Era Critics

Progressive era critics of Article V viewed the amending procedure as overly difficult, cumbersome, and ultimately undemocratic, in its use of supermajorities. The "rigid" nature of Article V was seen as an unyielding obstacle to evolving social realities and an uncompromising enemy to the Progressive cause. In that vein it endured a significant amount of criticism by Progressive politicians and scholars alike. As Progressive ideas gained traction amongst the populace and among academic political elites, there were increasing calls for altering Article V to make it less "rigid" and easier to use. Since Article V was seen as a major impediment the Progressive agenda, it seemed reasonable to try and amend Article V and update it to meet the needs of modern American society, something to which Progressives were acutely attuned.

One key Progressive intellectual, Herbert Croly, articulated these Progressive themes very well. Croly argued that Article V was "the most formidable legal obstacle in the path of Progressive democratic fulfillment."[5] Indeed, Croly did not simply restrict his criticism to Article V; rather, like most fellow Progressives, he was highly critical of the entire constitutional edifice,

> The traditional system possessed one specific form which, just as a matter of political mechanics, did more than anything else to convert a constitutional democracy into semi-democratic constitutionalism. This form consisted in the amending clause of the Constitution, which made the process of amendment almost insuperably difficult.[6]

Not only was Article V difficult, but it was seen as an obstacle to the larger Progressive political reform agenda. On this point, Croly quotes another scholar, "'that the first article of any sincerely intended progressive program must be the amendment of the amending clause of the Constitution.'"[7]

Progressives, like Croly, charged that Article V's supermajority requirements made constitutional amendment impossible, and as evidence, they pointed to the paucity of amendments passed since the founding. Indeed, the *infrequency* of amendment was a common Progressive refrain and could be found in a quote by Justice William P. Potter of the Pennsylvania Supreme Court who lamented, "We are taught by a century of our history that the Constitution can no longer be . . . amended."[8] Australian Henry B. Higgins remarked that, "the federal constitution has become practically unalterable," and "Except as the result of the volcanic upheaval of the great Civil War and by the use of such devices after the war as were, to say the least, unprecedented, there has been no change since 1804."[9] Frederic Johnstone, of the Chicago bar commented, "since the decade in which the constitution was adopted, but five amendments have been made, two of which, of comparatively minor importance, are over 100 years old, and the last three of which were written in blood."[10] Herman Ames, in chronicling over 1,700 proposed amendments argued that the Article V process had proven "unwieldy and cumbrous."[11] In a 1905 essay comparing the American Constitution with other constitutions in the world, Lord Bryce concluded that, "the Constitution which it is the most difficult to change is that of the United States."[12] Bryce declared that the United States Constitution was "rigid" and in doing so introduced the distinction between "rigid" and "flexible" constitutions that would be used by constitutional scholars for years to come.[13]

Another Progressive theme was that Article V was so difficult, that it endangered the public peace. Herman Ames argued that the majorities required for constitutional change were too large and he warned that such a rigid process could encourage revolution and violence.[14] Likewise, Progressive scholar John Burgess argued that the majorities required by Article V were "artificially excessive" and he opined that such inflexibility opened up the national possibility of "revolution and violence."[15] Furthermore, he argued that, "the safeguards against too radical change must not be exaggerated to the point of dethroning the real sovereign."[16] Woodrow Wilson commented that Article V was "so slow and cumbersome" that it could be moved by "no impulse short of the impulse of self-preservation, no force less than the force of revolution."[17]

This fear of "revolution," while perhaps genuinely felt given the social upheaval of the times, does not seem to stand up to any measure of thoughtful scrutiny. Surely Wilson and others would not have us believe that majorities would find it easier, and more desirable, to overturn the entire government through violent force of arms at extensive loss of blood and treasure than to muster supermajority support in Congress and majority support in three quarters of the states? Even restating their position in those terms highlights the impropriety of the charge and suggests that perhaps a certain measure of hyperbole crept into the Progressive analysis of the time. Nevertheless, the Progressive consensus was that Article V was indeed so rigid as to threaten the internal stability of the entire government.

Not only did Article V's difficulty threaten political violence, but according to early Progressives, it was forcing the courts to improperly respond to pressures for constitutional change. Woodrow Wilson commented, "The process of formal amendment was made so difficult by the provisions of the Constitution itself that it has seldom been feasible to use it; and the difficulty of formal amendment has understandably made the courts more liberal, not to say more lax, in their interpretation than they would otherwise have been."[18] Frederic Johnstone noted that the rigid nature of Article V had led to the courts expanding the constitutional powers,

> Neither the court nor the instrument gains respect when by construction it is forced to speak a language different from that which the plain meaning of the words convey. Wresting unspecified power from an ancient grant would seem almost a waste of judicial energy. The grantor is alive and might reasonably be expected to make another deed, especially as he would be the real beneficiary of the instrument.[19]

To avoid such judicial overreach, Johnstone favored eliminating the supermajority requirements of Article V, which would then allow a majority of the people to make alterations to the Constitution and relieve the need for the courts to try and keep the Constitution up to date with modern needs. Similarly, Henry B. Higgins confirmed that the "rigid" nature of the amending process had indeed led to judicial expansion of the Constitution, "the constitution has not merely been unfolded by the courts; it has been amended by the courts."[20] While Higgins argued for an easier amending process he wondered whether extra-constitutional interpretation might lead to the demise of the Constitution or whether, by "some almost superhuman effort of patriotism and self-effacement all parties may unite to amend the amending power."[21]

One major irony of the Progressive critique, during the early part of the twentieth century, is that it came just prior to and during one of the most prolific periods of constitutional amendment in American history. In the twenty years between 1913 and 1933 Article V was utilized five times. While this wave of Article V amendment did dampen Progressive proposals to reform Article V it did not eliminate the Progressive critique that Article V was still too difficult.

The democratic passion and political organization unleashed by the Progressive movement provided the raw material to mobilize coalitions to pass

Article V amendments. Progressives utilized Article V effectively to achieve wide ranging and transformative social reforms such as the federal income tax, direct election of senators, and women's suffrage. Yet even with these considerable successes utilizing Article V to bring about Progressive reforms, the supermajority requirements were still seen as too rigid and undemocratic by Progressive intellectuals and political actors alike; so much so that they would soon seek the aid of the least democratic branch.

Thus, in another grand irony, while early Progressives like Higgins and Johnstone seemed to lament the Supreme Court bending or adapting the written Constitution, in a few decades, it would be New Deal Progressives who would willingly orchestrate a revolution in Supreme Court doctrine and behavior that would seek to legitimate the Supreme Court adapting the Constitution to fit perceived changes in social conditions. Brad C. S. Watson has observed,

> One progressive understanding never changed: all social understandings are in flux, and in the face of this flux, the Constitution must necessarily be plastic. In light of this view, the Constitution, and liberal constitutionalism itself, had to respond incessantly to changing social circumstances. . . Progressives failed to perceive any irony because judicial restraint was never essential to their enterprise, but rather a mere tactical consideration in pursuit of a Constitution supporting social and individual change, experimentation, and growth.[22]

New Deal Progressives would see this new court and its "flexible" interpretations and adaptations, not as the bending of written law, but as a laudable victory for Progressive change. If the court could simply adapt the Constitution then Progressive reform might come more quickly and easily.[23] As the court asserted itself, it seemed to remove the need for Article V reform. This was certainly the case with regard to the child labor amendment which saw momentum for ratification wither after the Supreme Court issued its *United States v. Darby Lumber Co.*—thus overturning its earlier *Hammer v. Dagenhart* decision—which effectively cleared the way for Congress to legislate child labor regulations as part of the Fair Labor Standards Act of 1938. Startling court reversals on long held doctrines which opened the way for sweeping legislation and activist government soon became the familiar pattern. In fact, as we shall see in a coming chapter, Franklin Roosevelt consciously chose to rely on control over Supreme Court personnel to legitimate his New Deal rather than use Article V. Despite their early claims of fidelity to democratic and Constitutional form, the Progressive willingness to follow an increasingly ambitious Supreme Court into the thickets of counter majoritarian constitutional change show that the Progressive commitment to pragmatism ran deeper than their commitment to written constitutionalism, at least as written constitutionalism had heretofore been defined in America.

Contemporary Critics

Despite an increased role of the Supreme Court in "adapting" the Constitution to the felt needs of the time, Progressive era concerns over Article V's difficulty still remain and can be seen in what one might refer to as the *neo-progressive* scholarship of today. For example, Sanford Levinson points out that the courts have been very useful in adapting the Constitution, but it is not enough to facilitate necessary changes in the Constitution, "Clever adaptive interpretation is not always possible . . . and Article V has made it next to impossible to achieve such adaptation where amendment is thought to be necessity."[24] Another author, Daniel Lazare, has gone so far as to label our Constitution a "Frozen Republic" partly due to Article V and other difficult mechanisms.[25] Similarly, Robert Dahl while resisting attacking Article V openly, does identify Article V as the culprit in thwarting his most cherished democratic reforms.[26]

Sanford Levinson, perhaps the leading critic of the amending process sees Article V's difficulty as a major problem in American democracy. In fact, Levinson goes so far as describe the American public as "trapped inside" an "iron cage."[27] The bars of this cage are constituted significantly by Article V: "Article V constitutes what may be the most important bars of our constitutional iron cage precisely because it works to make practically impossible needed changes in our polity . . . no other country—nor, for that matter, any of the fifty American states—makes it so difficult to amend its constitution."[28]

For Levinson it is an "unfortunate reality" that Article V "practically speaking, brings us all too close to the Lockean dream (or nightmare) of changeless stasis."[29] Furthermore, he cites Donald Lutz's determination that, "the U.S. constitution is the most difficult to amend of any constitution currently existing in the world today".[30] For Levinson, the supermajority requirements of Article V are simply too rigid, "as a practical matter, though, Article V makes it next to impossible to amend the Constitution with regard to genuinely controversial issues, even if substantial—and intense—majorities advocate amendment."[31]

Levinson dismisses the flurries of amendments throughout history that might otherwise reflect well on the efficacy of Article V. For instance, he is dismissive of the Fourteenth Amendment as evidence of Article V's effectiveness, because it was only achieved "at the point of a gun."[32] In addition, he is critical how much time it takes for amendments to be added. For instance, while supportive of the Seventeenth Amendment itself, Levinson points to it, as an example of failure on the part of Article V. While Levinson would concede that with the passage of the Seventeenth Amendment, Article V did help produce significant Constitutional change; yet Levinson is highly critical of the fact that it took "many decades" for the Seventeenth Amendment to achieve after calls for such a measure since the Jacksonian period.[33] Levinson points out that the House of Representatives proposed constitutional amendments for the direct election of Senators five times between 1894 and 1911 and only once—

the last time—did the Senate even allow a vote. Once the vote was finally allowed the Senate continued its opposition as that vote did not achieve the necessary two-thirds majority in the Senate.[34] The Senate did not yield until it was forced to in May 1912 when the measure finally passed both houses of Congress. The problem for Levinson was that Senate's passage of the amendment only came as a forced concession. After decades of stonewalling by the Senate, finally at least nineteen state legislatures had exercised their Article V prerogative of petitioning Congress to call for a constitutional convention. When faced with a looming threat of a convention the Senate finally conceded as these efforts forced its hand. It seems that "hold out" Senators feared a constitutional convention more than conceding to the reform proposal. For Levinson, the reluctance of the Senate, and the necessity of the states forcing the Senate's hand, is not in the least satisfying. After an examination of this narrative Levinson concludes, "The Seventeenth Amendment at most proves that the structural change is possible, if all of the stars are aligned correctly. It scarcely demonstrates that the Constitution allows needed changes when time may be of the essence."[35]

Article V by the Numbers: Difficulty or Stability?

The Progressive critique of Article V, Roosevelt's rejection of it for the advancement of the New Deal, and more recent criticism from respected scholars such as Levinson do raise a valid question. Is Article V simply too difficult? As we have seen in part I, the Founders saw Article V as a perfecting mechanism that brought stability. It was meant to be "difficult" in the sense that the Constitution represented *fundamental law* or *higher law* that superseded mere normal legislation. The Constitution embodied foundational principles and sought primarily to secure the rights articulated in the Declaration of Independence. It sought to secure rights via institutional arrangements rooted in the sovereignty of the people. Thus, on a theoretical level one might not be surprised to find that Article V does erect barriers to "light or transient" impulses in an effort to provide stability to the founding document and to ensure that the government benefits from that ". . . veneration which time bestows on everything, and without which perhaps the wisest and freest governments would not possess the requisite stability."[36] The Founders' desire for stability might give one pause, nevertheless, the persistent criticism that Article V is too difficult demands that we take a closer look at the broad charge and its several facets.

Amendments are too Infrequent

One of the "proofs" of Article V's difficulty is the observation that there have been "only" twenty seven Amendments in over 220 years of the Constitution;

worse yet there have only been seventeen since the original ten Bill of Rights were passed. Such observations clearly insinuate that the Constitution should have been amended more than it has been. The assumption is that a healthy regime would undergo more frequent alterations of its fundamental law. On the surface this critique backed by the numbers does seem to suggest Article V's difficulty. For example, Donald Lutz produced a quantitative study that showed the United States with a comparatively low rate of amendment when compared to other countries.[37] Lutz's study uses a composite index to determine an amendment rate based upon factors such as how many amendments have been made relative to the duration of a constitution. Lutz assumes that constitutions that have been around longer should have more amendments; thus a successful constitution should have a "reasonable rate" of amendment. What is a "reasonable rate"? That is entirely relative to the rates of other countries. While Lutz's study is interesting it seems to rest on the philosophical assumption that the rate of amendment for the United States must be in line with the rates of other countries. In his defense, Lutz's purpose in his study is not necessarily to provide a philosophical defense of that premise. Instead this premise is simply assumed; but this assumption seems key to our purposes here. It might well be that amendment rates aren't things that can universalized so easily. It might well be that they are very particular phenomena just as the constitutions and the political cultures they reflect are very particular expressions.

Despite these considerations, Levinson eagerly picks up Lutz's study to make his point, "no other country . . . makes it so difficult to amend its constitution. This is yet one more instance where Americans should ask themselves what the rest of the world (and American states) know that the framers, whatever their brilliance and dedication, did not."[38] One might ask Levinson the reverse, what is it that the Framers knew that the rest of the world does not; why must he immediately assume the United States has missed something here? Levinson seems to rely too much here on an assumption that in matters of government it is better to "keep up with the proverbial Joneses" than to have institutions which reflect the principles, traditions, and history of the country and the people who live there. As we have seen in part I of this book the United States Constitution and Article V grew out of very unique circumstances and were established along with the political development of the American people. In contrast, Levinson fails to put forth a sustained argument on why the United States must conform to international norms of European social democracies. Are they more stable? Are they better at protecting rights? Have they preserved a philosophical and moral foundation for rights? Are their economics thriving? Have they created sustainable governing structures that will last over two hundred years? Even if one could answer "yes" to these questions and more, it does not necessarily follow that the European method of amendment would serve our uniquely American history, traditions, or principles. Or perhaps on the other hand such Europeans models would be better; but the case has to be made not simply asserted. One might add that according to Lutz, while the United States may have comparably the most difficult amending process it also has the longest existing Constitution. Therefore, one might as easily link apparent difficulty with stability.

Another way to ask the difficulty question might be, "Is Article V too difficult for the American people?" as opposed to "Is Article V too difficult for the Swedes?" Has Article V proven to be too difficult for the purposes of the American people and the stated ends of their government? If the ends of government are the preservation of rights rather than responsiveness to change then the American people might well find a virtue in Article V's difficulty rather than a vice. If Americans instinctively fear the tyranny of the few or of the many and—as we have seen—were skeptical of frequent or unseen alterations to the fundamental law then a difficult amending process might serve their purposes quite well.

That being said, it is still a fair question to ask whether or not Article V has proven to be too difficult even by American standards. One way to gain a different perspective on this matter is to examine how many amendments there have been relative to the longevity of the Constitution. In terms of frequency of amendment there have been twenty seven amendments in 223 years (1789-2012) which results in one amendment for every 8.2 years of the Constitution's existence. At first glance one amendment per every eight years does not immediately strike one as unduly infrequent. Eight years certainly does not strike one as an unduly long period of time especially if a main purpose of the amendment process is to support the stability of the Constitution. If critics find this too infrequent, one is left wondering exactly what the desired frequency of amendment is. Would critics prefer one amendment for every six years, or every two years, or every year? And if so on what basis do they make that judgment?

Critics may respond that the *average* number of years doesn't matter so much as the *actual* time between amendments. Indeed there have been lengthy periods without any amendments and critics point out that such gaps suggest long periods of unhealthy stasis in which Article V is preventing vital constitutional change from taking place. The longest time period between amendments is sixty-one years. This gap appeared between the Twelfth Amendment, ratified in 1804, and the Thirteenth Amendment, ratified in 1865. The second longest gap is forty-three years between the Fifteenth Amendment in 1870 and the Sixteenth Amendment in 1913. The third longest gap is twenty-one years between the Twenty-sixth and Twenty-seventh Amendments from 1971 to 1992; and as of 2013 it will be twenty-one years since the Twenty Seventh Amendment was finally ratified.[39] Now, to be sure, a sixty-one year *actual* gap is far longer, and perhaps more important than, an *average* of eight years so critics would seem to have a point. In addition, the current period of twenty years without an amendment is worthy of note as in a few years it will be the third longest time period without an amendment.[40]

These long periods without amendment do raise questions. Is a sixty-one year period without an amendment a sign of a flaw in Article V? Are sixty and forty year periods of time without an amendment signs of disease? The answer isn't immediately clear. Again, if the goal of a fixed written constitution is to produce stability in the fundamental law, then sixty years without amendment is not *ipso facto* proof of unhealthy stagnation. The answers to these questions lay in the purpose and design of Article V and its role in the constitutional system.

While the lengthy time gaps between amendments are noteworthy it would be helpful to examine how normal such gaps in time are. Thus, rather than dividing years of the Constitution's existence by the number of amendments, it might be helpful to assess the average time between amendments. Thus, by starting in 1791, the year the Bill of Rights was passed, what has the average time between amendments been? It is interesting to find that, even with the large periods of amendment inactivity, the average time between amendments has only been 12.2 years; again not a number at first glance that would suggest an overly restrictive amending process.[41] Again, one wonders what the critics of Article V would view as an appropriate average amount of time between amendments? Would a better average of years between amendments be ten years, or five years, or two?

The long periods of amendment inactivity contrasted with the relatively low average of years between amendments highlight the fact that amendments have tended to come in *amendment surges* or *clusters*; such as the initial Bill of Rights (1789-1791), the Civil War amendments (1865-1870), the Progressive Era amendments (1909-1933), and the Civil Rights Era amendments (1960-1971). If 12.2 years is the average time between all amendments, what is the average number of years between amendments if one factors out the long "gaps" and only calculates the average during these clusters of amendment? The result of this calculation results in a finding of a mere 5.4 years between amendments. Thus, it seems that when the American public is in the mood to demand changes to the Constitution the average time between amendments is quite rapid. Or put another way, when amendment surges take place it takes less time to alter the fundamental law than it does to serve out a single term in the United States Senate.

But don't the few large gaps of time still signal a defect of some sort? These amendment *surges* are relatively rare. To be sure the periods of inactivity do account for a large part of American history. In fact, added together the periods of inactivity account for 145 years (64%) of the Constitution's 223 year history. The charge is that such long periods without constitutional change are a sign of an ineffective amending process. However, the fact that the American people go through prolonged periods where they do not deem it necessary to adopt changes to their fundamental law is not necessarily evidence of a flaw. In fact, it might suggest quite the opposite: that long periods without amendments are periods of constitutional stability not crippling stagnation. To be sure, during these periods of Article V inactivity there were large issues that characterized public debate, such as slavery in the early nineteenth century, or growing industrialization in the late nineteenth century; but the existence of important public policy debate does not automatically suggest the need for a Constitutional amendment. What critics often overlook about the very nature of Article V is that its purpose is to provide a means of registering a political consensus once it emerges not to grant a constitutional victory to a slim or even comfortable majority. By its very design, Article V will tend not to allow amendments before the hard work of crafting a political consensus has been done via normal political institutions such as state legislatures and the Congress. The underlying assumption of critics seems to be that these long periods of inactivity, in and of themselves, prove that something is defective with Article V. Whatever the merits of such an assumption they are not readily apparent or unassailable and seem to reflect more of the Progressive bias towards constant reform rather than the Founders' preference for political stability. Thus, to simply grant critics their unstated assumptions is to gloss over deep philosophical divisions about human nature and the purpose of government.

Progressives seek constant reform in order to keep pace with vague notions of historical progress. For Progressives, stasis is deadly while for the Founders stasis was seen as healthy stability. The Founders saw fixed principles of natural right as guiding beacons and thus changes to the fundamental law should be rare as long as the government was adequately securing the natural rights of its citizens. By contrast, the Progressives are motivated by vague notions of historical progress, so for them a lack of change is by definition unhealthy. This assumption that change is healthy is often uncritically absorbed by critics and often operates as an unstated and undefended premise in their critique.

Another common observation along these lines is that the Civil War amendments came only "at the point of a gun" and only after the bloodiest war the nation's history. For example, Stephen Griffin holds that the Civil War, "was one of the greatest political failures in world history that can be linked to a constitution."[42] For him the difficulty of amendment and the rigidity of a written constitution have made the Constitution a failure and claims that it has been a success for over 200 years, upon close inspection, begin to look "fraudulent."[43] Isn't the Civil War and the irregular means used to pass the fourteenth amendment suggest that Article V, and the Constitution for that matter, did not serve the country well by not providing a means of avoiding such a horrible conflict?

It is hard to know what to make of this point. It seems to assume that some less difficult amending process would have allowed the sectional rivalry over slavery to be resolved peaceably. One is hard pressed to find any evidence for this. Abraham Lincoln made it very clear that the Civil War was an argument over first principles of the regime. The war was fought over deep divisions regarding the status of the Declaration of Independence and its claim that "all men are created equal." Indeed in Lincoln's memorable words at Gettysburg, America was a "nation, conceived in Liberty, and dedicated to the proposition that all men are created equal." Furthermore, Americans were "engaged in a great civil war, testing whether that nation, or any nation so conceived and so dedicated, can long endure." In a country so deeply divided over first principles and where those divisions manifested themselves in such a pervasive and noxious institution such as slavery, it is hard to imagine *any* institutional arrangements that would have resolved that conflict. Indeed one could argue that it was constitutional arrangements that kept such deep regional differences at bay for decades. Constitutional elements that are now commonly ridiculed as "difficult" such as separation of powers, bi-cameralism, the electoral college, and the emergence of a strong party system, either allowed for partisan coalitions that crossed regional boundaries or prevented regional interests from capturing the entire government at any giving time. More to the point, not having an easy amending mechanism forced the divergent parties to compromise in Congress over and over in order to postpone and perhaps avoid bloodshed altogether. Neither should it be overlooked that Article V's "difficulty" guarded against the many efforts to amend the Constitution in a manner that sought to entrench slavery.[44]

In the end, blaming Article V, or the Constitution, for the rupture of the Civil War or blaming it for not preventing the rupture is akin to blaming the existence of a vehicle code for causing auto accidents by negligent and reckless drivers. The Constitution as fundamental law structures politics and political conflict, but it doesn't, and can't, fully compensate for the irresponsible politics of specific interests or actors. In binding majorities to certain institutional procedures it seeks to mitigate majority tyranny but it simply cannot prevent the inevitable repercussions of years of accumulated personal and political vice. Similarly, Article V provides a means of altering the fundamental law provided there is a political consensus but it does not *produce* the consensus. It is perhaps the height of understatement to say that there clearly was no political consensus during the period leading up to the Civil War, thus it seems strange to lay that conflict at the feet of the amending process and the Constitution.

Punctuated Equilibrium

Ultimately, this tendency in critics to assume that lengthy periods without amendment are signs of an Article V defect, seem to disregard notions of "punctuated equilibrium" that have had an impact both in the world of science and in public policy literature.[45] Theories of punctuated equilibrium hold that in social and political systems it is common to observe long periods of stasis that are then "punctuated" by periods of rapid social and political change. If such theories are correct then we would expect to see exactly what we do when we look at the frequency of amendment.

Political scientists Baumgartner and Jones describe long periods of equilibrium held in place by "policy monopolies" which are "structured arrangements that are supported by powerful ideas."[46] They further describe how the "agenda-setting process implies that no single equilibrium could be possible in politics."[47] Those who are disadvantaged by the equilibrium in place may over time, perhaps decades, convince "others that their view of an issue is more accurate than the views of their opponents" and upon such success in the deliberative process, "they may achieve rapid success in altering public policy arrangements, even if these arrangements have been in place for decades."[48] In sum, Baumgartner and Jones "depict a political system that displays considerable stability with regard to the manner in which it processes issues, but the stability is punctuated with periods of volatile change" furthermore, "any study of the dynamics of American political institutions must be able to account for both long periods of stability and short, violent periods of change."[49]

These patterns of *punctuated equilibrium* are normal patterns that are observable in both the natural and the political world and such patterns are exactly what one observes in the patterns of amendment over 220 years. Certainly one could argue that the amending process needs to be more "responsive" to immediate changes in society and politics, but one would have to make a case for why some higher level of responsiveness is desirable, necessary, or even feasible. The issue of responsiveness is something that will be looked at more closely in the next chapter. In the end, the theory of *punctuated equilibrium* lays the burden of proof at the feet of Article V critics. Why should we have more frequent amendments? Why should the American political system behave differently than other social or political systems? It seems critics need to provide more analysis than has heretofore been offered on the issue of *infrequency*.

Three-Fourths Ratification

Another key element in the critique of Article V is the concern of critics over the demanding requirements of the three-fourths ratification process. Again the unstated assumption is that such a high supermajority requirement has contributed to amendments not being ratified at all, or not being ratified in a timely manner. As par for the course regarding criticisms of Article V's difficulty, the three-fourths requirement is often treated as so obviously "rigid" that no argument or proof need be offered in support of this claim. On the surface, critics of the three-fourths majority requirement do seem to have a point. Rarely if ever is such a high standard employed, even in the United States Constitution where two-thirds is usually the standard supermajority standard. Here again however, the requirement *seeming* too difficult and *actually being* too difficult might be different matters. Perhaps again a different perspective is in order.

Over the 220 plus years of the Constitution there have been thirty-three amendments proposed by Congress to the states; of those, twenty-seven have been ratified. Put another way 81 percent of the amendments proposed by Congress have been ratified by the states.[50] Given an 81 percent success rate it seems difficult to argue that the three-fourths ratification standard is much an impediment to amendments being ratified. Would critics rather have 90 percent or 100 percent of the amendments ratified?

But critics might still point out that passing *eventually* and passing in a *timely manner* are two different issues. In terms of timeliness, if one excludes the Twenty-seventh Amendment as an outlier (it took more than 202 years to ratify), then the average time of ratification is one year, eight months, and seven days.[51] Based on this method, the longest period for ratification was the Twenty-second Amendment regarding presidential tenure which took three years, nine months, and four days.[52] The shortest amendment was the Twenty-sixth Amendment (the right of eighteen-year old citizens to vote) took a mere three months, and ten days.[53] Therefore, by this method, in the entire history of constitutional amendment in the United States, the average amendment takes just under two years to get three-fourths of the states to ratify and it has never taken longer than four years to ratify.[54]

For all of the critics' angst over the difficulty of Article V requiring three-fourths of the states to ratify, the numbers seem to suggest that ratification is not the "rigid" impediment it is made out to be. Indeed, it is hard to imagine how much more quickly Croly, Levinson, and other Article V critics would rather have these amendments ratified. When the American polity must wait four years to replace a president and six years to replace a sitting senator, it seems quite reasonable to expect to achieve the consent of three-quarters of the states to a Constitutional amendment in less time. In fact in the eighteenth and nineteenth centuries the average amount of time it took to ratify an amendment was 811 days or about 2.2 years, just longer than a House Congressional term. In the Twentieth century it has taken only an average of 394 days, or 1.07 years to ratify. So not only has the time it takes to ratify amendments become less over time, but it takes, on average, less time to ratify an amendment in the 20th century than it does to replace a member of the House of Representatives at the federal level (although with an over 90 percent incumbency rate House Representatives incumbents are rarely replaced); more precisely it takes nearly half the time to ratify an amendment than it does to replace a member of the House of Representatives. Here again, we find that the suggestion that the three-fourths requirement is "too difficult" not to be backed up sufficiently by actual political experience. Once there is a consensus in Congress to propose amendments then it seems to take very little time to ratify, provided the political groundwork for change has been laid.

One might further note the irony that according these figures, the higher of the two supermajority requirements—three-fourths of the states—turns out not to impose any severe time limitation at all once amendments have been proposed by Congress. As already mentioned, the obvious reason for this is that more often than not, by the time an amendment is proposed, a national consensus has already developed around the proposal. Again oddly critics might have less of a problem with the three-fourths ratification standard but more of a problem with the time it takes to propose amendments rather than simply ratify them.

Two-Thirds Requirement in Proposing Amendments

Now to be sure, some critics don't focus on the time it takes to *ratify* amendments but on the length of time it takes to actually *propose* an amendment. For example, Levinson's full critique was not centered on ratification *per se* but rather his main concern was that it took decades for Congress to even propose the Seventeenth Amendment. Recall further that Levinson is concerned that it took immense pressure from the states to finally achieve a two-thirds majority in Congress.

> By 1911, at least nineteen state legislatures had exercised their Article V prerogative of petitioning Congress to call a constitutional convention for the purpose of proposing such an amendment. The fear of such a convention was enough to generate the required two-thirds majority of the Senate to send the amendment on to the very quick ratification by the states.[55]

As Levinson correctly notes, once the amendment was proposed by Congress it enjoyed a "quick ratification" that took only eleven months. Again, for Levinson the example here is, "The Seventeenth Amendment at most proves that structural change is possible, if all of the stars are aligned correctly. It scarcely demonstrates that the Constitution allows needed changes when time may be of the essence."[56]

Certainly partisans favoring the direct election of Senators would have preferred that the Seventeenth Amendment be proposed decades earlier, but upon deeper reflection, one is hard pressed to see what Levinson is upset about here. It seems that the amending process worked splendidly. First, Article V provided a means of registering the emergent political consensus regarding the popular election of Senators. The fact that it took decades for that political consensus to emerge and gain power in the national and state legislatures is more a commentary on the politics of that particular amendment than a reflection on Article V. Second, when the Senate used its in-built position to resist the amendment, Article V provided the states with a means of going around the Senate by petitioning Congress for a constitutional convention. This pressure forced the Senate to concede to the popular will and vote to propose the amendment.

Levinson views this as a, decades long, stifling of democratic will via Article V supermajority requirements in the Congress. However, an alternative narrative also might observe that it took several decades for a firm political consensus to emerge regarding a fundamental change to the constitutional structure. However, once that consensus achieved adequate saturation of the polity the people did not need to march on Washington D. C. in a spirit of violent revolution, rather they calmly and deliberatively utilized the Article V process which in turn allowed a change to the fundamental law to be promulgated. This might best be viewed as a slow yet stable building of a democratic consensus over time that was able, in the end, to use Article V's varied amendment provisions to overcome a resistant Senate.

What Levinson seems to be most critical of is that if an amendment is "needed" and time "is of the essence" then Article V simply won't do. Yet, surely Levinson would acknowledge that assessments regarding which proposed amendments are "needed" and whether time is truly "of the essence" are not purely objective; rather such assessments are often subject to deep political divisions and are based upon complex prudential valuations that are best worked out through a free and democratic processes. It is not uncommon for American representative institutions to engage in deliberation over time, even decades if necessary before reaching political consensus.[57]

Levinson also seems to be exhibiting some of what might be called, "history is written by the winners" syndrome. That is to say, even if there is largely contemporary agreement on the beneficial nature of the Seventeenth Amendment, the historical fact is that it took the American electorate decades of deliberation and debate before enough citizens came to have the same view of the matter.[58] Just because it passed does not mean it was easy or inevitable. Levinson seems to imply that there is some objective basis upon which to make these highly prudential judgments that would allow a simple majority to truncate the deliberative process required by supermajorities.

Responsiveness Versus Deliberation

Progressives and Levinson seem to have committed themselves to a system that simply reacts to immediate impulses in society. This inclination towards "responsive" politics seems to be the unstated premise that allows critics to confidently make determinations about the timeliness or relative necessity of a given amendment proposal. Certainly Article V prevented direct election of senators until the public deliberations had convinced significant majorities in the U.S. Congress and the states that such a change was indeed "needed" and "timely." Yet, it must be acknowledged that same Article V process that made it "difficult" to enact the direct election of senators has also prevented a great many amendments that parties on both sides of the political spectrum would now acknowledge were foolhardy or imprudent. Indeed the historical *zeitgeist* that led political actors to introduce controversial or ill-conceived measures may also have allowed such measures to pass had it not been for Article V's stringent requirements.[59] For example, Article V's requirements prevented moves to entrench slavery in the Constitution and prevented at least three amendments that sought to entrench bans on interracial marriage.[60] Surely, critics would concede that preventing slavery and miscegenation amendments are a virtue of Article V not a vice. Even contemporary partisans would find comfort in Article V's rigor. Those on the left might find solace in the continued failure of proposed prayer in school amendments, balanced budget amendments, or flag burning amendments while those on the right might find comfort in the failure of efforts to end the electoral college or death penalty abolition amendments.

Preventing undesirable amendments only highlights the inherent difficulty in designing an amending process that prevents undesirable change and allows desirable change. Madison argued that, "a coalition of a majority of the whole society could seldom take place on any other principles than those of justice and the general good".[61] If this is so then it would seem that institutions should be designed to ensure such "coalitions of a majority of the whole society" are formed. It is worth seeing Madison's fuller argument here:

> Justice is the end of government. It is the end of civil society. It ever has been and ever will be pursued until it be obtained, or until liberty be lost in the pursuit. In a society under the forms of which the stronger faction can readily unite and oppress the weaker, anarchy may as truly be said to reign as in a state of nature, where the weaker individual is not secured against the violence of the stronger; . . . In the extended republic of the United States, and among the great variety of interests, parties, and sects which it embraces, a coalition of a majority of the whole society could seldom take place on any other principles than those of justice and the general good.[62]

To be sure Madison refers to "majorities" here but Madison elsewhere sings the praises of "constitutional majorities" not simply popular majorities.

> It may be objected to majority governments, that the majority, as formed by the Constitution, may be a minority when compared with the popular majority. This is likely to be the case more or less in all elective governments. It is so in many of the States.[63]

Remember, for many of the Founders and especially for Madison political rights were best protected when shielded from raw popular majorities.[64] Thus, in simply asserting that Article V is too slow and impeded "necessary" and "timely" change, Levinson begs several important questions and glosses over the political reality that "necessity" and "timing" are essentially prudential political decisions rather than objective forms of unassailable knowledge.

The Difficulty of Consensus

Given this analysis, the picture that emerges is that frustration with Article V seems, upon closer examination, to be frustration with the deliberative process itself. To be sure critics would likely prefer that only simple majorities in Congress were required to propose amendments—as long as such majorities only proposed the amendments they desired and not the ones they don't desire—yet while such a change would certainly increase the number of amending proposals that pass Congress there is no guarantee that it would still be responsive enough for critics.

It is worth pointing out that, Article V aside, political consensus on any matter in such a diverse and vigorous democracy isn't easy. For instance, even when Congress has achieved a majority consensus, it is still difficult to build on that consensus to override a presidential veto. In fact, Congress has only overridden a presidential veto 110 times out of 2,562 vetoes.[65] Put another way, Congress has only overridden 4 percent of the presidential vetoes it has been faced with. Thus, 96 percent of the time Congress cannot muster the two-third majority needed to override the president even on measures that have been fully debated and have mustered clear majorities in both houses. Why then wouldn't we expect similar difficulties proposing amendments?

What about the passage of normal legislation? In Congress, where simple majorities are usually the norm, less than 4 percent of bills, introduced into a given Congressional session, ever become law.[66] If normal legislation fails to pass 96 percent of the time, it is no wonder that even fewer proposed amendments to the Constitution are able to command a two-thirds majority in both houses of Congress. Wouldn't one expect proposals for alterations of the fundamental law to take time to develop in the public mind, and wouldn't one expect that such proposals would undergo vigorous scrutiny and debate in Congress, perhaps over decades if need be?

What about the initiative process? Even in forward looking California an examination of that state's initiative process—a creation of the Progressive movement—out of the 910 provisions circulated for adoption between 1912 and 1995 only a mere 8.5 percent ever achieved adoption.[67] Thus, 91.5 percent of the time even directly democratic initiatives do not muster even majority support.

What each of these examples illustrate, is that it is inherently difficult to form a public consensus—even simple majority consensus—on many matters let alone a proposal that seeks to alter the fundamental law regarding important or controversial matters. It takes time and effort to develop political coalitions and to foster public deliberation in a diverse and vigorous democracy. Could it be that the impatience of Progressives and contemporary critics is less impatience with Article V but rather impatience with the deliberative process in Congress and amongst the citizens in the states? Could it be that critics are bothered by having to engage in sustained and persuasive debate on those issues they deem "necessary" even when significant and powerful minorities of fellow citizens do not deem such issues "necessary"? Could it be that elites get impatient with having to engage in the rough and tumble of political debate and would simply prefer that their opponents immediately see the wisdom of their position and then quickly concede? One wonders. The impatience of those offering the "Article V is difficult" critique seems to suggest they have a certain level of ambivalence with the realities of democratic deliberation.

One might further observe, that not only do critics seem to have an unstated and underlying frustration with the deliberative process, but they also seem to have a deep ambivalence and sometimes disdain for much of the larger constitutional structure. For instance, Robert Dahl wants wide ranging alterations to the Constitution, such as the removing of the Electoral College and the ending of equal suffrage in the Senate. Likewise, Levinson is very clear he would like to do away with the entire Senate and Bicameralism.[68] It seems then, that critics of Article V are usually dissatisfied with—or at least ambivalent towards—much of the larger constitutional structure. In this context, Article V is just one of many "difficult" elements that stand in the way of critics' reformation—or deconstruction depending on one's perspective—of the entire constitutional order. Thus, Article V is not always the main target of constitutional reformers, but it does serve as a gateway of sorts that prevents access to, and reform of, the rest of the Constitution. In the end, critics are often exasperated by Article V because it stands like a citadel at the narrow bend in the river preventing them from entering the bay and wreaking havoc on the entire constitutional edifice of ordered liberty.

Conclusion

This examination of Article V's difficulty reveals a couple of key things. First, a closer look at the actual frequency of amendments does not reveal an outlandishly infrequent amending process and theories of *punctuated equilibrium* suggest that long periods of stasis with rapid periods of change are the norm in human society. Second, upon an even cursory examination the three-fourths requirement for ratification has never been a serious impediment to amendment once amendments are proposed. Third, the two-thirds requirement, while preventing many amendments from being proposed or delaying other amendments, when put in context, does not seem to be out of step with the frequency and timing of even majoritarian deliberative processes. As we have seen political consensus requiring even bare majorities are not easily achieved in a diverse republic such as America and the two-thirds requirements have halted many imprudent amendments while requiring that a firm and extensive national coalition was assembled before proposing amendments.

Again, it is also important to remember that a written constitution demands a higher standard for amendment than is required for normal legislation. Furthermore, it is important to keep in mind that if the purpose of an amending process is to provide a means of constitutional change while still maintaining stability, then Article V seems to acquit itself rather well. For those whose political philosophy commits one to constant, rapid change and the deconstruction of a Constitution that binds—rather than caters to—popular majorities it is obvious why Article V has come under some measure of criticism for its difficulty. Instead if one desires a stable, regular means of registering changes to the fundamental law once a firm and national coalition has formed on a particular issue, then Article V has served the polity rather well.

In the end, it is worth reiterating that the stock critiques of Article V usually consist of nothing more than a mere mention of the supermajority requirements as self-evident proof that Article V is too difficult. Rarely if ever is further analysis even attempted. Yet as we have seen even cursory examinations reveal deep problems with the assertions of Article V's difficulty. At a minimum, critics gloss over deep philosophical issues about constitutionalism and democracy. At a maximum, critics engage in hyperbole and unsubstantiated assertions. Indeed, it seems that reports of Article V's difficulty, like Mark Twain's death, "have been greatly exaggerated."

Notes

1. Herbert Croly, *Progressive Democracy* (New York: The MacMillan Company, 1914), 230.

2. John R. Vile, *Encyclopedia of Constitutional Amendments, Proposed Amendments and Amending Issues, 1789-2002.* 2nd ed. (Santa Barbara, CA: ABC-CLIO, 2003) 111.

3. David Kyvig, "The Road Not Taken: FDR, the Supreme Court, and Constitutional Amendment," *Political Science Quarterly,* (Autumn, 1989), 464.

4. Sanford Levinson, *Our Undemocratic Constitution: Where the Constitution Goes Wrong (and How We the People Can Correct It)* (New York: Oxford University Press, 2006) 21.

5. Herbert Croly, *Progressive Democracy* (New York: The MacMillan Company, 1914), 230.

6. Ibid.

7. Ibid., 230-231.

8. Kyvig, *Explicit and Authentic Acts,* 193.

9. Henry B. Higgins, "The Rigid Constitution," *Political Science Quarterly* 20 (March 1905), 203-22; quoted in Vile, *The Constitutional Amending Process,* 141.

10. Frederic B. Johnstone, "An Eighteenth Century Constitution," *Illinois Law Review* 7 (December 1912), 281; quoted in Vile, *The Constitutional Amending Process,* 146.

11. As quoted in Vile, *The Constitutional Amending Process,* 140-41.

12. James Bryce, "Flexible and Rigid Constitutions," *Constitutions*, (Germany: Scientia Verlag Aalen, 1980) reprint of New York and London 1905 edition; as quoted in Vile, *The Constitutional Amending Process,* 138.

13. Ibid., 138.

14. As quoted in Vile, *The Constitutional Amending Process,* 140-41.

15. John W. Burgess, *Selections from Political Science and Comparative Constitutional Law* (Farmingdale, NY: Dabor Social Science Publications, 1978), 22; quoted in Vile, *The Constitutional Amending Process,* 139.

16. Ibid., 22; quoted in Vile, *The Constitutional Amending Process,* 139.

17. Woodrow Wilson, *Constitutional Government* (Boston: Houghton Mifflin, 1885 and 1913), 242; quoted in Vile, *The Constitutional Amending Process,* 139.

18. Wilson, *Constitutional Government* (New York: Columbia University Press, 1908) 193.

19. Johnstone, "An Eighteenth Century Constitution," 274; as quoted in Vile, *The Constitutional Amending Process,* 145.

20. Higgins, "The Rigid Constitution," 210; as quoted in Vile, *The Constitutional Amending Process,* 141.

21. Higgins, "The Rigid Constitution," 222; as quoted in Vile, *The Constitutional Amending Process,* 142; it is interesting to note that these early progressive critiques showed some measure of concern about the role of judicial "amendment" and its impact on the Constitution and its authority. They accepted the reality that courts would utilize such power rather than resisting the court's usurpation in this manner. Their Progressive impulse led them to seek changes to Article V rather than demanding courts restrain themselves to judging rather than legislating.

22. Brad C.S. Watson, *Living Constitution Dying Faith: Progressivism and the New Science of Jurisprudence* (Wilmington, DE: ISI Books, 2009) 195.

23. See Bruce Ackerman, *We The People*, for an account of what he calls "structural amendments." The New Deal shift by the court to re-interpret the commerce clause to allow unprecedented Congressional intervention in the economy.

24. Sanford Levinson, *Our Undemocratic Constitution*, 160.

25. Daniel Lazare, *The Frozen Republic*.

26. Robert A. Dahl, *How Democratic is the American Constitution?* (New Haven, Yale University Press, 2001)

27. Sanford Levinson, *Our Undemocratic Constitution: Where the Constitution Goes Wrong (And How We the People Can Correct It* (New York: Oxford University Press, 2006), 20, 96.

28. Levinson, *Our Undemocratic Constitution*, 160.

29. Ibid., 21.

30. Ibid.

31. Ibid.

32. Ibid., 160.

33. Ibid., 161.

34. Ibid., 162.

35. Ibid.

36. The *Federalist No. 49*.

37. Donald Lutz, "Toward a Theory of Constitutional Amendment." *Responding to Imperfection*, 237.

38. Levinson, *Our Undemocratic Constitution*, 160.

39. I believe it is accurate to count the Twenty-seventh Amendment here as it did take states engaging in Article V activity to ratify the amendment. Even if one disregards it as an outlier it will have been forty-one years since the Twenty-sixth Amendment, still less, but not much than the forty-three year gap between the Fifteenth and Sixteenth Amendments.

40. One might briefly note that this current gap partially overlaps with a period where the Supreme Court has seen itself empowered to "adapt" the Constitution on its own, thus alleviating the need for new amendments. On the other hand some of its rulings, such as *Roe v. Wade*, have precipitated moves to "amend" the Constitution as a means of overturning decisions that are perceived as "wrong" by a significant group of citizens. As far as the current period, we would have to go another twenty-three years without an amendment for this period of inactivity to reach the second longest period of amendment inactivity (forty-three years) and another forty-one years to equal the longest period of inactivity (sixty-one years) prior to the Civil War. Even if one disregards the Twenty-seventh Amendment in this analysis, as of 2012, the gap from 1971 till now will be in a dead heat with the second longest gap and sill nearly twenty years away from becoming the longest time without an amendment.

41. 13.8 years if one excludes the ten amendments in the Bill of Rights.

42. Stephen Griffin, in Levinson, *Responding to Imperfection*, 47.

43. Ibid., 59.

44. Herman Ames, *The Proposed Amendments to the Constitution of the United States During the First Century of its History* (Washington, Government Printing Office, 1897) 193. Ames notes that there were numerous attempts to entrench slavery, to prevent the abolition of slavery, and entrench the fugitive slave laws. President James Buchanan proposed three such amendments in his annual address in 1860.

45. For the landmark study in public policy see Frank R. Baumgartner and Bryan D. Jones, *Agendas and Instability in American Politics* (Chicago: University of Chicago Press, 2009) 2nd ed.

46. Ibid., 4.

47. Ibid.

48. Ibid.

49. Ibid.

50. One might note that this 81 percent is just shy of the incumbency re-election rate for sitting Senators but far short of the 90 percent plus incumbency rate for House Members. I am not suggesting any relationship here, but rather just mentioning it as a matter of perspective.

51. Library of Congress, Congressional Research Service, CRS Report 97-922 GOV, *Ratification of Amendments to the U.S. Constitution, David C. Huckabee, September 30, 1997.*

52. CRS Report, , *Ratification of Amendments to the U.S. Constitution, 1.*

53. Ibid.

54. Ibid.

55. Levinson, *Our Undemocratic Constitution,* 162.

56. Ibid.

57. Again the literature on punctuated equilibrium is instructive here.

58. For evidence that not all view the Seventeenth Amendment as sound, see Ralph Rossum, *Federalism, the Supreme Court, and the Seventeenth Amendment: The Irony of Constitutional Democracy* (Landham, MD: Lexington, 2001).

59. See Herman Ames, *The Proposed Amendments*, for a list or early amendments proposed in Congress.

60. Vile, *Encyclopedia of Constitutional Amendments,* 243.

61. *Federalist No. 51.*

62. Ibid.

63. James Madison, *Letters and Other Writings of James Madison, Fourth President of the United States*, 4 vol. (Philadelphia: J.B. Lippincott & Co, Published by Order of Congress), IV: 333. Cited in the American Reference Library [CD-ROM]. Orem, Utah: Western Standard Publishing Company, 1998. Hereafter cited as *Writings of James Madison.*

64. For example see chapter 5 of this volume.

65. CRS Report, *Regular Vetoes and Pocket Vetoes: An Overview*, Order Code RS22188, Updated July 18, 2008.

66. Roll Call reported that only 3.3 percent of bills became law in the 110th Congress. Paul Singer, "Members Offered Many Bills but Passed Few," Roll Call December 1, 2008. http://www.rollcall.com/issues/54_61/-30466-1.html (accessed September 2, 2012)

67. CRB Report: California Research Bureau, CRB-97-006, *California's Statewide Initiative Process*, May 1997, 4.

68. Levinson, *Our Undemocratic Constitution,* 29-30.

Chapter 7
The Critics: Article V is Undemocratic

> A government is democratic just in proportion as it responds to the will of the people; and since one way of defeating the will of the people is to make it difficult to alter the form of government, it necessarily follows that any constitution which is democratic in spirit must yield readily to changes in public opinion.
>
> J. Allen Smith[1]

Intertwined with, and underlying, the charge that Article V is "difficult" is the argument that Article V is "undemocratic." By utilizing representative institutions, rather than direct democratic forms, and by requiring supermajorities rather than simple majorities, Article V has been criticized for not being sufficiently responsive to democratic majorities. Critics maintain, that by restraining contemporary simple majorities from altering their fundamental law, Article V prohibits the American people from controlling their own destiny; it makes them beholden to the "dead hand of the past" and ignores Thomas Jefferson's maxim that "*that the earth belongs in usufruct to the living.*"

Progressive Era Critique

Progressive era intellectuals and activists argued that Article V was ultimately undemocratic because it stifled popular majorities by "rigidly" requiring supermajorities and channeling popular will through representative institutions rather than directly democratic ones. In their view, such supermajority requirements in reality empowered entrenched reactionaries, or selfish interests, thereby stifling popular will and the public good.

For example, progressive scholar J. Allen Smith argued that the entire Constitution was an exercise in creating a government devoid of popular control and the Article V process was a key element in such an aristocratic and undemocratic document. Regarding the purpose of his book, *The Spirit of American Government,* he had this to say, "It is to call attention to the spirit of the Constitution, its inherent opposition to democracy, the obstacles which it has placed in the way of majority rule, that this volume has been written."[2] For Smith it was vital to call attention to the undemocratic nature of the Constitution if the American people were to move forward, they must realize "the fact that the so-called evils of democracy are very largely the natural results of those constitutional checks on popular rule which we have inherited from the political system of the eighteenth century."[3] Smith believed that the Constitution should never thwart the public will, rather it should simply be a "means" of "securing the supremacy" of public opinion.[4] For Smith, "All democratic constitutions are flexible and easy to amend" and a truly democratic constitution would not erect such obvious obstacles to the immediate popular will, such as Article V.[5] By such standards the amending process, was a blot on the democratic nature of the Constitution:

> A government is democratic just in proportion as it responds to the will of the people; and since one way of defeating the will of the people is to make it difficult to alter the form of government, it necessarily follows that any constitution which is democratic in spirit must yield readily to changes in public opinion.[6]

Rather than a process to register political consensus, Article V is seen as "defeating the will of the people." Lest one should think that Article V was an oversight, Smith is also very clear that Article V was an intentionally undemocratic feature of the constitution specifically designed by the framers to thwart democratic intent: "This feature of the Constitution, which nominally provides for amendment, but really makes it an impossibility, is perhaps the best proof we could have that the Constitution as framed and adopted represented the views of a minority who intended by this means to perpetuate their influence."[7] Thus, Article V was seen by Smith as an intentional restraint on true democracy and a means to advance the interests of the political elite at the people's expense. Ultimately for Smith "a constitution is in no proper sense the embodiment of the will of the people unless it recognizes the right of the majority to amend."[8] Smith's views are reflective of the general Progressive position that any institutional restraint on the will of the people was suspect and, for Progressives, Article V was the lynchpin of the Constitution's undemocratic nature.

Smith's arguments are indicative of large scale Progressive critiques of the amending process. John Burgess argued that the amending process is "ordinarily unworkable" and hampers "the will of the undoubted majority of the whole people in a democratic republic from realizing its well considered and well determined purposes in its organic law."[9] Herbert Croly referred to Article V as, "the least democratic article in the Constitution" and explained that, ". . . the machinery of amendment provided by the Constitution did more than anything else to emancipate that instrument from popular control. Its revision required such an emphatic preponderance of approving public opinion that no proposed amendment could be carried by any one political group."[10] Furthermore, the amending process ". . . did more than anything else to convert a constitutional democracy into semi-democratic constitutionalism," and he saw Article V as "unquestionably the most formidable legal obstacle in the path of progressive democratic fulfillment."[11] Article V was a gatekeeper preventing large scale reform and its strictures unduly empowered the Supreme Court: "In practice the monarchy of the Law hangs suspended to the nail of this particular bit of writing, and as long as it remains intact the political destinies of the American people will have to rest to an unnecessary and unwholesome extent upon the dicta of a board of judicial trustees."[12] Croly was clear that the progressive cause could not wait to meet the requirements of Article V:

> But in the long run progressive democracy cannot possibly submit to the abridgment of popular political responsibility which is implied by the present amending clause. It cannot wait until two-thirds of a Congress and the legislatures of three-fourths of the states are convinced of the desirability of any proposed modification. The existing method calls for amendment practically by unanimous consent. It removes proposals to revise the Constitution from the realm of partisan political controversy, and it necessitates the retention of means, similar to those which have been used in the past, to give the needed flexibility to the development of the Constitutional system—means which, as we have already seen, placed the political destinies of the American people under the immediate direction of a group of benevolent guardians.[13]

Croly was clear that Article V must be altered and the new amending process must be more permissive of the popular will, "The new machinery of amendment ought to be very much more easily worked than the old. It must make the Constitution alterable at the demand and according to the dictates of a preponderant prevailing public opinion."[14] Croly saw the amending mechanism as an important battleground and he sought to make sure that the public was "aroused to the plain fact that the amending clause is the most formidable legal obstacle to the democratizing of the American political system, that article of the Constitution will become the centre [sic] of attack."[15] As Progressive "Generals" such as Croly and Smith identified Article V as a key target and a strategic priority, the Progressive "lieutenants" in Congress mobilized to reform and "democratize" Article V according to their new progressive standards of government.

Efforts at Amending Article V

John Vile points out that there were eighteen proposals for reform of Article V between 1911 and 1929, most of these seeking to liberalize and "democratize" Article V.[16] M. A. Musmanno, building off the efforts of Herman Ames, produced an account of amending proposals that had been introduced in Congress since the founding. His research revealed an unprecedented surge in efforts to make Article V less "rigorous" and more "democratic." Musmanno recalls that,

"Prior to 1911, although the matter was much discussed in Congress, especially during the consideration of other amendments to the Constitution, but very few resolutions exclusively directed to the altering Article V were presented."[17]

A brief survey of measures introduced into Congress, between 1864 and 1928, shows a wide variety of proposals to alter Article V. In a nod towards direct democracy, some measures sought to make use of popular referendums. One 1919 proposal called for amendments being initiated by 500,000 or more voters and ratified by a majority of voters in the states via referendum.[18] Progressive Senator Robert La Follette famously proposed reforms to Article V in both 1912 and 1913. His proposal sought to have amendments proposed by only ten states or a simple majority in Congress and then ratified by a majority of citizens in a majority of states via referendum.[19] Referenda were seen, by Progressives, as more legitimate forms of democracy that allowed the people to directly express their will on a given measure.

Some measures proposed giving the states control over the amending process, while other proposals sought to ensure some form of popular mandate for constitutional amendments by requiring that intervening elections in the state legislatures were held before amendments could be ratified. Four proposals sought a blend of majoritarian and supermajority requirements for either the proposal or ratification stage of the amending process. Ten proposals sought to make the whole amending process subject to majority rather than supermajority consensus.

Not only did these proposals seek to move in the direction of a lower standard of consensus, they also sought to utilize different institutions. Some of the reform measures called for state conventions while others called for national conventions. Still others opted for national and state direct popular votes. Some still kept the supermajority requirements but made the votes more directly democratic via referendum. In short, almost all of the measures introduced sought to make Article V more democratic in some way, whether they proposed making the amending process more directly influenced by simple majorities in representative institutions, or by direct popular involvement through referendums and the like.[20]

None of these attempts at making Article V more democratic were ultimately successful. In fact none of these proposals even passed the Congress, but they did represent real political efforts at reforming Article V. The irony is that after all of the angst over the difficulty of Article V as an impediment to social change, the Progressive movement successfully utilized Article V to make historic transformations to the constitutional text and to American politics. As one might expect, criticism of Article V and the amending process did abate considerably after the successful passage of the Sixteenth, Seventeenth, Eighteenth, Nineteenth, and Twentieth Amendments. Yet as we have already seen, Progressives were still very ambivalent about Article V and when push came to shove during the New Deal the Progressive instincts of Franklin Roosevelt led him to abandon Article V in favor of a pliable Supreme Court. Thus, while Progressive forces were unable to formally alter Article V, the impact of Progressive legal philosophy and Progressive "constitutionalism," led to a shift away from utilizing Article V.

The natural tension, inherent in American Constitutionalism, between popular sovereignty and constitutionalism was difficult for the Progressives to reconcile. Their passion for reform and direct democracy created an impatience for social and political change, an impatience created by their frustration with traditional constitutional norms and provisions that sought to harness and channel raw public opinion. For Progressives, it was not enough to simply allow this tension to exist they sought to resolve it by relaxing the authority of the Constitution and its ability to limit popular authority. Rather than allowing the tension to be worked out through Congress and the State legislatures as prescribed by Article V, Progressives sought to resolve the tension by moving the amending process either to elite judges, or simple majorities in Congress or direct democratic forms such as referendums. One could say that their deep belief in social progress and pursuing the immediate desires of public opinion, in many respects trumped their commitments to written constitutionalism. The Progressive commitment to pragmatism over constitutionalism led them to simultaneously criticize Article V as "impossible" and "undemocratic" all the while utilizing it to advance their populist agendas. It also led them to criticize the "conservative" Supreme Court as anti-democratic only until they were able to capture the Supreme Court during the New Deal, at which time the court became the new champion of the Progressive cause and the court's "counter-majoritarian" nature was minimized and rationalized.[21]

Contemporary Critics

Criticism of Article V's undemocratic nature did not end with the Progressive era. While the New Deal Court led the nation in a new direction regarding constitutional change via judicial adaptation, still there are limits to how far the court is willing to bend the plain meaning of the constitutional text. Thus, there are still calls for abandoning Article V in favor of simple majorities or more directly democratic procedures.

For example, Robert Dahl is very critical of the undemocratic nature of the Constitution, especially the Electoral College and the equal representation in the Senate. While he never attacks Article V head on, his criticism of the Senate and his frustration with the non-directly democratic features of the Constitution suggest by extension a certain natural hostility on his part towards Article V:

> Why should we feel bound today by a document produced more than two centuries ago by a group of fifty-five mortal men, actually signed by only thirty-nine, a fair number of whom were slaveholders, and

> adopted in only thirteen states by the votes of fewer than two thousand men, all of whom are long since dead and mainly forgotten?[22]

Dahl is concerned that Americans have never "had an opportunity to express our considered will on our constitutional system . . . For example how many readers of these lines have ever participated in a referendum that asked them whether they wished to continue to be governed under the existing constitution? The answer, of course, is none."[23] For Dahl our Constitution only serves Americans well if it is able to "meet *democratic* standards of the present day."[24] One can sense Dahl's frustration with Article V when he complains that over 700 proposals have been submitted to amend the Constitution with regard to the Electoral College and yet every one of them died in the "graveyard of constitutional amendments altering the Electoral College . . . the Senate."[25] Dahl is deeply critical of the equal representation in the Senate since, for him, it is inherently undemocratic and a constant impediment to democratic will and reform. Dahl's fundamental dislike of equal representation in the Senate must certainly transfer to the Senate's role in the amending process; especially since the "undemocratic" equal representation in the Senate is magnified by Article V's two-thirds supermajority requirement. Dahl's masked frustration with Article V is even more apparent when one is reminded that Article V itself is the location in the Constitution where the equal representation of the Senate is entrenched via the following Article V language, "no State, without its Consent, shall be deprived of its equal Suffrage in the Senate." The point is that Dahl has deep reservations about the democratic nature of the Constitution and he seeks foundational reform of the government, yet Article V and the Senate's equal representation stand in the way. In the end, Dahl is representative of a class of contemporary Progressive scholars who are frustrated with the non-directly democratic aspects of the Constitution and Article V certainly fits, like the Electoral College, into that category of *insufficiently democratic* institutional provisions.

Sanford Levinson, on the other hand, takes more direct aim at Article V. In his intelligent and provocative work entitled *Our Undemocratic Constitution: Where the Constitution Goes Wrong (and How the People Can Correct It)* he devotes an entire chapter to Article V, entitled "The Impermeable Article V" and in the previous chapter we saw that Levinson describes Article V as an "iron cage."[26] Levinson realizes that the surge of Progressive era amendments has the potential to undercut his argument about Article V being undemocratic. As we have already seen Levinson dismisses the Seventeenth Amendment, as evidence that Article V can facilitate important democratic reforms. The decades long delay in the Seventeenth Amendment's passage was due to the two-third proposal requirement and the Senate's stubborn resistance, all of which for Levinson is a sign of the inherently undemocratic nature of Article V. In short, the issue for Levinson is responsiveness to the raw immediate popular will. To make amendments more responsive, Levinson, like Dahl, suggests that a national popular referendum would be a legitimate and more preferable way in which to alter the Constitution.

Another supporter of a national popular referendum is Akhil Reed Amar. Amar draws deeply from the wells of popular sovereignty in his analysis. In this way Amar displays on the Progressive elements such as *anti-formalism*, *pragmatism*, and he embraces the notion of deference to direct popular majorities as opposed to representative majorities. Like the Progressives, Amar seems not to fear the excesses of direct democracy and majority tyranny and animated much of the Founders' concerns over such measures being relied upon in the American system of government. Amar argues that Article V is not the exclusive manner in which to amend the Constitution, because "We the People" are sovereign and thus *we* can alter the Constitution with a simple majority at any time we want. He argues that the ratification of the current Constitution in 1787 was an example of a legal and legitimate exercise of popular sovereignty. Just as "the people," acting in state conventions, were able to supersede the Articles of Confederation, and the individual state constitutions, "We the People" in the current year onward can similarly alter our established constitutional arrangements at will. From this premise Amar advocates a national referendum as a legitimate alternative to Article V.

In the end, Article V critics from the Progressive era until now hold to the premise that simple majorities and referendums are more democratic, and thus more preferable, as amending procedures than the supermajorities or representation that characterize Article V. This preference is driven by a much deeper desire for responsive government. Not only is Article V undemocratic in and of itself, but it also shields other undemocratic elements in the Constitution like the equal representation of the Senate and the Electoral College. Instead of Article V's use of supermajorities and representation, most modern critics favor a national referendum that would allow "We the People" to alter their form of government via a simple numerical majority vote. Yet again, critics raise a fair question: why wouldn't a more majoritarian, more directly democratic amending process be preferable? Can anything be wrong with more democratic and more responsive government?

National Referendums and Simplistic Democracy

What critics overlook, or do not adequately address, is that there are very good reasons to avoid directly democratic forms such as a national referendum. Dahl, Levinson, and Amar operate on the assumption that direct democratic numerical majorities are somehow more legitimate and more desirable than public opinion that has been sifted through representative institutions and supermajority consent requirements. As we shall see there is a strong case to be made that such "impulses" towards direct democracy are imprudent and a potential danger to the rights of citizens.

As a mode of amendment national referendums do not provide an institutional setting that allows for adequate deliberation by the citizens, it bypasses deliberative institutions such as conventions and legislatures, and it undermines the tapestry of state and local voices that are traditionally given a place in American pluralistic democracy. In the end, the call for national referendum reflects a deeper philosophical shift away from the natural rights of the Declaration of Independence in favor of a rather constricted and thin view of democracy.

These seemingly instinctive calls for a more direct and responsive democratic reform characterize what Herbert Storing referred to as "simplistic democracy."[27] *Simplistic democracy* holds that government is good, "so far as it is *responsive* to popular wishes" and Storing admits that "there is a great deal to be said for these principles. Government *should* be responsive. . . Any gross departure from . . . these principles would surely and properly be resisted by all Americans."[28] However as Storing points out, "the great architectural principle of the American government as it was conceived by its framers is precisely that responsiveness to public opinion is a necessary but *not* a sufficient condition of good government" and Storing worries that moves toward simplistic democracy will "weaken further our already loose grasp on this vital principle."[29] But in what way is responsiveness not enough? Responsiveness, while vitally important, is not the ultimate end of government and restraining responsiveness in some ways may provide better government and guard against abuses of government:

> To say that democratic responsiveness is necessary but not sufficient implies that government ought to be responsive to public opinion in general and over time but that it need not be—indeed that it should not be—merely responsive. A merely responsive government is likely to tend toward instability, ignorance, and indifference to individual and minority rights.[30]

For Storing, limits on responsiveness are not inherently "undemocratic" because, for one thing, the people placed such limits upon themselves. Indeed this is what constitutionalism is in some elemental sense, limits on a polity placed by the polity on itself; "The 'antidemocratic' or nondemocratic devices in our Constitution are democracy's own inventions of prudence to deal with its own harmful tendencies."[31]

According to Storing, advocates of "simplistic democracy" focus too much attention on the *inputs* of the constitutional system and not enough attention on the *outputs*.[32] That is to say critics spend a lot of energy decrying perceived deficiencies in the democratic nature of certain devices in the Constitution, such as Article V, but they ignore the outcomes of such devices, such as the preservation of rights and the establishment of political stability. The focus on trumped-up issues of "legitimacy" is too narrow and simplistic. In addressing attacks on the Electoral College that are nearly identical to the attacks on Article V, Storing points out that there is more to democracy than simple majorities:

> Legitimacy is considerably more complex than numbers of votes. It depends on those qualities the founders tried to build into the American system and that we have on the whole enjoyed: stability, charac-

> ter, a capacity to govern well, as well as popular responsiveness. In no one of these respects is the present system . . . perfect; the main reason for that is that they are to some extent in tension. We are trying to have the best of several worlds—the world of political stability, the world of social diversity, the world governmental confidence, as well as the world of democratic responsiveness. The proponents of direct popular election seem bent on resolving this complex set of worlds into the single one of numerical preponderance.[33]

Like the Electoral College, Article V is designed to be responsive to popular will but it is also designed to promote stability, deliberation, and a commitment to the Constitution as fundamental law. A simplistically majoritarian amending process would threaten each of these essential elements of good government. For Storing, simplistic democracy may sound appealing in theory, but the reality would likely be much different, "That world, the world of simplistic democracy, would be, I am confident, a good deal less satisfactory than what we have now. It would also turn out to be a good deal less simple than it seems to be on the surface."[34]

Similarly, Robert Goldwin responded to Progressive historians, such as Charles Beard, who cast the Constitution as fundamentally undemocratic and the Founders as hopelessly self-interested. Goldwin argued that perhaps the institutions utilized by the Framers, to channel but not stifle, popular will were, in the end, sound and admirable:

> if Beard was not correct—if the Constitution is in fact democratic, or if it was designed to secure rights for all through representative institutions—then we would have to understand the relationship between our ideals and institutions differently: perhaps the institutions that Beard and others have denounced as obstacles to majority rule in fact ensure that majorities rule in a sober, decent fashion.[35]

What Goldwin points out and that critics of Article V often overlook is the potential danger of majority tyranny and the importance of institutional devices to encourage and demand some measure of deliberation. Indeed, Framers such as Madison sought to rescue democratic government from being *too* responsive. The great threat to democracy was simple majority power unhinged from any institutional restraints, the very restraints that critics of Article V wish to undue. Recall the famous passage from *The Federalist:*

> When a majority is included in a faction, the form of popular government, on the other hand, enables it to sacrifice to its ruling passion or interest both the public good and the rights of other citizens. To secure the public good and private rights against the danger of such a faction, and at the same time to preserve the spirit and the form of popular government, is then the great object to which our inquiries are directed.[36]

The "great object" then of American democracy is not responsiveness but the protection of rights from minority and majority tyranny alike. Similarly, Joseph Bessette reminds us that the Framers sought to "refine and enlarge" the public will and in doing so realized that public opinion could take different forms:

> There are, then, two kinds of majority sentiments, two types of public voice. The one is more immediate or spontaneous, uninformed, and unreflective; the other is more deliberative, taking longer to develop and resting on a fuller consideration of information and arguments. It is the second type that the famers sought to promote; this is what they meant when they talked about the rule of the majority.[37]

Critics of Article V seem content with "spontaneous" and "unreflective" majorities rather than deliberative ones and they seem to undervalue legislatures and representation as "adding value" to the quality of democratic decision-making.

Refining public opinion in this way requires representation. Only through representation can you get consistently informed people who are in an environment that encourages deliberation.[38] The institutions and institutional arrangements of the Constitution allow elected officials to deliberate in a capacity that is simply not possible with directly democratic means. Such institutional arrangements are designed to allow the "cool and deliberate sense of the community" to prevail and they seek to help the people to rise above the swirling intrigues of interest and faction to ensure that the laws conform to "the mild voice of reason, pleading the cause of an enlarged and permanent interest."[39] Modern and Progressive critics do not adequately address these concerns; in their rush to be uncritically responsive to immediate public opinion they hastily move to dismantle the very devices designed to curb the excesses of direct democracy and the eventuality of majority tyranny.

Deliberation and Representation

At first glance a national referendum would seem to deprive the amending process of adequate and sound deliberation, or that "mild voice of reason" the Founders sought to ensure when they relied upon representative institutions and required prudent supermajority consensus. National popular referenda by contrast seem to open amendments up to raw public opinion creates space for demagoguery of the worst kind. But surely there would be *some* deliberation during a referendum. Perhaps, but what would the quality of that deliberation be? Joseph Bessette finds the deliberative qualities of referenda lacking:

> No doubt a kind of communitywide deliberation would accompany any referendum contest, but such popular consideration is likely to be influenced profoundly by slick advertising campaigns, the most immoderate voices on each side of the controversy, and the passions of the moment. To repeat an earlier point, sound deliberation requires both extensive knowledge and a setting which promotes collective reasoning about common goals. Although Congress is far from the

> perfect deliberative institution, it more closely approximates the requirements for sound deliberation than could be expected in most any legislative contest conducted in an assembly of two hundred million.[40]

Thus, a referendum abandons the institutional devices that are designed to facilitate deliberation. In general the people, while inherently capable of good decisions, cannot *en masse* extract themselves enough from the vicissitudes of daily life to accumulate adequate expertise and information to be fully deliberative. Now certainly technology might aid in the more efficient accumulation of information and expertise, but general apathy and time constraints of interested persons would likely not ensure a majority that is fully prepared to deliberate. Second, a national referendum does nothing to ensure a truly deliberative environment. Mass communications are more the domains of incivility and demagoguery not sustained and civil deliberation. Representative institutions are designed to foster expertise, information, and deliberation. Representative institutions seek to balance the needs of responsiveness with the needs of deliberation, moderation, and wisdom; all of which help contribute to a regime that secures the rights of its citizens. Referendums may secure the *will* of the majority, but there is little guarantee that they will secure the *rights* of the minority or the "permanent and aggregate interests of the community"[41]

Not only would a national referendum lose the moderation instilled by such measures, but it would deviate also from the principle of federalism. In some respects, replacing Article V with a national referendum would have similar effects on the federal system as would replacing the Electoral College with a direct national popular election of the president. For this reason it is worth considering Michael Uhlmann's arguments against a direct national election of the president due its negative effects on the federal principle. Uhlmann points out that, "Because the presidency is connected to the rest of the constitutional system, candidates must think about the unique structure of the nation they seek to lead."[42] In the same way the amending process would do well to fit "the unique structure of the nation" that is governed by the fundamental law. For example, "because the states, whether small or large, are the principal presidential battlegrounds, candidates accommodate interests that might otherwise be ignored if the size of the popular vote were the only criterion for election."[43] Again, in the same way a campaign to pass an Article V amendment must be attuned to the diversity of state communities and interests. Conversely, a national referendum would free advocates of a given amendment from having to appeal to the diverse fabric of communities that is the United States, and instead allow them to focus on the large population centers which were be few and more uniform. Ultimately for Uhlmann a direct national election for president simply, "ignores the federated nature of the American republic."[44] Likewise a national referendum for amendment weakens the voice of the people by ignoring the historic and contemporary tapestry of diverse communities that are the life and sinew of the American republic.

If presidential elections should reflect the varied geography and local politics of the American political landscape, what argument would there be for abandoning this federal principle in the area of constitutional amendments? Would not constitutional amendments potentially threaten the concerns of different states of various sizes, shapes, and regions? Shouldn't the "unique structure of the nation" also shape a campaign for an alteration to the fundamental law of the nation? As Uhlmann points out, "Campaigning in New Hampshire is very different from campaigning in California, and representing 'all the people' means representing them no less as Texans or New Yorkers than as citizens of an undifferentiated whole."[45] Similarly, amendments will effect citizens of New Hampshire and Texas differently and there would seem to be a strong argument for having those differences adequately reflected in the amending process.

Furthermore, ignoring the traditional and organically federal nature of the American polity will have profound effects on the marketing of constitutional amendments for, "Voters in the less populous states, indeed in any area that cannot be readily subsumed in a mass media market, will be of decidedly secondary importance . . ."[46] Just as political candidates would be drawn to the larger media markets where the "cost-per-voter" is the lowest, so too would activists for constitutional amendments be drawn to the large media markets thus excluding the diversity of smaller local markets; "To be sure, mass marketing of this sort already occurs, but it is constrained by the necessity of reaching voters outside the big media markets. With a national plebiscite, national television campaigning will become the order of the day."[47] According to Uhlmann you would say goodbye to distinctive local politics and, "Say hello to slick admen and spinmeisters who will care little about voters at the state and local level, except insofar as they can be melded into poll-driven sub-categories of national voter sentiment."[48] In such national media campaigns designed to mold and shape public sentiment, "the media mavens will not have to leave their offices in New York, Washington, or Los Angeles to run a presidential campaign. Why should they?"[49] The same would go for a national referendum regarding a constitutional amendment. Powerful moneyed interests on either side would seek to play to the lowest common denominator in moving public opinion one way or another and it would all be done from America's three most important cities.

The fact is that *Madison Avenue* just isn't very *Madisonian*. In *Federalist No. 10* and *No. 51* James Madison argues that majority tyranny will be defused through a "multiplicity of interests" spread across the "extended sphere" of the entire country. Madison was relying upon the natural regional, cultural, and political diversity of the country to counteract the natural tendencies for majority factions to form in more homogenous polities. Madison sought to answer the Anti-Federalist arguments that republics could only exist in small homogenous societies. Madison turned such arguments on their head pointing out that eventually such homogeneity allowed a majority faction to form at the expense of the rights of minorities and the "permanent and aggregate interests of the community." Modern advertising however seeks to undo this tapestry of communities, this multiplicity of interests, this bulwark against majority tyranny in favor of homogenous and manageable demographic blocs. The point of national campaigns and national advertising is to mold public opinion around one or a few easily grasped political slogans or ideas not to facilitate deliberation. The goal is to form a majority around a single issue or candidate to reflect a multiplicity of interests. The goal is not to respond and reflect diversity but rather to erase or obscure diversity of opinion. For Madison what would secure the diversity was the "extended sphere" which was his term for the large expanse of the country. However, national ads directed at rather homogenous urban markets with conformist images and slogans seek to undo or cover up the regional and cultural diversity of this vast geographic land. Rather than a rich and variegated natural tapestry, such campaigns seek to produce shiny uniform and moldable plastic voting blocs. Yet it is this diverse tapestry or "multiplicity of interests" that Madison relies upon to prevent majority tyranny. How is tyranny avoided or deliberation aided by such means that would of necessity be part of any national referendum?

In the end, should Madison Avenue be the biggest shaper of changes to the fundamental law? Shouldn't alterations to the higher law of the nation involve the geographic and political diversity of the country? Should it be reduced to media campaigns and manipulative television and radio ads. Surely such demagogic devices have always played a role in American politics (at least in the form of newspapers) but representative institutions are somewhat insulated from the worst of such manipulations. The information available to legislators or convention delegates along with the attention to providing for relatively deliberative settings would negate the worst of such raw public manipulation through mass media marketing devices. By requiring representative institutions at the state and the national level, Article V reflects the organic historical reality of the United States. The United States despite its many national characteristics is still a quilted patchwork of local and state communities. The mosaic diversity of such communities ought not be so easily obliterated in the homogenizing stultifying conformity inducing impulses of a media driven national referendum process. The drive for democratic "purity" and a nationalizing "homogeneity" should give thoughtful observers pause before eschewing Article V in favor of such questionable devices.

Critics might respond that "refining" public opinion may be an admirable goal and a good talking point, but it is one thing to take majority opinion and improve on it, but quite another thing to deny the will of a numerical majority all together. Constitutional devices such as the Electoral College and equal representation in the Senate do thwart numerical majorities from time to time. How can defenders of Article V legitimize institutional constraints on the majority that actually thwart or prevent the actual numerical majorities from determining constitutional change? Why are institutions such as Article V, which sometimes allow minority will to be decisive, not patently undemocratic and illegitimate? The obvious answer is that such complaints are a subtle rejection of any constitution that seeks to bind any majority. As such it is a veiled critique of written constitutionalism itself. The more complex and interesting answer lies again in James Madison's analysis of *constitutional majorities.*

Constitutional Majorities

Madison was fully aware that the constitutional mechanisms may from time to time stifle immediate popular will. A *constitutional majority* is produced naturally when adhering to the forms prescribed in the constitutional text. For example, the Electoral College will produce a constitutional majority for the purposes of electing the president, congressional elections may produce a constitutional majority for the purposes of passing legislation, and the Article V will produce a constitutional majority for the purposes of changes to the fundamental law. These *constitutional majorities* may very well not represent a *popular majority* of the whole population, due to many factors such as voter apathy, equal representation in the Senate, and different voting patterns in congressional districts, or states electoral votes.[50]

For James Madison this distinction between *constitutional* and *popular* majorities naturally flows out of elective government and is not something that can be avoided,

> It may be objected to majority governments, that the majority, as formed by the Constitution, may be a minority when compared with the popular majority. This is likely to be the case more or less in all elective governments. It is so in many of the States.[51]

While this is certainly a problem in Confederacies, who provide each member with an equal vote regardless of population the republican system in the United States may also produce disparities between constitutional and popular majorities.[52] Madison admits that this disparity could be abused or result in abuse, but such risks are ultimately unavoidable in a constitutional system of government:

> That this departure from the rule of equality, creating a political and constitutional majority in contradistinction to a numerical majority of the people, may be abused in various degrees oppressive to the majority of the people, is certain; and in modes and degrees so oppressive as to justify ultra or anti-constitutional resorts to adequate relief is equally certain. Still the constitutional majority must be acquiesced in by the constitutional minority, while the Constitution exists. The moment that arrangement is successfully frustrated, the Constitution is at an end.[53]

Madison is pointing out that the reality of constitutionalism is that the majority may from time to time be thwarted and indeed there is a risk that injustices may occur under such a system. However, greater injustices are *more* likely without adequate constraints on the majority. In addition, such injustices must be weighed against political life outside of the Constitution or under a different constitution. A people cannot claim adherence to a constitution as a binding force only to ignore it when it is inconvenient. Nor should they deprecate the Constitution because it does not always produce clean numerical majorities in messy political matters. Madison is quick to point out that there are natural political checks on constitutional majorities. Constitutional majorities (that aren't a numerical majority) are, in the end, checked by the fact that they are indeed a numerical minority. Majority opinion will eventually predominate over time as more elections or more votes are taken. In other words a constitutional majority that happens to be a numerical minority will be short lived:

> It is a favourable consideration, in the impossibility of securing in all cases a coincidence of the constitutional and numerical majority, that when the former is the minority, the existence of a numerical majority with justice on its side, and its influence on public opinion, will be a salutary control on the abuse of power by a minority constitutionally possessing it: a control generally of adequate force, where a military force, the disturber of all the ordinary movements of free governments, is not on the side of the minority.[54]

For Madison, the expectation that constitutional majorities will always coincide with numerical majorities is utopian at best. A commitment to republican government and constitutional government requires sober expectations and a perspective that gives the constitutional observer a clear vista into the less desirable alternatives that have been offered up by history and experience:

> The result of the whole is, that we must refer to the monitory reflection that no government of human device and human administration can be perfect; that that which is the least imperfect is therefore the best government; that the abuses of all other governments have led to the preference of republican government as the best of all governments, because the least imperfect; that the vital principle of republican government is the lex majoris partis, the will of the majority; that if the will of a majority cannot be trusted where there are diversified and conflicting interests, it can be trusted nowhere, because such interests exist everywhere.[55]

Critics of Article V would do well to reconsider the sage advice of Madison here, for the search for perfection in government leads to dangerous expectations. Madison is cautioning critics to realistically assess the tradeoff between constitutional republican government and its protections (which inherently includes the occasional disparity between constitutional and numerical majorities) or other governmental forms which history has shown to be much more of a threat to individual liberty.

The founding generation clearly rejected notions of direct democracy that seem to permeate modern politics. They feared the chaotic impact of subjecting government to the waves of popular passions that were so endemic to popular government. Recall the descriptions in *Federalist No. 9,* of republics that produced, "sensations of horror and disgust at the distractions with which they were continually agitated, and at the rapid succession of revolutions by which they were kept in a state of perpetual vibration between the extremes of tyranny and anarchy."[56] The founding generation preferred to insulate government from such instability while still making it ultimately accountable to the popular will. Representative institutions such as the state legislatures and the U.S. Congress serve to channel popular sentiments and reflect a "cool and deliberate" sense of public opinion in their legislation. This deliberation of the legislatures would serve to "refine and enlarge" public opinion thus dispensing the popular will in a manner more consistent with good government than the raw democratic impulses that could often sweep a democratic society wreaking havoc on sound public policy and individual liberty.

In the end, any amending process must set up procedures that require the formation of an authentic voice of the people via the creation of a constitutional majority. For critics of Article V, "authenticity" is only measured by responsiveness. Yet such responsiveness is a threat to the deeper purposes of the Constitution. The Constitution is meant to "secure" rights, not to provide simplistic democracy. As we have seen, there are complex and persuasive arguments for the reliance on institutions that are representative and deliberative rather than merely responsive. In the end, by trusting the amending process to legislative bodies at the state and national level or constitutional conventions, the Framers sought to ensure that alterations to the fundamental law would receive the requisite deliberation due such acts. They sought to ensure that not only would amendments to the Constitution be enacted by the authentic voice of the people but also their reasoned and deliberative voice. It was not enough that the people choose, but they must choose well.

Natural Rights

But choosing well suggests there is a standard by which to judge the choice made. Yet, the commitments of many critics to modern and post-modern philosophical premises that exclude the ability to "know" the good in any definitive form leave many critics with no standard by which to judge the acts of the majority as legitimate or illegitimate. In the absence of such a standard then it seems to follow that there is no sound basis upon which to thwart will of a majority. The majority will must prevail for on what grounds do we say that the majority is wrong?

Indeed for the Progressives such as Woodrow Wilson, the belief in the rationality of history and the historical and cultural relativity of truth undermined the belief in natural rights that animated the Founders. The Progressive impulse was to deny that such rights existed and to assert that the Founders were motivated by pecuniary interests rather than a sense of justice. Institutional devices that were meant to foster prudence and deliberation were in this light seen as unjust attempts to tip the balance of power in the favor of elite moneyed interests against the people. In the modern era of Progressives, moral skepticism was the order of the day, thus there was not basis upon which to judge majority will as right or wrong. Popular majorities were always right. Thus a government that was meant to secure rights against an overpowering majority made no sense. Popular will working through majorities determined the very nature of truth and thus restraints on such will were anachronistic remnants of a bygone era.

Yet moral skepticism in a democracy simply won't do; for democracy itself becomes incoherent when separated from the reality of natural rights and natural law. Human equality is itself a moral proposition; therefore if one then moves to exclude moral assessments from politics, and political decisions, then the very basis of democracy is undercut and becomes incoherent. Walter Berns makes this point well:

> Except on the basis of natural right, it is not easy, and may even be impossible, to provide a principled defense of majority rule, or, stated otherwise, to defend majority rule on the level of principle. Presumably such a defense would rest on an assertions of the equality of men; but in what respects are men equal—naturally equal—one to another? We all know that they are not equally intelligent, virtuous, godly, handsome, white, yellow, or black. Nor are they equally strong; unless the stronger can be taught that strength is not a legitimate claim to rule, they will rule. Not only will they rule, but the weak, in addition to being unable to resist in practice, will be unable to object in principle. The only respect in which all men are equal is in their possession of natural rights. It is from the fact of this equality of rights that the majority derives its right to determine the form of government under which all will live. The question put to the people on this founding occasion is, and can only be, under what form of government will rights best be secured?[57]

Indeed, majority rule makes no sense when severed from the reality of natural right for when natural law is denied majority will is reduced to naked power and the position of "might makes right." When it is not clothed in the eternal and universal principles of natural right, ". . . majority rule can be justified only if men are equal; they are equal only in their possession of rights. A politics of equality must, therefore, be a politics concerned with rights . . ."[58] Indeed, James Madison in *Federalist No. 51* argues that "justice is the end of government" and when the "stronger faction can readily unite and oppress the weaker, anarchy may be truly said to reign as in a state of nature."

Thus, the Progressive desire for responsiveness is a significant deviation from the Founders' constitutionalism, in fact one could argue it is a departure from the foundational premises behind written constitutionalism altogether. That is to say a truly "responsive" government would not be bound by any constitutional restraints on the majority will. Something more akin to the Athenian demos would seem to be the ideal form for those critics of Article V who resist restraints on public opinion. To be sure, critics likely want some minimal restraints on the majority but what is their principled basis for such restraints? From what theoretical or philosophical reservoir can such resources be drawn? As we have seen a position that pushes for raw majoritarianism undercuts the very moral basis for democracy.

In Book I of Plato's *Republic* the character Thrasymachus asserts that justice is nothing more that the "advantage of the stronger" and that such a principle is operative in democratic regimes as well as tyrannies or oligarchies. Socrates in response argues and illustrates that "justice" cannot simply be subject to the will of the strongest whether that will be exerted by the one, the few, or the many. Plato illustrates through his dialogue that since "justice" is elusive it can only hope to be obtained by dialogue and deliberation. For similar reasons, the Founders opted for a written constitution that provided institutional space and incentives for sound deliberation and as we have seen, Article V is a key part of this system. The Progressives, perhaps unknowingly, have sided with Thrasymachus and would have the Constitution yield to the immediate impulse of the strong as long as the strength comes from democratic majorities who are not restrained long enough to respect the interests or rights of minorities.

Conclusion

In the end, not only is Article V more consistent with the tradition, history, and ideas that are central to the uniquely American form of constitutionalism and federalism, but Article V provides a superior form of amendment that restrains the human tendency towards majority tyranny. Critics of Article V will resist that they want to pave the way for majority tyranny, yet they must concede that one of the dangers of majority tyranny is that those in the majority rarely recognize their policy impositions as a violation of rights of the minority. There is always a public rationale for the policy in question and often that public rationale is terribly convincing to the majority, but that does not change the fact that someone's rights are being violated or that the public good is being eviscerated by the blind arrogance of a mere majority swept up in passionate defense of their brand of "justice." The Framers sought to compensate for potentially dangerous popular impulses by requiring deliberative supermajorities to consent to changes in the fundamental law. As we have seen there is nothing inherently undemocratic in these requirements. Indeed such requirements were created democratically by the people themselves in order refine the democratic principle in a manner that saves it from its own potential excesses.

As water gives life to human communities so does democracy. Water, by itself, nourishes human bodies and, through its use in agriculture, provides communities an essential element of human flourishing. In the same way, democracy nourishes the human soul that seeks liberty and it also provides communities with the ability to flourish though self-determination and ordered liberty. Yet, an excess of water that comes through unexpected storms can produce flash floods and can be deadly. An excess of water at the wrong time in the wrong form can be devastating to human lives and communities. Thus, it is better when water is harnessed in reservoirs and its impact in the community is moderated through channels, canals, irrigation, and pipes. Similarly, an excess of democracy driven by floods of raw majority opinion untethered from principles of moderation and prudence can be similarly devastating to individual lives and the fabric of once thriving communities. Likewise, it is best when pools of democratic power are stored up in reservoirs and prudently released in an orderly and systematic manner. When the democratic principle is allowed to irrigate (rather than flood) the fields of politics it provides cool liberty to individuals in a moderation that allows the community to flourish. Article V represents a vital element of the constitutional system in this regard. It is designed to allow the constitutive power of the people to alter the fundamental law—a potentially chaotic and destructive power—in a peaceful and regular manner. Article V allows for democratic change that is prudent and directed at securing the rights of the governed all the while still allowing the people to exercise their sovereign power.

But is it impossible to channel the democratic impulse into constitutional forms and formalities? Won't the democratic impulse naturally overflow the forms provided for it? Won't it naturally shape the American polity in a flowing organic manner like a river shapes a landscape over centuries as it ebbs and flows and cuts deep channels in the land? In short, isn't Article V too formal and therefore essentially irrelevant given the march of history? To these questions we now turn.

Notes

1. J. Allen Smith, *The Spirit of American Government: A Study of the Constitution: Its Origin, Influence and Relation to Democracy* (Norwood, MA: Norwood Press, 1911; reprint of 1907 edition), 40.
2. Ibid. vii.
3. Ibid.
4. Ibid., 40.
5. Ibid.
6. Ibid., 4.
7. Ibid., 49.
8. Ibid., 63.
9. John W. Burgess, "Present Problems of Constitutional Law," *Political Science Quarterly* 19 (1904), 548; also quoted in Kyvig, *Explicit and Authentic Acts*, 193.
10. Herbert Croly, *Progressive Democracy*, 130.
11. Ibid., 230.

12. Ibid., 231.
13. Ibid., 232.
14. Ibid., 231.
15. Ibid., 246.
16. Vile, *The Constitutional Amending Process*, 147.
17. M.A. Musmanno, *Proposed Amendments to the Constitution* (Washington: GPO. 19. 29; Brooklyn, NY: Central Book Company), 189-190. For an example of a Pre-Progressive attempt at amending Article V: In 1826, After the large number of amendments seeking to alter presidential elections (after the defeat of Jackson in 1824), "Mr. Herrick, of Maine, offered a resolution proposing to prohibit the introduction of amendments to the Constitution except in every tenth year." Also, Rhode Island proposed that "after 1793 no amendment to the Constitution should be made 'without the consent of the 11 of the States heretofore united under the Confederation.'" This was done in hopes of protecting the small states. This would have given a preponderance of amending power to the original thirteen states.
18. Vile, *Encyclopedia of Constitutional Amendment*, 14.
19. Vile, *Encyclopedia of Constitutional Amendment*, 15.
20. M.A. Musmanno, *Proposed Amendments to the Constitution* (Washington: GPO. 1929; Brooklyn, NY: Central Book Company).
21. For more on the Progressive commitment to Darwinism and Pragmatism see Brad C. S. Watson, *Living Constitution Dying Faith: Progressivism and the New Science of Jurisprudence* (Wilmington, DE: ISI Books, 2009).
22. Robert A. Dahl, *How Democratic is the American Constitution?*, Kindle edition, Chapter 1, location 33 of 1570.
23. Dahl, *How Democratic is the American Constitution?*, Kindle edition, Chapter 1, location 37.
24. Ibid.
25. Dahl, *How Democratic is the American Constitution?*, Kindle edition, Chapter 4, location 714
26. Levinson, *Our Undemocratic Constitution*, 160.
27. Herbert Storing, "In Defense of the Electoral College," in Joseph Bessette, ed. *Toward a More Perfect Union: The Writings of Herbert Storing* (Washington, D.C.: The AEI Press, 1995), 395. Storing made these arguments in defense of the Electoral College but they seem very useful and appropriate in defending Article V as well.
28. Ibid., 395.
29. Ibid., 396.
30. Ibid.
31. Ibid.
32. Ibid., 397.
33. Ibid., 402.
34. Ibid., 402.
35. Robert A. Goldwin ed., et. al., *How Democratic is the Constitution?* (Washington, D.C.: AEI Press, 1980), i.
36. *Federalist No. 10.*
37. Joseph Bessette, "Deliberative Democracy: The Majority Principle in Republican Government," in Goldwin, *How Democratic is the Constitution?*, 106.
38. See Joseph Bessette, in Goldwin, 105; or Joseph Bessette, *The Mild Voice of Reason.*
39. *Federalist No. 42*; for an excellent discussion of deliberative democracy see Joseph M. Bessette, *The Mild Voice of Reason*, (Chicago, University of Chicago Press, 1994).
40. Bessette, in Goldwin, *How Democratic is the Constitution?*, 115.
41. *Federalist No. 10.*
42. Uhlmann, "As the College Goes, So Goes the Constitution," *Claremont Review of Books*, (Winter 2001). http://www.claremont.org/publications/crb/id.1135/article_detail.asp, (accessed September 2, 2012)
43. Ibid.

44. Ibid.
45. Ibid.
46. Ibid.
47. Ibid.
48. Ibid.
49. Ibid.
50. The distinction between popular majorities and constitutional majorities has certainly been a controversial issue in modern American politics. One has only to remember the rancor over the 2000 Presidential election and the fact that Al Gore won a popular majority while Bush won a constitutional majority. It is to Gore's credit that he was able to clearly understand and accept this distinction. Gore eventually recognized and honored the modes prescribed in the Constitution for establishing a constitutional majority for the purposes of presidential election.
51. James Madison, *Letters and Other Writings of James Madison, Fourth President of the United States*, 4 vol. (Philadelphia: J.B. Lippincott & Co. Published by Order of Congress), IV: 333. Cited in the American Reference Library. [CD-ROM] Orem, Utah: Western Standard Publishing Company, 1998. Hereafter cited as *Writings of James Madison.*
52. *Writings of James Madison*, IV: 333.
53. Ibid., IV: 333.
54. Ibid., IV: 333.
55. Ibid., IV: 334.
56. *Federalist No. 9.*
57. Walter Berns, "Does the Constitution 'Secure These Rights?'" in Goldwin, *How Democratic is the Constitution?*, 75-76.
58. Ibid., 76.

Chapter 8
The Critics: Article V is Too Formal

> Men living in democratic centuries do not readily understand the importance of formalities and have an instinctive contempt for them . . . Formalities arouse their disdain and often their hatred. As they usually aspire to none but facile and immediate pleasures, they rush straight at the object of any of their desires, and the slightest delay exasperates them.
>
> Alexis de Tocqueville[1]

Another common argument against Article V is that Article V is simply too formal, that it does not allow for the inevitable expression of America's "unwritten constitution" to evolve and adapt to changing social circumstances. Such arguments are rarely use the term "formal" nor do they make this critique in a direct or open fashion; rather they are usually the clear implication of attempts by scholars to deconstruct Article V's formal requirements in favor of informal evolution of constitutional provisions. As we have seen in previous chapters early Progressives worried that Article V's difficulty might push constitutional changes into the less democratic courts. To alleviate these concerns they sought to use Article V's procedures in efforts to amend Article V itself; to make Article V less difficult and more democratic, as they saw it. As we have seen these efforts failed but they did respect the formality of Article V and for a time Progressives made peace with Article V. Progressives found Article V a powerful tool in remaking the Constitution in very important ways; such as the income tax provision, the direct election of senators, and extending women's suffrage to a national level. However, over time the inherent pragmatism at the core of Progressive thought led "New Deal" era Progressives to reject legal forms and formalities including those of Article V in an effort to remake the Constitution in more fundamental ways. To achieve their programmatic reforms New Deal Progressives led by Franklin Roosevelt abandoned Article V's democratic consent requirements in favor of the counter-majoritarian power of the Supreme Court.

By the time of Franklin Roosevelt's "constitutional revolution" of 1937 the stage was set for ignoring the forms and formalities of Article V in favor of judicial adaptation of the Constitution. Roosevelt believed that Article V was too difficult and he feared his preferred amendment might be thwarted by an active minority of citizens. Instead of utilizing Article V, Roosevelt sought rather to remake the courts or intimidate them into compliance. Once Roosevelt had secured a powerful and active court, Article V seemed superfluous, "judicial Review rendered most change by amendment unnecessary and comparatively difficult, thus unattractive."[2] The forms and formalities of Article V were thus abandoned at important moments for the informal adaptation of the Constitution by Congress allied with the president and sanctioned by the Supreme Court.[3]

Now few judges today would openly or publicly admit that they are skirting Article V formalities, but legal scholars who are in many ways less subject to public scrutiny have more freedom to make the public case for judicial, legislative, or executive adaptation instead of formal amendment. The reticence of sitting judges to view their wide ranging and often strained rulings as amendments suggests that Franklin Roosevelt's so called constitutional revolution was not as successful or complete as some might like to assert. Nevertheless, the public arguments for abandoning Article V's formalities come largely from legal scholars in the academy and not from judges themselves. Accordingly, let us look at the views of a few such scholars and assess their arguments for informal alternatives to Article V.

Contemporary Critics

Bruce Ackerman

Bruce Ackerman is an accomplished and noted legal scholar who is concerned with weaving a new post-modern narrative about our constitutional "foundations"—for Ackerman there have been three American "regimes"—and a key part of his new narrative is that "the people" are not and never have been bound to the Article V amending procedure under the Constitution, "the critical question is . . . Should modern Americans read Article V as if it described the only mechanisms they may appropriately use for constitutional revision at the dawn of the twenty-first century?"[4] Ackerman thinks not for "The text does not answer this question explicitly. None of its 143 words says anything like 'this Constitution may only be amended through the following procedures, and in no other way.'"[5] According to Ackerman, since Article V does not declare its own exclusivity its claim as the sole legal means of amendment cannot hold up to scrutiny. From this textual premise Ackerman builds a historical case against Article V arguing that it is merely "sufficient" but not "necessary" for the enactment of a valid constitutional amendment.[6]

For Ackerman, Article V is really only one way to amend the Constitution, but it is certainly not the "exclusive" way to amend that document. Much of Ackerman's argument rests on his assertion that the founding in 1787 was technically illegal under the Articles of Confederation since the mode of ratification demanded by the *Articles*—which called for unanimous consent among the states—was jettisoned in favor of a nine state standard for ratification of the new Constitution. Since this unanimous consent provision of the Articles was not followed, Ackerman believes that this move by the Founders established a precedent for irregular modes of amendment thereafter. Ackerman further argues that both the Reconstruction era amendments and the New Deal jurisprudence were also technically "illegal" under Article V's provisions and yet they have been accepted as legitimate today. Although these developments are "illegal" according to Ackerman, he further argues that they were necessary and ultimately legitimate forms of constitutional change. These irregularities are examples of an alternative form of *higher lawmaking* or what he calls a "structural amendment," which should be considered part of normal constitutional development, and embraced as legitimate. For Ackerman, these "structural amendments" essentially amount to "re-foundings" of the American regime.

In explaining structural amendments Ackerman describes a process whereby a constitutional impasse between competing branches of government is decided by popular mandates via intervening elections. These mandates in turn give the popular institutions enough power to "force" competing institutions into submitting to a new constitutional order. First, there is the "signaling phase" where a popular movement gains sufficiently deep and widespread support that their issue is put at the forefront of the public agenda.[7] The second phase is the "proposal" phase where the movement seeks some element of constitutional reform. The third phase is the "mobilized popular deliberation" phase in which the reform movement provokes a silent majority to respond by defending the constitutional status quo. If the movement emerges from the "deliberation" phase deeper and stronger then they may achieve the reform they have sought. Thus we arrive at the fourth phase of "legal codification" where the Supreme Court translates "constitutional politics into constitutional law."[8]

In Ackerman's assessment these non-Article V "structural amendments" more adequately describe what happened during Reconstruction and the New Deal. Given that the tragic reality of Civil War radically broke existing legal norms one surely would make allowances for any irregularities that were necessary in reconstituting the ruptured union. However, the New Deal is another matter and it is the real focus of Ackerman's attention and his argument.

Ackerman is trying to make sense of the radical nature of the New Deal and its political transformation of the federal government into an activist arm in the service of Progressive visions. He is trying to provide a narrative explanation of this transformation within the American constitutional tradition. It is clear to Ackerman that FDR's court packing plan and the New Deal transformation of the Supreme Court into the final arbiter of the Constitution certainly exceeded the constitutional forms that had existed until that point. Given the scope of this irregularity he is trying—in post-modern fashion—to legitimize these changes *post hoc* by using language and imagination to smooth over the legal abnormalities. To the extent that Ackerman is attempting to provide a historical explanation of "transformative" periods in American constitutional history, then he may have some interesting observations. However, Ackerman is doing much more than that, for he does not merely provide an explanation of the past, but he provides a pathway to the future. He is not describing irregularities, rather he is recommending them. Ackerman seeks to legitimate and perpetuate non-Article V "usurpations" of the constitutional amending process. Rather than seek to restore the exclusive form of Article V he seeks to weaken it. In the end, Ackerman's structural amendment seeks to undo the formality of constitutional change in favor of informal unrestrained adaptation. One keen observer put it this way,

> Ackerman prescribes a four-step process for enacting unofficial constitutional "amendments." This process requires signaling, proposing (not to be confused with Article V's proposal process), mobilizing and deliberating, and codifying (which Ackerman writes will be done by the courts 'in the modern system' of codification). In essence, Ackerman's view represents an unofficial amending of the constitution's amendment provisions; but his view has not been signaled to, nor proposed to, the American people; it has not mobilized them, nor has it been deliberated by them; and it has not been codified.[9]

Thus, in the end Ackerman's sweeping narrative attempts to render Article V an extraneous part of the Constitution rather than a vital means of preserving both popular control of the government and the rule of law.

Sanford Levinson

Sanford Levinson's anti-formalistic tendencies reveal themselves in the very terminology he uses to describe constitutional alterations. For Levinson an examination of Article V and the numbered textual amendments to the Constitution are insufficient to explain or account for constitutional change as he defines it.[10] Levinson argues that some items labeled as amendments in the constitutional text might be better described as interpretations, while certain interpretations by the Supreme Court could be better labeled as amendments, "[t]here is not reason . . . to call a numbered textual addition a genuine 'amendment' unless it truly changes the pre-existing legal reality."[11] According to Levinson we should reserve the term "amendment" to reflect broad and fundamental changes to our governmental system and not just changes to the constitutional text. For instance, he argues that the Supreme Court rulings in decisions such as *McCulloch v. Maryland* and *Home Building & Loan v. Blaisdell* are legitimately viewed by some as amendments to the Constitution rather than interpretations. Levinson argues that the subtle and complex difference between an *interpretation* and an *amendment* cannot be consistently determined by any formal criteria. If one cannot consistently distinguish between the two by utilizing formal criteria, then one cannot argue that courts have not made amendments. Furthermore, if courts can make, and have made, amendments then certainly Article V cannot claim to be the exclusive means of constitutional amendment.

Based on this premise that Article V cannot be, and has not been, the only source of "amendment" within the American system of government, discussions of constitutional change must move beyond Article V. The implications of Levinson's argument are that non-Article V changes to the Constitution are a natural result of the evolution of the law, and should be accepted as such. By carefully and loosely defining amendments as changes in the "pre-existing legal reality" Levinson, like Ackerman, deftly demotes Article V from the exclusive means of amendment into simply one of many amendment options. In short, Levinson argues for the existence, and emergence, of an evolutionary unwritten constitution as the preeminent force in American Constitutionalism. In Levinson's scheme the written text is neither authoritative, nor does it accurately reflect the changes in American politics and governmental institutions. Levinson seems to take no issue with the Supreme Court exercising the authority of constitutional amendment in its decisions. Such actions are pragmatic responses to changing social and political conditions and therefore unavoidable given the nature of law and politics. In the end, Levinson carefully defines the term "amendment" such that Article V is rendered a historical artifact. Under his new terms, many "amendments" have already been made without the use of Article V, and likely in the future we will see more non-Article V "amendments."[12] Similarly to Ackerman, Levinson employs a post-modern sensibility that sees the use of language as the key challenge for scholars. The unabated adaptation of the constitution can be allowed to continue with the simple redefinition of amendment from something formal and explicit into something informal and indefinite.

Stephen Griffin

Lastly, Stephen Griffin, outright rejects the notion of a written constitution as a legally binding document and he sets out to "debunk claims of the Constitution's success."[13] Stephen Griffin's approach to Article V rests on his conclusion that the current constitutional order is deeply flawed. These deep flaws demand radical changes to the American constitutional structure and yet an adherence to Article V's formalistic process prevents such needed changes, "The Constitution that the framers created may well prevent Americans from making the kind of structural reforms that may be necessary to cope with the policy challenges of the next century."[14]

Griffin directly questions the viability of traditional American Constitutionalism and argues that the U.S. Constitution is, contrary to common opinion, a historical failure because it was unable to prevent the political division leading to the Civil War. Nor was the Constitution able to accommodate the need for government growth during the depression prior to the New Deal. For Griffin these failures are the result of America's misguided theoretical belief in "rule-of-law" constitutionalism—where the Constitution has the legal force of law—which cannot work because the Constitution as a governing legal document is too rigid to accommodate the necessities of social and historical change. Because of the rigidity inherent in "rule-of-law" constitutionalism there are only two possibilities, "Change can only occur by loading the Constitution with regulative rules that reflect the political compromises of the day, or through non-

Article V means."[15] The dilemma is that either approach erodes the Constitution's authority as fundamental law. Based on this analysis, Griffin asserts, "The whole idea that the Constitution has worked fairly well, to say nothing of being an outright success, begins to look quite fraudulent."[16]

In the end, Griffin argues that history has made Article V irrelevant as the source of serious constitutional change, and with the demise of Article V, so goes the demise of the Constitution as a legal written document. Thus, for Griffin, "It appears that the eighteenth-century concept of constitutionalism is compatible only with the kind of limited government the framers were familiar with. The Constitution the framers created may well prevent Americans from making the kind of structural reforms that may be necessary to cope with the policy challenges of the next century."[17] According to Griffin, viewing Article V as the exclusive means of amendment ignores historical reality and perpetuates the false assumption that "rule-of-law" constitutionalism is a viable approach in the modern world.

Griffin takes the premises of Levinson and Ackerman to their logical conclusion. If formal amendment cannot be maintained and has been abandoned then indeed a written constitution with the force of law cannot be maintained. A written constitution seeks to use the tool of positive law to limit and control government. If that tool is inadequate then written constitutionalism will indeed fail.

Criticisms Examined

The Founding was Illegal

Much of Ackerman's anti-formalism rests on his claim that the Constitution itself rests upon an illegal abandonment of the Articles of Confederation. If the creation of the Constitution itself was "illegal" then why should future adaptations of the Constitution adhere strictly to legal form? Much of Ackerman's argument of illegality rests upon Article XIII of the Articles of Confederation which stipulates that all of the states must ratify changes to the Articles. Of course as we have seen the delegates at the Constitutional Convention in Philadelphia in 1787 rejected this mode of ratification and settled upon only nine states as needing to ratify before the proposed Constitution became operational. Thus, indeed the ratification procedure for the new Constitution was inconsistent with the procedure laid out in Article XIII of the Articles of Confederation; yet as Akhil Reed Amar points out, ". . . inconsistency is not illegality. The Articles of Confederation were nothing more than a tight treaty among thirteen otherwise independent states—a self-described 'firm *league* of friendship' in which each state expressly 'retains its sovereignty.'"[18] Indeed as we have seen in chapter 3, during the Constitutional Convention, Madison argued that the amending mechanism of the Articles of Confederation was defective in its requirement of unanimity. Thus it was imperative that the new Constitution not tie itself down to the flawed amending process of the Articles of Confederation. In addressing this point Madison indeed argued at the convention that the Articles of Confederation were a treaty and thus they were not as legally binding as would a proper constitution.[19]

Madison in *Federalist No. 43* elaborates on the key point that the Articles of Confederation were in reality not much more than a treaty and as a treaty that has been breached on numerous occasions, its legal authority dims in proportion.

> It has been heretofore noted among the defects of the Confederation, that in many of the States it had received no higher sanction than a mere legislative ratification. The principle of reciprocality seems to require that its obligation on the other States should be reduced to the same standard. A compact between independent sovereigns, founded on ordinary acts of legislative authority, can pretend to no higher validity than a league or treaty between the parties. It is an established doctrine on the subject of treaties, that all the articles are mutually conditions of each other; that a breach of any one article is a breach of the whole treaty; and that a breach, committed by either of the parties, absolves the others, and authorizes them, if they please, to pronounce the compact violated and void.[20]

As a treaty the Articles were simply not legally binding in the same way that the Constitution since breaches of the treaty—of which there had been many—would reduce the binding nature of the agreement to the point that each state had enough legal grounds to leave the Articles of Confederation should they have wished to do so.[21] While the Articles did declare that the union it created was "perpetual" that was simply not enough:

> Nor does Article XIII's declaration that "the Union shall be perpetual" change the analysis, for in fact this clause was itself yoked to a mandate that the Articles "shall be inviolably observed by every state." Under standard principles of international law, each of these yoked mandates was a condition of the other. When inviolable observation lapsed, so did perpetual union under the Articles.[22]

As a league, even a very strong league, each state could dissolve its participation on its own terms if other states had breached the agreement. Thus there was no legal impediment to any of the states leaving the Articles of Confederation anytime they wished.

Also, in *Federalist No. 43* Madison addressed this issue of the legality of ratifying the proposed Constitution outside the provisions of the Articles of Confederation in natural law terms, "The express authority of the people alone could give due validity to the Constitution. To have required the unanimous ratification of the thirteen States, would have subjected the essential interests of the whole to the caprice or corruption of a single member."[23] In a way, Madison is making the point that being bound to an unreasonable tenet of positive law would violate core tenets of the natural law. To adhere blindly to the unanimous requirements of the Articles of Confederation would be to violate common sense and principles rooted in nature. Instead Madison urged an adherence to "the great principle of self-preservation; to the transcendent law of nature and of nature's God, which declares that the safety and happiness of society are the objects at which all political institutions aim, and to which all such institutions must be sacrificed."[24]

So the natural law establishes the people as the source of authority for the Constitution and their survival, safety, and happiness as the ends of the Constitution. Thus a breach of the Articles of Confederation was not "illegal" in the deepest sense for there was a natural legal footing for abandoning the unanimous consent of the Articles. Thus, Ackerman's position does not fully account for the legal nature of popular sovereignty. Despite the states' commitment to the Articles the people still retained the ultimate right under natural law to alter or abolish their government should it not be conducive to their safety and happiness. Again as we have seen this point was made by the delegates at the Philadelphia Convention. As Madison had argued in Philadelphia the new Constitution must reach beyond the state authorities directly to "supreme authority of the people themselves."[25] Ackerman's critique does not adequately address the natural law authority of the sovereign people which ultimately trumps the positive law authority of the Articles of Confederation.

However, if the people in their sovereign power could trump the Articles of Confederation why can't they trump the existing Constitution? First, if a polity is seeking to throw off their old constitution and begin a fresh with a new one, then the term *amendment* does not really apply. An *amendment* is an improvement to an existing constitution. In a very vital sense ending an old constitution and beginning another is a very different question than amendment. Leaving the positive law framework of an existing constitution—as Blackstone noted in chapter 2—puts a people back in a state of nature and no longer subject to the old positive law. Thus they are bound by the natural law but no longer the old positive law. Reason demands that such changes are done explicitly or they have no legitimacy. Ackerman's theory does not adequately account for the explicit nature that such fundamental changes require. Second, if a people want to *amend* their constitution the answer is that they can, but they must adhere to forms and formalities and precedent, both of which are already provided by Article V.

In the end, Ackerman's assertion that the ratification was illegal simply does not to account for the very nature of the Articles of Confederation, "the Constitution did not 'illegally' depart from Article XIII because that Article and the other Articles of Confederation were by 1787 no longer legally binding for any state that chose to exercise its legal right to rescind the compact."[26] One must remember that it was the very weakness of the Articles that led to the Philadelphia convention in the first place and therefore ignoring the frail legal footing of the Articles by not establishing a new government on firmer footing would have been imprudent and extremely unwise. In the end, the abandonment of the Articles ratification procedure for the new one was indeed bold, creative, and assertive, but it was in no way illegal.

Structural Amendments

A large part of Ackerman's analysis depends upon a founding precedent for not being formally bound by established law and therefore opening the option of abandoning the positive law of the Constitution when it becomes "necessary." Thus by showing that the Founders did not simply engage in an illegal abandonment of the Articles of Confederation, Ackerman's theory takes a severe blow because it is deprived of a foundational precedent that clears the way for later "illegal" actions.

However, Ackerman's theory of structural amendment deserves to be responded to on its own terms. Ackerman strains to justify his break with formal amendment by clothing it in the robes of democracy. For instance the key transformation for Ackerman is the New Deal break with the previous constitutional order. For Ackerman the American people "ratified" the New Deal constitutional order in the 1936 election, and thus took Roosevelt's side in his constitutional impasse with the Supreme Court. Did Roosevelt really have a mandate for constitutional change? How are we to characterize Roosevelt's actions surrounding the New Deal transformation and the infamous "court packing" plan? Are his actions a model for a new post-modern constitution or are they best seen as a usurpation of long held tenets of America's written constitutionalism? To gain a better perspective on Ackerman's theory we must re-examine this momentous transformation of American politics.

The New Deal Rejection of Article V

What is clear from careful histories of the period is that Roosevelt actively considered an Article V alteration to the Constitution but ultimately decided against it, "Roosevelt considered and rejected constitutional amendment as a means of resolving a fundamental dispute over the extent and limits of federal power. Roosevelt's perception of the amending process as impossibly difficult and amendment itself as unnecessary outweighed any evidence or argument to the contrary."[27] As Ackerman would have it, Roosevelt didn't need Article V because the American people had already democratically endorsed a new constitutional order, yet as we will see, clarity is not the strength of informal procedures. In the end, rule of law through democratic institutions depends critically on formal processes that ensure clarity. When the people speak it needs to be clear that they have spoken and it needs to be clear what they have said. Such clarity can only be achieved when "the people" are empowered and required to communicate in a formal manner.

Franklin D. Roosevelt's battles with the Supreme Court over implementation of his New Deal during his first term are a familiar episode in American history. Roosevelt had targeted the Federal Courts for conflict very early in his term. As early as 1933, Roosevelt began to think about a total transformation of the Supreme Court and commented on how few Democrats were on the federal bench.[28] As he proceeded with his New Deal project the showdown with the courts became inevitable.

In a key decision in January of 1935 the court in its 8-1 decision in *Panama Refining v. Ryan* struck down the "hot oil" provisions of the National Industrial Recovery Act.[29] Later that spring in March, the Supreme Court seemed to soften its stance and Roosevelt's administration benefitted from a series of close 5-4 decisions that upheld New Deal programs. However, by May the court stunned Roosevelt when it struck down a whole series of New Deal measures: the Railroad Pension Act (*Retirement Board v. Alton Railroad Co.)*, the Frazier-Lemke Act (*Louisville Bank v. Radford*), presidential removal of regulatory commission members (*Humphrey's Executor v. U.S.*), and the National Industrial Recovery Act (*Schechter v. U.S.*); the last three of which were unanimous decisions.[30] In the cases where the court narrowly construed the commerce clause, Roosevelt reportedly commented angrily that the court was using a "horse-and-buggy definition of interstate commerce."[31] Six months later in 1935 and again in the spring of 1936 the court struck down an array of legislation that threatened the very heart of the New Deal.[32] Thus, the court's rejection of New Deal legislation threatened Roosevelt's entire program and resulted in a showdown between the presidency and the Supreme Court. This inter-branch conflict set up the 1936 presidential elections as a test of popular support for Roosevelt's New Deal and offered the potential to provide Roosevelt with added resources in his battle with the court. Roosevelt's decisive victory over Alf Landon in the 1936 election was an absolute landslide and provided Roosevelt with an unprecedented victory and a firm electoral mandate supporting his New Deal.

It is hard to overstate the completeness of Roosevelt's victory in 1936. Roosevelt won nearly 61 percent of the popular vote, which is second highest percentage in modern presidential history.[33] Roosevelt carried every state except Maine and Vermont and his 523 electoral votes to Landon's 8 (a 97% margin) was the greatest electoral landslide in modern presidential history. Roosevelt also had lengthy coattails, and his 1936 victory gave him a staggering Democratic majority in Congress. In the House of Representatives Roosevelt had 331 Democrats to a measly 89 Republicans and 13 others (establishing Democratic control for nearly sixty years until 1994); while in the Senate he had 76 Democrats to 16 Republicans. This gave him a three-fourths majority in both houses of Congress and the ability to pursue the New Deal agenda with virtually little to no opposition. Roosevelt's Democrats also had amazing success at the state level. By 1936 Democrats controlled 39 of the 48 governorships (more than three-quarters). Democrats also completely controlled 29 of 48 state legislatures with Republicans only controlling 8, with the two parties sharing control of 9 other legislatures.[34] Thus, Roosevelt had three-fourths majorities in both houses of Congress and over three-fourths control of governorships. While Democratic control of 29 of 48 legislatures did not represent three-fourths it still represented a powerful New Deal presence at the state level. Clearly the American people had spoken in the 1936 election. They decisively chose Roosevelt and the Democratic Party to lead them for the next four years. Yet according to Ackerman they had done much more than that. They had chosen to amend the United States Constitution, not formally but structurally. They had deliberated over the constitutional proposition and they had chosen the New Deal order over the old order. Or had they?

Had Roosevelt and the New Dealers clearly signaled and proposed their intentions to fundamentally transform the regime and abandon the Article V amendment process in favor of Supreme Court administered "structural amendments"? Clearly the people signaled their support for the New Deal programs, but it seems a stretch to suggest that the people knew they were voting to "re-found" the regime and abandon Article V as the exclusive means of amendment. By implication Ackerman's theory suggests that the people knowingly chose to allow Roosevelt to fully implement his New Deal even if that meant the American people relinquished control over the amending process in favor of elite driven changes to the Constitution. Where these choices and trade-offs made clear to the voters in 1936? The evidence suggest that such choices were not clear at all.

One major flaw in the theory that the American people sanctioned constitutional change outside of Article V is that Roosevelt and the Democratic Party seemed to signal just the opposite intention in 1936. Indeed, the 1936 Democratic Party Platform explicitly called for "clarifying" amendments to the Constitution, amendments which were intended to clearly empower Congress to regulate the economy and give constitutional legitimacy to key elements of the New Deal.[35]

> If these problems cannot be effectively solved by legislation within the Constitution, we shall seek such clarifying amendment as will assure to the legislatures of the several States and to the Congress of the United States, each within its proper jurisdiction, the power to enact those laws which the State and Federal legislatures, within their respective spheres, shall find necessary, in order adequately to regulate commerce, protect public health and safety and safeguard economic security. Thus we propose to maintain the letter and spirit of the Constitution.[36]

Therefore, Roosevelt ran on a platform that promoted the notion of amending the Constitution to allow for the aggressive and transformative New Deal project. Rather than clearly proposing an irregular and informal change to the Constitution outside the auspices of Article V, it seems instead that Roosevelt and the Democratic Party promised a formal and regular amendment to the written Constitution. It seems more likely that the landslide, among other things, was endorsing such a change. This fact seems to muddy the waters a bit regarding what the people were actually intending when they handed a mandate to Roosevelt in the 1936 election. Perhaps the electorate had decided they were open to amending the Constitution via Article V, just as the Democratic Party Platform had advocated. It is indisputable that the American people in large majorities supported the New Deal and Roosevelt; what isn't so clear is what that meant *vis à vis* their desire to fundamentally alter the United States Constitution.

Furthermore, Roosevelt's historic and overwhelming electoral mandate seemed to give him the political capital he needed to take on the Supreme Court via an Article V amendment, and it seemed logical for him to take the next step and secure a firm constitutional and legal basis for his movement with the clear backing of the American people. Article V had enabled recent Progressive movements to codify major changes in the Constitution, now seemed like the final culmination of this Progressive outburst in the first half of the century.

Yet at the height of his political power, armed with immense political capital and the American public firmly behind him and his policies, Roosevelt rejected the Article V option and went in an entirely different direction. Instead, of formal amendment Roosevelt took legislative aim at the Supreme Court. Shortly after his inauguration Roosevelt introduced his infamous "Court Packing Plan," in February of 1937. This legislation would allow for up to six additional Supreme Court justices to be added by the president and effectively render the Supreme Court as an arm of the Executive branch.[37] The act was roundly criticized and, "widely perceived as a sly attempt to evade the Constitution's provision of lifetime tenure for members of the Court, to diminish their influence by permitting the President to 'pack the court' with sympathetic justices."[38]

In a dramatic showdown with Congress, Roosevelt's plan proved very unpopular, even among Democrats in Congress. Due to strong resistance in Congress by May of 1937 Roosevelt's court packing bill was seen by many political observers as dead, since he simply did not have the votes to enact the plan.[39] Yet fate would intervene and with the retirement of Justice Van Devanter that spring—thus allowing Roosevelt to alter the balance of the court—and the March decision that saw Justice Owen J. Roberts vote to uphold Washington's minimum wage laws in *West Coast Hotel Co. v. Parrish,* (the famous "switch in time that saved nine"), the court seemed ready to comply with the New Deal program.[40] With these developments there seemed to no longer be a need to alter the Supreme Court's composition; Roosevelt had achieved victory over the court via retirement and intimidation. There seemed to be no need for the court packing plan now.

However, despite the power to replace Van Devanter and the court's new support of the New Deal legislation, Roosevelt was still determined, for some reason, to re-shape the Court. In June, Roosevelt unveiled a second—but not very different—version of the scheme.[41] Yet even this second version still faced enormous opposition from within his party.

Yet if Bruce Ackerman's account is correct Roosevelt's actions seem odd. According to Ackerman, the 1936 election had given decisive democratic support for deep changes in the constitutional order. If that were true then we would expect to find unequivocal support for Roosevelt's first court packing plan let alone the second; and yet we find instead deep division within the Democratic Party in Congress. For example, one need look no further than a biting Senate Judiciary Committee Report issued by fellow Democrats that thoroughly condemned Roosevelt's aggressive plan. The report issued a scathing attack on Roosevelt's plan, "[w]e recommend the rejection of this bill as a needless, futile, and utterly dangerous abandonment of constitutional principle . . . It is a measure which should be so emphatically rejected that its parallel will never again be presented to the free representatives of the free people of America."[42] It is curious that fellow Democrats saw Roosevelt's actions as a "dangerous abandonment of constitutional principle" given that the 1936 elections had supposedly given Roosevelt the democratic imprimatur to make whatever changes he saw fit. This report and Democratic resistance to the court packing plan do not seem to fit within Ackerman's scheme. In fact, Roosevelt's bill was risking open rupture within his party's legislative delegation; this should not be happening if indeed the 1936 election had legitimized Roosevelt's actions as Ackerman claims.

Despite such a derisive rejection of this bill by fellow Democrats in the spring, Roosevelt reached out in June to rekindle warm relations with congressional Democrats. Roosevelt used his considerable political acumen to reconnect with resistant Democrats in Congress and his efforts helped establish conditions for one more push on the court packing plan.[43] Once Roosevelt had laid the groundwork then a delicate coalition was skillfully assembled by the political weight and personal cajoling of Senate Majority Leader Joseph Robinson.[44] By the end of June, Robinson had secured the votes to pass the bill and its prospects for passage looked bright.

The "general opinion" was that the bill would pass, but those prospects "rested wholly on the ability of Joe Robinson to bully, persuade, or cajole enough reluctant Democrats to go along with him. Without the majority leader, FDR's cause was doomed."[45] The proximate challenge was to get enough votes for cloture in the Senate. As part of his plan to break the opposition, Robinson intended to use the stifling summer heat of Washington, D.C. to wear down opposition and perhaps bring the aging Senatorial opponents quite literally to their knees.[46] Ironically, a mere week into the intense floor debate over the bill, the heat and stress that was meant to bring the opposition to heel, seemingly, and sadly, led to the untimely death of Senator Robinson himself.[47]

With the loss of Robinson the fragile majority he had crafted quickly broke apart and a coalition of conservative Democrats and Republicans drove a stake through the heart of Roosevelt's plan and it was defeated. The embattled Republicans still stinging from the 1936 elections, greatly relished this unexpected victory and took the opportunity further embarrass Democrats and Roosevelt by to insisting on a roll call vote thus recording in detail the defeat President's cherished bill in the records of the Senate.[48]

Roosevelt's loss in the court packing plan revealed cracks in his heretofore impenetrable Congressional support. A coalition of conservative Democrats and Republicans had been able to fight Roosevelt to a standstill and in subsequent showdowns that coalition was able to re-emerge from time to time to blunt Roosevelt's power. The weakened New Deal was dealt a decisive blow the next year with the 1938 midterm elections which gave Republicans historic gains in the Congress; gains that would not be equaled again until seventy-two years later in

November 2010 when Republicans took back the House from Democrats during Barack Obama's presidency. In addition to huge losses in Congress the Democrats lost control of eight state legislatures dropping their control to only twenty-one, while Republicans picked up ten legislatures to control eighteen, while seven remained split. With vastly weakened majorities at the federal and state levels, Roosevelt was unable to advance the New Deal any further, let alone press for an amendment. The high water mark of the New Deal had passed and the opportunity to achieve an Article V amendment seemed to have been lost as well:

> Thereafter the administration enjoyed very few of the legislative successes that had been so frequent before the Court fight. Roosevelt's huge 1936 electoral triumph was dissipated, its congressional majority never to produce the legislation that had seemed so easily within reach. In many respects, the New Deal had come to its end.[49]

Roosevelt purposely chose not to pursue Article V amendment in favor of a court packing plan; the results of this fateful decision would ultimately erode the congressional legislative coalition in support of his New Deal project. Here again Ackerman's thesis seems strained. If Roosevelt had so clearly "signaled" his intent to transform the constitutional order and "proposed" then why did he not succeed in passing his court packing bill? Why was there so much opposition even within his party to his efforts? According to Ackerman the country had just deliberated on this transformation and democratically sanctioned Roosevelt's efforts. So then why did Roosevelt encounter such obstacles and defeat of his bill? Could it be that the 1936 election had not so clearly signaled the peoples' desire for presidential intimidation and control of the Supreme Court? This is one key problem with informal change. Because changes are not formally proposed and formally ratified, it is not clear what the people are endorsing. Formally the American people elected Roosevelt to four more years as the president. Formally the American people gave the Democratic Party control of Congress and a vast majority of the state legislatures and governorships. That much is clear. Yet trying to claim informal democratic legitimacy for wholesale constitutional change seems difficult in the least. Formal procedures clarify and focus the democratic energy and legitimacy of the American people; *post hoc* justifications of informal processes are very problematic for it is not entirely clear what the people were saying "informally" with their vote. Nor was it entirely clear—especially given the Democratic platform's endorsement of a clarifying amendment—that the people wanted to abandon Article V in the way Roosevelt did.

Given this lack of clarity, another question that lingers is why Roosevelt made the choice that he did. Why choose to legislatively alter (and intimidate) the court rather than draw on his unprecedented popular mandate to seek an Article V "clarifying" amendment as was called for in the 1936 Democratic national platform?[50] It would seem that with such an overwhelming electoral mandate—one that according to Bruce Ackerman is the equivalent of a new founding of the country—Roosevelt would have been better served utilizing Article V to give him clear constitutional sanction for the New Deal, "Not only opponents of the President but also a number of his friends and supporters expressed the belief that a more forthright and defensible approach to the Court problem would have been to seek one or more amendments to the Constitution to give the New Deal's federal initiatives an unquestionable and lasting legitimacy."[51] The Article V option would have resulted in a clear national debate regarding a new role for federal power which, had it been engaged in, might have provided a more solid political footing for Roosevelt's transformative agenda. Again with three-fourths of Congress in Democratic control and 46 of 48 states supporting Roosevelt for reelection, surely there was enough national and local support for at least one major amendment. For example, one poll at the time revealed that three-fourths of the voters in New Jersey would support a constitutional change to make the New Deal effective.[52]

Roosevelt had been very involved in amendment politics during his days as a state senator in New York and as a member of Woodrow Wilson's cabinet. As a state senator he had personally supported the Sixteenth and Seventeenth Amendments. He had also supported the women's suffrage amendment and had witnessed the prohibition amendments first hand.[53] These experiences gave Roosevelt an appreciation of the promise and the peril of the amending process. His experience gave him second thoughts about pursuing it in the case at hand.[54] As we know, Roosevelt did take a serious look at an amendment approach but was ultimately convinced it was too difficult and ultimately unnecessary.[55]

Roosevelt publicly stated that an amendment was not necessary as the Constitution already provided the power to do what he was proposing. However, this position seems a bit hollow given that Roosevelt and the Democratic Party thought that they needed to endorse an Article V amendment in the party platform. If Roosevelt and the Democrats were so convinced that no formal amendment were necessary, then why did they push to have it put in the platform? Perhaps Roosevelt thought it wasn't necessary, but put the plank in the platform to placate the many who thought it was. However, even with that explanation, it makes it hard to argue that the American people were clear about the choices being put before them. If they were truly endorsing a new political order and a new means of altering the Constitution, then how come the dominant party explicitly endorsed formal changes to the Constitution? It all seems very confusing.

Ackerman's theory assumes that the choices before the electorate are clear, and that the American people are knowingly choosing to utilize normal presidential elections to alter the written Constitution via "transformative appointments" to the Supreme Court. However, in 1936 it seems difficult to discern such specific intent from the election. Perhaps instead of sanctioning a non-Article V informal amendment, the people were signaling, given the platform, that they wanted Roosevelt to pursue an Article V amendment. Or perhaps the people were very particular in their desires, perhaps they wanted Roosevelt to serve as president, but perhaps they did not want foundational changes to the constitutional order. It is very difficult to tell. If Roosevelt pursued the Article V option, the people would have had the opportunity to make the distinction between who they wanted to serve as president and how they wanted the Constitution structured; by conflating the two as Ackerman does, we have no idea exactly what the people desired.

Again, it seems very difficult indeed to assume that the American people were "choosing" informal amendment when the people elected a president and party on a platform promising formal amendment. It is also perhaps telling that Roosevelt did not reveal his court packing plan until the February after he was safely reelected. The timing of his plan's unveiling and its discontinuity with the party platform certainly raises questions. This sequencing strongly suggests something more like constitutional "bait and switch" by Roosevelt rather than open and honest deliberation about a re-founding of the republic. Yet in the midst of all this uncertainty Ackerman would have us believe that the people were soberly deliberating and endorsing fundamental changes to the constitutional order via informal constitutional amendment; how he knows this for certain one can't be entirely clear.

While Roosevelt did say he felt an amendment was unnecessary he also worried openly about the Article V process itself. He complained that "too much time was required to win agreement on an amendment from among the many different proposals put forth and to overcome obstacles to ratification."[56] Privately, he also feared that strong interest groups were amassing war chests to fight his amendment at the state level and that it would be extremely difficult to get both houses to agree on amendment language.[57] Roosevelt saw Congressional success as fifty-fifty odds and he gave ratification in the states "little chance."[58] Even his recent electoral mandate did not provide comfort, "Despite his recent electoral triumph, the political challenge of amendment seemed formidable to Roosevelt. It appeared to daunt him more than the problem of choosing appropriate New Deal-affirming language."[59] In fact, Roosevelt revealed to his confidant on such matters Felix Frankfurter that if he were in opposition to the amendment and had ample finances, he could ". . . guarantee that an amendment would not be ratified prior to the 1940 elections. In other words, I think I could prevent ratification in thirteen states."[60]

Roosevelt reiterated similar remarks multiple times including a fireside chat where he was defending his court packing plan.[61] In his March 9, 1937 fireside chat Roosevelt made the following remarks in defense of his court packing plan. This particular fireside chat is quite revealing and provides a solid account of Roosevelt's perspective on the matter. For one thing, from the substance of his remarks, he clearly wasn't confident that a public mandate for formal change existed:

> I have thus explained to you the reasons that lie behind our efforts to secure results by legislation within the Constitution. I hope that thereby the difficult pro-

> cess of constitutional amendment may be rendered unnecessary. But let us examine that process.
>
> There are many types of amendment proposed. Each one is radically different from the other. But there is no substantial group within the Congress or outside the Congress who are agreed on any single amendment.
>
> I believe that it would take months or years to get substantial agreement upon the type and language of an amendment. It would take months and years thereafter to get a two-thirds majority in favor of that amendment in both houses of the Congress.[62]

Here again, one is hard pressed not to question Roosevelt's political calculus considering his massive electoral mandate, total control of Congress by the Democratic Party, and his impressive personal appeal. It seems to strain credulity that he could not produce an amendment proposal for "months or years" or at all. Did Roosevelt truly believe that it would be more difficult to agree to wording on a proposed amendment—an amendment that was part of the party platform he was elected upon—than it would be to assemble a congressional majority to support his unprecedented and controversial court packing plan? This seems dubious. Not only was achieving agreement on the proposal of an Article V amendment an apparent concern for Roosevelt, but so was ratification:

> Then would come the long course of ratification by three-quarters of all the states. No amendment which any powerful economic interests or the leaders of any powerful political party have had reason to oppose has ever been ratified within anything like a reasonable time. And remember that thirteen states which contain only 5 percent of the voting population can block ratification even though the thirty-five states with 95 percent of the population are in favor of it.
>
> A very large percentage of newspaper publishers and chambers of commerce and bar associations and manufacturers' associations, who are trying to give the impression today that they really do want a constitutional amendment, would be the very first to exclaim as soon as an amendment was proposed, "Oh! I was for an amendment all right, but this amendment that you've proposed is not the kind of an amendment that I was thinking about. And so, I am going to spend my time, my efforts, and my money to block this amendment, although I would be awfully glad to help to get some other kind of an amendment ratified."

Here we see Roosevelt lamenting the consent requirements of Article V by arguing that the ratification process could prove fatal even if he were to usher a proposal through Congress. Yet again this "narrative" is not so easily believed. As we saw in chapter 6 nearly every amendment that has been proposed has been subsequently ratified; thus ratification has not proved to be the obstacle that it is often made out to be. We also saw that ratification generally does not take very long once a majority coalition has been assembled to propose the amendment.

Surely just after the most lopsided election in modern presidential history Roosevelt could have navigated the ratification process. The Progressive movement had been very successful in achieving ratification of its multiple amendments, why now would such efforts prove problematic? Roosevelt had built a formidable political coalition at all levels of government and yet this coalition could not pass a foundational amendment to alleviate the constitutional concerns over its agenda? This is hard to believe. In addition, if indeed Roosevelt was correct that he did not have a popular mandate for an amendment, then it seems to weaken Ackerman's claim that there was a mandate for even more fundamental changes in the constitutional order.

On another level Roosevelt's words in this "chat" seem to be very strange talk in a constitutional republic. It seems a bit at odds with the principle of the rule of law and of written constitutionalism itself, to have the chief executive publicly making such an extensive case for the difficulty of the heretofore exclusive means of constitutional amendment and yet still insisting that he press on with his agenda. Roosevelt indeed seems to be signaling that he is prepared to deviate from the traditional constitutional norm of adhering to Article V for such changes. Clearly the dominant understanding of the Constitution up until this point had been that Article V's standards are difficult because it requires a large level of democratic consent, but such levels of consent are necessary to ensure adequate deliberation and popular authority before altering the fundamental law. The Founders had implemented the Article V consent requirements in order to respect minority opinion, to ensure wisdom and deliberation in majorities, and guard against majority tyranny. And yet, here Roosevelt is clearly taking umbrage with these consent requirements in a public manner without addressing any of the principled reasons that those requirements were created in the first place. It also seems odd that a president who thinks an amendment unnecessary must spend such effort to publicly justify ignoring those very clear formal standards for amendment. Ackerman puts a lot of weight on signaling in his theory. One can't help but shake the thought that Roosevelt is indeed signaling a profound constitutional change, but one that is neither legal in the purest sense, nor one that fits the constitutional practices and traditions of the American people. Recall that this fireside chat is taking place *after* Roosevelt's reelection and after the "deliberation" period that is very important to Ackerman's scheme. This key fact would seem to undermine the democratic legitimacy of Ackerman's structural amendment if the people reelected Roosevelt with the understanding that he would pursue an Article V amendment and then he reveals afterward that he thinks such a course unnecessary and too difficult. Again this sequencing suggests something of a "bait and switch" by Roosevelt where he does not reveal his true constitutional path until safely reelected. These realities seem to severely undercut Ackerman's argument that a democratically legitimate "structural amendment" took place via the 1936 election.

If that weren't enough, Roosevelt further publicly concedes that he indeed does not have adequate public support to formally amend the Constitution.

> Two groups oppose my plan on the ground that they favor a constitutional amendment. The first includes those who fundamentally object to social and economic legislation along modern lines. This is the same group who during the recent campaign tried to block the mandate of the people. And the strategy of that last stand is to suggest the time-consuming process of amendment in order to kill off by delay the legislation demanded by the mandated. To those people I say, I do not think you will be able long to fool the American people as to your purposes.
>
> The other group is composed of those who honestly believe the amendment process is the best and who would be willing to support a reasonable amendment if they could agree on one.
>
> To them I say, we cannot rely on an amendment as the immediate or only answer to our present difficulties. When the time comes for action, you will find that many of those who pretend to support you will sabotage any constructive amendment which is proposed. Look at these strange bedfellows of yours. When before have you found them really at your side in your fights for progress?

Progressives may admire this passage as a testament to Roosevelt's pragmatism. Yet another way to view this passage is that Roosevelt the astute politician is publicly declaring that he does not have a clear public mandate for constitutional amendment, yet he is going to proceed to legislatively alter or intimidate the offending branch into submission nonetheless. By Ackerman's theory the period for public debate should be over. Arguments on both sides have been made and fully deliberated upon and the reform movement has convinced enough Americans to join them in their reform of the constitutional order. If the New Deal call for constitutional change was truly successful then there certainly would have been a supermajority ready to overrule the Supreme Court via Article V. It isn't clear why the constitutional impasse must be resolved via extra constitutional means when Article V provides a means for a clear public repudiation of an obstinate and obstructionist court. It seems either that the deliberations were not as decisively in favor of a new constitutional order as Ackerman would have us believe or they were, but the leadership of the movement was too squeamish to put their majorities to the test in a formal setting.

Again the ambiguity involved in Ackerman's informal amendment is indeed the very point of utilizing legal forms and formalities. The forms of Article V ensure a clear articulation of the public mind on important matters of constitutional amendment. It ensures adequate levels of democratic consent and it does so in an explicit and prudent manner and yet the President who had just won a most decisive reelection chose not to avail himself of the power and clarity of Article V. Given all of this, how are we supposed to be convinced by Bruce Ackerman that the 1936 presidential election was such a clear and unequivocal mandate for constitutional transformation when Roosevelt himself did not believe the public would support such a transformation formally?

The real answer seems to come at the end of Roosevelt's fireside chat when he engages in an astounding ode to legal realism and judicial fiat:

> And remember one thing more. Even if an amendment were passed, and even if in the years to come it were to be ratified, its meaning would depend upon the kind of justices who would be sitting on the Supreme Court bench. For an amendment, like the rest of the Constitution, is what the justices say it is rather than what its framers or you might hope it is.[63]

What an incredible thing for a president operating under the rule of law and a written constitution to say. In essence, Roosevelt is saying that rule of law doesn't matter and the text of the Constitution doesn't matter rather only the raw power of judicial opinion really matters. Roosevelt's cynicism about the role of judicial review is startling. He seems to view judicial review as a naked exercise of power for the purposes of pursuing ideological policies rather than a legally bound form of interpreting the constitutional text. In this context, his move to the court packing plan makes perfect sense. Why bother with the messiness of democratic legitimacy, when the real game is usurpation though political elites? Ackerman is indeed right that a transformation occurred during the New Deal but try as he might the transformation does not seem to be a democratic one.

Perhaps it is important at this point to remember the words of George Washington which, when read in the context of Roosevelt's dealings with the New Deal seem to take on exceptional relevance and importance:

> It is important, likewise, that the habits of thinking in a free country should inspire caution in those entrusted with its administration to confine themselves within their respective constitutional spheres, avoiding in the exercise of the powers of one department to encroach upon another. The spirit of encroachment tends to consolidate the powers of all the departments in one, and thus to create, whatever the form of government, a real despotism. A just estimate of that love of power and proneness to abuse it, which predominates in the human heart is sufficient to satisfy us of the truth of this position. The necessity of reciprocal checks in the exercise of political power, by dividing and distributing it into different depositories, and constituting each the guardian of the public weal against invasions by the others, has been evinced by experiments ancient and modern, some of them in our country and under our own eyes. To preserve them must be as necessary as to institute them.[64]

One could certainly argue that Roosevelt was not prepared to "confine" himself within his "respective constitutional sphere." Indeed one could argue that "the spirit of encroachment" led him to engage in the court packing plan. Could it be that Roosevelt himself was not the best judge of how much his motives were tainted by "that love of power and proneness to abuse it, which predominates in the human heart"? Could it be that Founders knew this was a perennial problem that "men were not angels" and that the separation of powers that allowed the Supreme Court to pass judgment on New Deal legislation was a prudent device and that similarly Article V was designed to moderate the "love of power" and the "spirit of encroachment" that pervades human nature? But perhaps times had changed, perhaps the federal government needed to take a more active role in the economic and social life of the country. Washington addresses this potentiality, that there may come a time when the current distribution of powers is undesirable or inconvenient and there is pressure for reform.

> If in the opinion of the people the distribution or modification of the constitutional powers be in any particular wrong, let it be corrected by an amendment in the way which the Constitution designates. But let there be no change by usurpation; for though this in one instance may be the instrument of good, it is the customary weapon by which free governments are destroyed. The precedent must always greatly overbalance in permanent evil any partial or transient benefit which the use can at any time yield.[65]

One does not have to impute a spirit of despotism to Roosevelt to be hesitant to endorse his actions surrounding the court-packing plan. Indeed one may well concede his good intentions and one may well even agree with his policy prescriptions, but as Washington warns such "usurpation" while done in good will and for noble reasons will produce more "permanent evil" than it will "partial or transient benefit." Thus, at a crucial moment in American history where the people seemed hungry for change, their leaders lost faith in the democratic process and instead relied on usurpation to pursue the public good. They abandoned the rule of law and principles of written constitutionalism in order to avoid the messiness of democratic politics. Perhaps we should not be surprised by this, for as Madison warned us that "men are not angels" but it is because of the less than angelic nature that Article V requires the explicit public consent for alterations to the Constitution. It is because "men are not angels" that five votes on the Supreme Court were not empowered to alter the Constitution at will. It is because "men are not angels" that the Constitution was constructed to constrain the raw will of democratic leaders. In the end, as Washington points out, even well intentioned leaders with noble causes will produce "permanent evil" when they usurp the formal process of amendment.

Roosevelt's usurpation has sent shock waves through our constitutional system that are still being felt today. In fact, one could argue that a good majority of post New Deal constitutional scholarship in political science and law has been wrestling with Roosevelt's usurpation in one way or another. They have wrestled to smooth over the "counter-majoritarian" difficulty presented by the New Deal "revolution" and Roosevelt's outlandish public proclamation that the Constitution is merely "what the justices say it is". The founders would not agree with Roosevelt's stark legal realism that placed the Supreme Court at the top of the Constitutional food chain. For them the Constitution was not "what the justices say it is" but it was a legally binding fundamental law meant to ensure a republican form of government that protects the liberty of its citizens.

Interpretation v. Amendment

As we have seen, Sanford Levinson undermines Article V's exclusive role in constitutional amendment by intermingling the concepts of interpretation and amendment. The result of his analysis produces a framework where informal legal evolution becomes the equivalent formal Article V amendments. For Levinson the term amendment should not simply be reserved for the formalities of the Article V process, "[t]here is not reason . . . to call a numbered textual addition a genuine 'amendment' unless it truly changes the pre-existing legal reality."[66] According to Levinson, using his definition, some numbered amendments are simply interpretations of the constitutional text, while some court decisions are really amendments. To be sure there have been momentous Supreme Court decisions that dwarf the importance of some of the merely clarifying amendments to the Constitution, so at first glance Levinson would appear to have a point.

Levinson's point is that some of the Supreme Court's *interpretations* are so expansive that they seem to tread upon the turf of *amendments* by seemingly altering the text itself. For example, Levinson argues that the Supreme Court in its *Home Building & Loan Association v. Blaisdell* ruling in 1934 was in effect the court altering the constitutional provision that stipulated, no state could pass a law "impairing the obligation of contracts" to a provision that meant "states were prohibited only from passing laws *unreasonably* impairing such obligations, but that impairments deemed necessary to important state ends were legitimate."[67] Levinson's take on *Blaisdell* may well be right, but he seems to move very quickly from an *empirical* observation to a *normative* judgment. In other words, just because the courts have adapted the constitutional text in these ways, it does not necessarily follow that they should. Yet Levinson simply labels *Blaisdell* as an amendment without any hesitation at all over the propriety of such a determination given the American commitment to a written Constitution and formal amendment. If such changes should normally and legitimately be made via formal amendment using Article V, wouldn't the *Blaisdell* ruling be an usurpation by the courts? Levinson does not address this potential categorization of the ruling; for him since it significantly changed the pre-existing legal reality then it should properly be referred to as an amendment.

However, there are several problems with Levinson's argument. First, Levinson muddies the water regarding the distinction between *amendments* and *interpretations*. The word, *interpret* simply means, "to explain or tell the meaning of something."[68] Thus, a *constitutional interpretation* is properly defined as an explanation or a meaning of a constitutional text. By contrast to *amend* is to "put right, to change, or modify for the better, or to alter formally by modification, deletion, or addition."[69] Thus for an interpretation to remain an interpretation it must be tethered to an acceptable range of meanings regarding the constitutional text in question. However, by contrast an amendment is not bound simply by the words of the text but only by the implication that it must improve the text or be consistent with it. Generally speaking, this distinction shouldn't be difficult to maintain analytically. Now perhaps expansive or careless interpretations might have the impact or effect of amendments, but that would still not make them amendments by definition. The only way to totally confuse the two is to alter the definition of the term *amendment* which is exactly what Levinson does.

Levinson defines *amendment* from the very beginning in a manner that misconstrues its relationship to the constitutional text. In doing so Levinson arbitrarily undermines Article V's exclusivity from the very start. In other words, Levinson's initial move to define amendments as inherently informal, then leads him to dismiss Article V as the exclusive means of amendment, is inherently tautological reasoning. His argument seems to be that Article V cannot account for all amendments because Levinson has decided to define the term "amendment" in a manner that Article V cannot account for.

By incorrectly defining the term "amendment" Levinson also fails to adequately make the distinction between America's "unwritten constitution" and its written Constitution. In one sense every polity has an unwritten constitution; for every polity has "an assemblage of laws, customs, and institutions that collectively defined the proper form and functions of government."[70] This unwritten constitution is necessarily organic and evolutionary in nature. However, as we have seen the American constitutional experience led our nation's Founders to erect a written Constitution on top of the unwritten one with the purpose of defining and limiting governmental powers, as well as directing and binding the naturally unbounded evolutionary tendencies of the unwritten constitution. They also sought to empower the people via institutional devices such as elections, terms of office, separation of powers, formal procedures and the like which would allow the polity to reign in, bind, direct, or empower the elites that must engage in much of the day to day governing. These forms and formalities are like handles that allow the people to "grab hold" of the government in different places at different times and once they have grabbed hold they can direct the elites as they see fit. In this sense then, Article V is a very important "handle" in that it allows the people to control how the changes and pressures of the unwritten constitution impact the written Constitution. When faced with social change and political evolution over time, the American people can intentionally and deliberatively alter their fundamental law in accordance with these changes or choose not to alter their fundamental law if they want to resist or channel such organic impulses in different directions. What seems to be troubling Levinson is the apparent disjuncture between significant legal changes in the unwritten constitution, which are numerous, and the few formal amendments that have been created via Article V in the written Constitution. He is also wrestling with the fact that some formal amendments seem like nothing more than "good housekeeping" measures while others are more transformative.

Levinson is correct to point out areas of the law and constitutional practices that have indeed evolved over time. Yet court decisions that have altered the pre-existing reality of the law are not amendments, as Levinson insists, but merely the normal process of the evolution of the law and constitutional practice. Most of these (arguably not *Blaisdell* however) are simply the normal development of legal norms and principles over time. However, in a system with a written constitution great care is taken to ensure that expansive interpretations are judged against the standards inherent in the term "interpretation." That is to say, since an interpretation by definition must adhere to the meaning of the text, expansive interpretations must be judged by their plausibility and their faithfulness to the text. Interpretations that do not meet this standard of adhering to the text, cross the line into *error* or *usurpation*; both of which should be corrected if possible or if prudence dictates otherwise they should in the very least not be endorsed or repeated. To do otherwise is to erode the normative commitments to a written constitution and the legally binding nature of its text as fundamental law. For these reasons it is inappropriate to consider normal evolutions in the law the equivalent of formal amendments.

So what are we to make of Levinson's point? He seems to be stuck between the reality of important constitutional changes occurring outside of Article V and Article V's claim to be the exclusive means of amendment. To make sense of this apparent inconsistency he is prepared to dissolve the lines between amendment and interpretation and abandon Article V altogether as the sole means of constitutional amendment. In the end, to resolve this dilemma Levinson opts for informal adaptation and evolutionary constitutional change over formal amendment as outlined in Article V's text.

In wrestling with the same problem, Stephen Griffin gives up on the entire project of having a rule of law Constitution. As we have seen Griffin argues that a legally binding Constitution must yield to the currents of history and social change. To pick up the analogy between water and democracy again, Griffin counsels Americans to blow up the dam, the aqueducts, and the irrigation channels for they can't work to restrain the democratic push of history. While Griffin seems to abandon the notion that a written Constitution can serve as the fundamental law of the nation a bit too easily, he at least deserves credit for taking Ackerman and Levinson's premises to their logical extreme. Once you begin to erode the binding authority of Article V to administer changes to the Constitution, you begin to erode the legal authority of the written Constitution altogether.

Ackerman, Levinson, and Griffin are all a bit too eager to jettison the binding nature of Article V and the written Constitution when they constrain their preferred policy desires or the desires of the American electorate at any given moment; on the other hand there do seem to be significant changes in constitutional practice that are not accounted for by Article V. However this does not mean that the constitutional text cannot restrain the political branches from abandoning the rule of law or the Constitution as fundamental law. Changes over time in constitutional practice and constitutional norms that do not seek to extend beyond the plain meaning of the constitutional text, can be accounted for without undermining Article V or the authority of the written text.

Perhaps what Ackerman, Levinson, and Griffin are all wrestling with is what Keith Whittington would refer to as constitutional "construction."[71] Whittington makes the key distinction between *interpretations*, *constructions*, and *amendments*. In some ways, Ackerman, Levinson, and Griffin are all wrestling with how to highlight the difference between an interpretation and a construction. Yet to confuse a construction with an amendment is to undermine the written nature of the Constitution.

For Whittington, "Constitutional construction is one mechanism by which constitutional meaning is elaborated. It supplements other methods of determining constitutional meaning and provides a more complete and workable governing instrument."[72] Whittington lays out a hierarchy of "levels of constitutional deliberation" with mere "policymaking" at one extreme, followed by "interpretation," "construction," "creation," and "revolution" at the other extreme.[73] Constitutional amendment is an act of "creation" and only it and "revolution" can utterly transform the Constitution. While revolution entirely replaces the old text, "creation" or amendment modifies the old text but does not replace it. Policymaking operates within a general consensus of constitutional meaning and does not "extend the meaning of the constitution itself."[74] However, interpretation and construction both "elaborate the inherited text" while both still "assume a fidelity to the existing text." Put another way, they seek to clarify and extend the text while still being faithful to it, "Both seek to elaborate a meaning somehow already present in the text, making constitutional meaning more explicit without altering the terms of the text itself. As such, both methods of constitutional elaboration are subordinate to the text, which is understood as prior and more fundamental."[75] Both recognize the authority of the written text and both are in service of its meanings and intentions. Interpretations and constructions simply try to give practical meaning to abstract language or to clarify ambiguities in the language, however, "Interpretations and constructions can be abandoned without abandoning the text, and if a correct understanding of the text is seen as being in conflict with prior efforts at interpretation or construction, it is the earlier elaborations that must give way."[76] The key point here is that both are inferior to the true meaning of the text and they must not override the authority of the text as fundamental law.

So what distinguishes an *interpretation* from a *construction*? Where interpretation is an act of *discovery* construction is more *inventive*. Interpretation is meant to pursue a "preexisting if deeply hidden meaning" in the Constitution; "interpretation is understood to be a more technical activity, concerned with employing a set of analytical tools to unearth the meaning inherent in the constitutional text."[77] By contrast, constructions are an inventive political enterprise for they "elucidate the text . . . where the text is so broad or so underdetermined as to be incapable of faithful but exhaustive reduction to legal rules."[78] Constructions are forged by political actors articulating normative guidelines for practical action that is faithful to the Constitution even in the midst of confusion, disagreement, or lack of clarity on its exact application in a given political context. Whittington includes the creation of military colleges, judicial review, the military draft, congressional subpoenas, "no right to secession," and the Louisiana Purchase, among dozens and dozens of other examples of constitutional constructions that altered governmental behavior in relation to debated understandings of the constitutional text.[79]

Constructions differ from amendments in important ways for since constructions are in service to the constitutional text there are limits to how far political actors can construe the text, "Although different constructions will be plausible in different political contexts, and such shifts are appropriate, some proffered constitutional values will not be consistent with the constructed text. The availability of formal amendments institutionalizes this possibility, marking the fact that the text is not infinitely malleable or expansive."[80] Thus, political efforts to create constructions of the text simply cannot go beyond the plain meaning of the text and when they do they must avail themselves of the Article V amending process that has been established to formally alter the existing legal realities that may no longer serve the needs of the American polity.

Thus, where Levinson intentionally muddles the distinctions between interpretations and amendments, Whittington provides a compelling account of how to distinguish interpretations from both amendments and constructions. Whittington's account is faithful to the constitutional norms that grant fundamental legal authority to a written constitution; yet his account also provides a helpful accounting for the many examples of unwritten constitutional change that naturally happens in a polity over time.

In the end, Ackerman, Levinson, and Griffin to their credit, acknowledge the irregularities inherent in the New Deal constitutional revolution. Many scholars simply paper over the aggressive and expansive usurpations of the constitutional text engaged in by the New Deal Court and its immediate progeny. However in coming to terms with the usurpations of Roosevelt and Roosevelt's handpicked court, all three scholars move to undermine Article V and its authority to ensure that changes to the constitutional text are indeed explicit, authentic, and adhere to key constitutional norms as well as America's foundational commitment to the rule of law and a written constitution. Repeated references to the "unwritten constitution" or constitutional "evolution" only obscure rather than reveal. Of course all polities have an unwritten constitution in the sense that they have some regularity to governance no matter how informal; and yes, these unwritten constitutions do evolve or change over time. However, the very point of a *written* constitution is to shape and channel the evolutionary tendencies of the unwritten constitution. An inordinate focus by scholars on the unwritten constitution or on evolutionary change tends to mask the human agency directing the changes. It is this human agency that a written constitution is directed to restrain. Constitutional forms and formalities such as Article V are to provide clarity to constitutional change and to reveal the multiplicity of human agents that are required for such changed. Attempts to shroud constitutional change in cloudy evolutionary processes only prevent a clear understanding of how a move away from forms only advantages the privileged power of elites in shaping the constitutional future at the expense of the common citizenry. As Tocqueville warned us over a century ago such easy abandonment of constitutional forms and formalities come easily to those reared in a democracy.

> Men living in democratic centuries do not readily understand the importance of formalities and have an instinctive contempt for them . . . Formalities arouse their disdain and often their hatred. As they usually aspire to none but facile and immediate pleasures, they rush straight at the object of any of their desires, and the slightest delay exasperates them. This temperament, which they carry with them into political life, makes them impatient of the formalities which daily hold up or prevent one or another of their designs. But it is just this inconvenience, of which democracies complain, which makes formalities so useful to freedom. For their chief merit is to serve as a barrier between the strong and the weak, the government and the governed, and to hold back the one while the other has time to take his bearings. Formalities become more important in proportion as the sovereign is more active and powerful and private individuals become more indolent and feeble. Thus democracies by their nature need formalities more than other peoples, and by nature have less respect for them. This deserves most serious attention.

In the end, law is form and rule of law must include forms and formalities; furthermore a written constitution that serves as the fundamental law of a given polity must itself be subject to precedent, form, and formality. To abandon such form makes change subject to usurpation, manipulation, and raw power; the very type of politics that American Constitutionalism has always sought to minimize through the rule of law. Again as Tocqueville observes, such forms "serve as a barrier between the strong and the weak, the government and the governed, and to hold back the one while the other has time to take his bearings." In the end, abandoning the forms and formalities of Article V undermines the Constitution as the fundamental law and as such it undermines the rule of law as a core value of the American regime. The forms and formalities of Article V allow the people to explicitly decide whether or not to amend their Constitution and to do so in a clear and democratically decisive manner. Thus ultimately the forms of Article V support and sustain a written Constitution as the fundamental law of the polity.

Notes

1. Alexis de Tocqueville, *Democracy in America* (J.P. Meyer ed. Harper Perennial, 1969), 698.
2. Kyvig, *The Road Not Taken*, 464.
3. Ackerman, *Foundations*, 51-52.
4. Ackerman, *Responding to Imperfection*, 72.
5. Ibid.
6. Since Ackerman has not yet extended this logic to other articles of the Constitution, one is not clear on whether he believes there are multiple means of electing a president, or members of Congress, but it is clear he does not believe that a single formal process for amendment exists.
7. Ackerman, *Foundations*, 266.
8. Ackerman, *Foundations*, 266-267.

9. Jeffrey H. Anderson, "Reserving Law-Making to Law-Makers: The American Founders' and Early Courts' Opposition to Judicial Policy-Making." Dissertation completed at the Claremont Graduate University, 2001.

10. In his highly theoretical essay Levinson makes no distinction between the Constitution as a written text, and the Constitution as a term to describe the alignment of government powers and institutions relative to one another. Consequently, Levinson makes no distinction between constitutional change in terms of factual developments regarding the alignment of powers and institutions, on one hand, and clear alterations to the constitutional text on the other. Clarification of this ambiguity is critical in moving discussions of constitutional amendment forward.

11. Levinson, *Responding to Imperfection*, 26.

12. Here Levinson illustrates the inherent confusion involved in this issue. I would make the distinction between "changes in the pre-existing legal reality" and changes to the constitutional text, while Dr. Levinson would not. Here Levinson confuses the American system with the British system. Certainly there are significant legal changes that can take place without requiring a change to the constitutional text, but these are not properly called amendments in a formal legal sense of the word. An amendment is simply any textual change to the Constitution.

13. Griffin, *Responding to Imperfection*, 38.

14. Ibid., 61.

15. Ibid., 58.

16. Ibid., 59.

17. Ibid., 60.

18. Amar, *Consent of the Governed*, 465.

19. Farrand, *Records*, I: 122-123.

20. *Federalist No. 43.*

21. See Amar, *Consent of the Governed*, 465.

22. Amar, *Consent of the Governed, 465.*

23. *Federalist No. 43.*

24. Ibid.

25. Farand's Records, I: 122-123.

26. Ibid., 466.

27. Kyvig, *The Road Not Taken*, 464.

28. Marian C. McKenna, (2002). *Franklin Roosevelt and the Great Constitutional War: The Court-packing Crisis of 1937.* New York, NY: Fordham University Press. 146.

29. Kyvig, *The Road Not Taken, 464.* The term "hot oil" refers to "contraband oil" that was produced out of compliance with state and federal regulations. The government was attempting to regulate the price of oil but "hot oil" resulted in over production and thus produced unwanted effects on the petroleum market. The court struck down this provision of the National Industrial Recovery Act (NIRA) because it held that Congress had unduly delegated legislative powers to the president thus violating the Constitution's separation of powers. See C. Herman Pritchett, "Panama Revining Co. v. Ryan" in *Oxford Companion to the Supreme Court*, Kermit Hall, ed., (New York: Oxford University Press, 1992), 619.

30. Ibid., 464-465.

31. Ibid., 465.

32. Ibid., 465.

33. Second only to Lyndon Johnson's defeat of Goldwater in 1964.

34. Michael Dubin, *Party Affiliations in the State Legislatures: A Year by Year Summary, 1776-2006* (Jefferson, NC: McFarland, 2007). The nine other legislatures reflect either shared partisan control or third party control. The exact breakdown was not readily available but it is safe to assume that most of the nine were shared between the two major parties.

35. See also Amity Shlaes, *The Forgotten Man*, 297.

36. Democratic Party Platform of 1936, at The American Presidency Project. University of California Santa Barbara, http://www.presidency.ucsb.edu/ws/ (accessed on September 16, 2011).

37. Kyvig, *The Road Not Taken*, 466.

38. Ibid., 466.

39. Leuchtenburg, *FDR's Court Packing Plan*, 674.

40. In *West Coast Hotel Co. v. Parrish* the court upheld a Washington State minimum wage law for women. This move by the court overturned its previous rulings in *Morehead v. New York ex rel. Tipaldo* (1936) and in *Adkins v. Children's Hospital* (1923). While it has been popularly held that Justice Owen Robert's vote was a "switch in time"; there seems to be some evidence that Robert's vote was not in response to FDR's bill, but it still may have been in response to the larger pressures on the court more generally, see Marian C. McKenna, *Franklin Roosevelt and the Great Constitutional War: The Court-packing Crisis of 1937* (New York, NY: Fordham University Press, 2002) and Charles A. Leonard, "West Coast Hotel Co. v. Parrish," in *Oxford Companion to the Supreme Court*, Kermit Hall, ed., (New York: Oxford University Press, 1992), 924.

41. Leuchtenburg, *FDR's Court Packing Plan*, 673; Leuchtenburg does not elaborate on what was different between the January court packing plan and the summer version. The main point at issue here is that while some details might have been altered the general thrust and designs of the plan were the same.

42. As quoted in Leuchtenburg, *FDR's Court Packing Plan*, 675.

43. Ibid.; Leuchtenburg's account provides a very dramatic retelling of this conflict.

44. Ibid.

45. Ibid., 682.

46. Ibid., 681-686.

47. Ibid., 684-686.

48. Ibid., 686-689.

49. Kyvig, *The Road Not Taken*, 466.

50. Democratic Party Platform of 1936, at The American Presidency Project. University of California Santa Barbara, http://www.presidency.ucsb.edu/ws/ (accessed on September 16, 2011). See also Amity Shlaes, *The Forgotten Man*, 297.

51. Kyvig, *The Road Not Taken*,467.

52. Ibid., 472.

53. Ibid., 467-468.

54. Ibid.

55. Kyvig, *The Road Not Taken*.

56. Ibid., 476-477.

57. Ibid., 477.

58. Ibid.

59. Ibid.

60. Ibid.

61. Ibid., 478.

62. Fireside Chat, March 9, 1937; accessed at The American Presidency Project, UC Santa Barbara, http://www.presidency.ucsb.edu/ws/; (accessed on September 23, 2011).

63. Ibid.

64. George Washington, *Farewell Address*, 1796, Yale Law School Avalon Project, http://avalon.law.yale.edu/18th_century/washing.asp (accessed December 20, 2012).

65. Ibid.

66. Levinson, *Responding to Imperfection*, 26.

67. Ibid., 24.

68. Webster's Ninth New Collegiate Dictionary (Springfield, MA: Merriam-Webster Inc. Publishers, 1987).

69. Ibid.

70. Definition borrowed from Kyvig, *Explicit & Authentic Acts*, 21.

71. Keith Whittington, *Constitutional Construction: Divided Powers and Constitutional Meaning* (Cambridge, MA: Harvard University Press, 1999).

72. Ibid., 3.

73. Ibid., 4.

74. Ibid.
75. Ibid., 5.
76. Ibid.
77. Ibid., 6.
78. Ibid., 5.
79. Ibid., 12.
80. Ibid., 14.

Chapter 9
Conclusion: The Case for Article V

> The basis of our political systems is the right of the people to make and to alter their constitutions of government. But the constitution which at any time exists till changed by an explicit and authentic act of the whole people is sacredly obligatory upon all. The very idea of the power and the right of the people to establish government presupposes the duty of every individual to obey the established government.
>
> George Washington[1]

> We shall have in this article an adequate provision for all the purposes of political reformation.
>
> Dr. Charles Jarvis[2]

> We have now sunk to a depth at which re-statement of the obvious is the first duty of intelligent men.
>
> George Orwell[3]

The Case for Article V

In some respects this book is, as Orwell might say, a re-statement of the obvious. It should be obvious that Article V has played a vital historical role in perfecting the United States Constitution. It should be obvious that Article V is an integral part of the constitutional architecture. It should be obvious that formal amendment is necessary to maintain a written constitution. Furthermore, it should be obvious that Article V is the only legitimate means of constitutional amendment and that it strikes a careful and prudent balance between preservation and progress allowing the people to deliberatively alter their fundamental law in a clear and sober voice. Yet, as we have seen, these things are not obvious to a prominent and influential segment of legal scholars. Article V is attacked by its critics for being too difficult, undemocratic, and too formal. These attacks seek to undermine, weaken, or replace Article V with modes of change that are more informal, less difficult, or more responsive. To its detractors Article V is an obstacle to progress rather than a vital element of the sound and stable United States Constitution. It is because Article V's role as an essential support for American Constitutionalism and liberal democracy is not obvious to all, that this book has been written.

In making the case for Article V as the only legitimate form of constitutional amendment, this book has attempted to lay out the history of ideas and principles that have shaped Article V and embodied its role in the American Constitutional system. It has been shown how, from their earliest days of European settlements, Americans have embraced written documents when constituting their polities. In fact, in large respects it is fair to say that the American Constitutional tradition has always embraced a written document as its source of fundamental law. The earliest state constitutions with few exceptions provided for written documents and formal amending procedures, and both the Articles of Confederation and the current United States Constitution made provision for formal amendment. As we have seen Article V was essential in the Federalist efforts to ratify the Constitution by providing a means of parrying the thrust of the Anti-Federalists in the state ratification conventions. One could make the case that without Article V the Constitution might not have been ratified. Immediately after ratification of the Constitution, Article V allowed the people to add the Bill of Rights to the document. After the devastating Civil War Article V provided a means of enacting the Thirteenth, Fourteenth, and Fifteenth Amendments that registered the nation's rejection of slavery as an institution and extended civil liberties and the right to vote to former slaves. During the Progressive era, Americans democratized the Senate through the popular selection of Senators, created the income tax, passed and repealed alcohol prohibition, and then they granted the franchise to women on a national level. During the Civil Rights era, Americans granted Electoral College votes to Washington D.C., ended the poll tax, and extended the right to vote to eighteen year olds. In all of these ways, the American people have used the orderly, regular, open, and deliberatively democratic process of Article V to perfect their Constitution. Public consensus was forged through messy democratic politics—sometimes quickly and sometimes over decades—but each time, Article V allowed each national consensus to be registered peaceably and effectively.

A necessary result of this amending history is that Article V has been naturally woven into the very fabric of American politics, and its constitutional status makes it the sole source of legal authority for amendment. The notion of Article V as the sole legitimate process for amendment was virtually unchallenged for over 200 years following the creation and ratification of the United States Constitution. While today Article V is under scrutiny by some, and declared obsolete, or superfluous, by others, it is nonetheless the only method of amendment clearly prescribed in the Constitution's text and is constantly utilized as a pathway for proposed amendments to the Constitution.

This book has shown that formal amendment, in some form, is a logical extension of written constitutionalism. A formal document that serves as the fundamental law requires formal changes. In some crucial sense, *amendment* is about preservation and progress. The formality of amendment allows a polity to preserve its written constitution while it also allows the polity to progress and change over time while maintaining certain fundamental changes registered in the written constitution. Put another way, the amending process gives the American people a means of altering their constitutional system in the interests of progress, and similarly it gives them a chance to preserve that system from usurpation or decline over time. Colonial American leaders lamented their inability to *preserve* the British constitution of customary constraint. The unwritten nature of the British constitution had "evolved" in a manner that saw colonial rights recede into the swirling waters of Parliamentary sovereignty. There were no means by which the American colonists could grab hold of the British constitution; or put another way, there were no institutional means by which to preserve the aspects of that system that they desired. In stark contrast, Article V does provide that opportunity for the American people, the chance to both preserve the elements of the Constitution that they find conducive to sustaining their rights and yet also pursuing progress in attempts to perfect their Constitution through formal amendment. In short, it meets George Washington's requirements of the amending process being "explicit and authentic."[4] Furthermore, it should be abundantly clear by now Article V is consistent with the American commitment to deliberation and prudence in its institutional framework. It requires that the public deliberate over time through their representative institutions; and in doing so, it prevents rash or unwise alterations to the fundamental law. Article V is consistent with the basic American political tradition of drawing on the authority of popular majorities via representative bodies. In this way Article V uses democratic reservoirs of power judiciously and responsibly.

Moreover, Article V respects the inherent federal nature of the American political tradition. It treats states as states, not as simple arms of the federal government. This federal nature of American politics is sewn into the history and experience of the American people and as such is engrained in the very nature of American politics and the American spirit. As long as local power and control is used responsibly (not as it was used to support Jim Crow laws, and African-American subjugation in the South) state administration of local government has given average Americans a critical voice over how their daily lives will be regulated by the government.[5] In this sense federalism provides the people with governments that are closer to their daily lives and therefore gives more control over the manner in which government interacts with them and their communities. Article V respects this American tradition of federalism and federalism's benefits to American political freedom and social innovation.

Article V also respects the American tradition of separation of powers. It keeps that which is an essentially creative power in its proper sphere. Whereas, executive power is a derivative enforcement power and judicial power is a derivative interpretive power, legislative power is the core governmental power, and is creative by nature. Accordingly, Article V draws its authority solely from legislatures or conventions at the national and state levels, thus avoiding any undue mixing of governmental power. Article V also strikes a balance between elite amendment (by judges, presidents, or bureaucrats) on one hand, and the potential excesses of direct-democratic amendment on the other. In sum, Article V has clearly served Americans well historically and it has proven to be an effective and prudent means of registering democratic consensus in a peaceful and clear manner.

Clearly the case for Article V as the sole legitimate form of amendment is compelling; and in contrast, the case against Article V has been shown to be quite weak. For example, the critique of Article V being *too difficult* rests largely on a series of unsupported and unstated assumptions. Critics usually fail to offer a clear standard for how often and how quickly amendments should be made; instead, they simplistically assert, without much analysis, that the frequency and timing of amendment under Article V are insufficient. As we have seen, these assertions do not hold up to even minimal examination. Furthermore, the criticism of Article V's difficulty also rests upon undefended assertions about responsiveness that do not fully account for the realities of democratic deliberation or the political models of "punctuated equilibrium" that reveal long periods of inactivity that are "punctuated" by periodic amendment bursts or clusters to be quite normal and expected. Building political consensus in a diverse pluralistic democracy takes time and requires both patience and a tolerance for untidy politics; critics seem to lack both qualities.

The criticism that Article V is *undemocratic* has been shown to rest on notions of responsive government that are inconsistent with the natural rights philosophy found in the Declaration of Independence and the limitations on impulsive popular decisions found throughout the Constitution. This view of responsive democracy has been called "simplistic democracy" in that it prioritizes responsiveness at the expense of other important ends of government, namely the rights of citizens, political stability, good government, and sound decision making. An excessive focus on responsiveness comes at the expense of deliberation which is necessary to "refine and enlarge" the public voice in a manner that will not threaten the rights of other citizens or the permanent interests of the community. Modes of amendment such as national referendums abandon critical modes of public deliberation that can only occur through representation at both the state and federal levels of government. The Constitution has always served the American desire not only for responsive government, but also for a government that makes sound decisions and protects the natural rights of its citizens.

The criticism that Article V is *too formal* and needs to be replaced by informal adaptation by the courts or the political branches has also been similarly found wanting. Informal adaptation clearly undermines the American commitment to a written constitution. If the written text of the Constitution is to maintain its legal authority, alterations to that text must be known to the governors and the citizens alike. The problem is that *adaptations* are by their very nature not explicit. This lack of explicitness makes it difficult to know whether an amendment to the Constitution has occurred and makes it difficult to know exactly what that change is. Informal adaptation also makes it difficult to know whether such amendments are indeed democratic or made in the authentic voice of the people. Again, this is due to the informality of adaptive change. The people don't know that a change has been proposed, which makes it difficult for the people to speak specifically on the proposed "amendment." Furthermore, models of adaptive change tend to rely on the courts to alter the Constitution based upon their perceptions of the public will or under pressure from the political branches. This inordinate reliance on the least popular branch for constitutional amendment sorely undermines the democratic credibility of the regime. When sitting presidents and Supreme Court justices can publicly proclaim that the Constitution is merely "whatever the Supreme Court says it is," then for some the Constitution's text has become a pretext for the assertions of raw political power unhinged from notions of rule of law rooted in popular authority.[6] Furthermore, the scholarly emphasis on some impersonal and inexorable "evolution of the law" only masks the human agency of political leaders who direct these informal alterations to advance their version of the public good. This "evolution" through human agency is what the founding generation (and Lincoln) might label "decay" or "usurpation" of the Constitution and its attending forms.

As solutions to such perceived inadequacies, Article V critics tend to argue either for national referenda or for adaptation by the courts. Put another way they tend to favor the people speaking en mass in a non-deliberative voice or by small groups of political elites who are not fully or reasonably accountable to democratic audit. Put another way, critics either justify excluding the people from constitutional change or they included them but only in a manner where the public mind is unduly vulnerable to manipulation and demagoguery.[7] Thus, they err in both directions and they exclude the moderate and stable course of entrusting and empowering popular majorities via representative institutions.

The picture that begins to form is that critics of Article V are deeply ambivalent about sound democratic deliberation. Deliberation requires institutional support that can only be found in public deliberative bodies such as conventions or legislatures. It is only in such settings that the people can hope, however imperfectly, to guard equally against demagoguery and public factions that riddle more directly democratic devices such as referendums. The Founders were clear that there were two types of public voice, "one more immediate or spontaneous, uninformed, and unreflective; the other more deliberative, taking longer to develop and resting on a fuller consideration of information and arguments."[8] Representative bodies allow the raw public impulses to be "refined and enlarged" so that the "cool and deliberative sense of the community" can rule.[9] Representative bodies provide critical elements of deliberation such as information, time, and structured forums that allow for arguments to be made and persuasion to take place based on notions of the public good.[10] Institutional settings such as ratifying conventions or legislatures allow for the people's representatives to overcome the obstacles to deliberation that the national referendums are simply unable to overcome due to the manipulations of media and the immense size of the public and their inability to deliberate face to face. In the end, critics of Article V implicitly give up on such deliberative institutions and devices and as a consequence they give up on deliberative democracy in any meaningful sense.

Part of the reason critics of Article V give up on deliberation is their impatience with the time it takes for deliberation to take place. Again there is a latent elitism in the criticism of Article V being too difficult. As pointed out in chapter 6, critics seem to "know" which proposed amendments are "necessary" and which ones are not and they are frustrated when the masses do not immediately agree with them. When it takes time, sometimes decades, for public deliberation to develop, then critics assume, often without argument, that Article V supermajority consent requirements have been stifling the "true" public voice. Yet how are they so sure which public voice is "true"? What ground are they standing on that allows them to "know" what the people should do before the people have deliberated on the matter? Philosopher kings in the Platonic vein might know; but in a liberal democracy, the people deliberate via their elected representatives in order to reach such conclusions. Furthermore, critics complain about the "rigid" requirements of Article V. But as we have seen, such requirements have over the years also prevented truly noxious and dangerous amendments from passing. What process would critics propose exactly that would weed out dangerous amendments while keeping sound or healthy amendments? Presumably they would like to make that determination themselves? Yet elites have poor record discerning sound constitutional principles. Most obviously, it is easy to recall that elite judges firmly embraced slavery in *Dred Scott v. Sanford,* segregation in *Plessy v. Ferguson*, and eugenics in *Buck v. Bell.* More directly democratic forms such as national referendums aren't likely to help with this dilemma either. We must remember that it is quite likely that bare popular majorities would have "amended" the Constitution in attempts to entrench slavery or prevent "miscegenation" or any other number of dreadful or outright silly amending proposals. Only the super majority requirements of Article V administered by the people deliberating in representative bodies rejected such measures. As we have seen, deliberation via representative assemblies was the best test of just public policy for the founding generation.[11]

In the end, critics imply that only they are in a position to judge which amendments are sound and which are not, yet they provide no sound argument as to why elites or the mass public would do that job well. It might be worth reminding them that, "Genuine deliberation directed toward wise policies is often a slow, untidy, and contentious process in which 'differences of opinion' and the 'jarring of parties' play a central role."[12] In this context, alternatives to Article V reveal themselves as short cuts to either avoid consent requirements—in the case of informal judicial adaptation—or attempts to avoid truly deliberative public endorsement—in the case of national referendum.

What has become apparent in this examination of the criticisms of Article V is that critiques of Article V take place in a larger context of antagonism towards the Constitution itself. Thus, it is not surprising that Article V critics often find additional fault with the equal representation in the Senate or the lack of national popular voting in the Electoral College. For a case in point, one need look no further than Sanford Levinson's *New York Times* editorial entitled "Our Imbecilic Constitution" that attacked the Constitution for generating "dysfunctional, even pathological" politics and he singled Article V out for specific opprobrium.[13] Levinson advocated large scale constitutional change and even suggested presidential appointments to the House and Senate as a desired reform. Recall that Robert Dahl advocates ending the equal representation of the Senate and Daniel Lazare called for a House of Representatives led popular *copu d' état.*[14] Thus, in many cases the critics' ultimate goal is not Article V per se but rather the deconstruction and transformation of the fabric of the larger constitutional order, but they find Article V as an inconvenient impediment to their efforts. One could say that critics are often frustrated with its provisions because Article V stands like a citadel at the narrow bend in the river preventing them from entering the constitutional bay and wreaking havoc on the entire edifice of ordered liberty. Thus to achieve their goal they must remove the stubborn citadel of Article V first.

In the end, much of these criticisms come down to a fundamentally different view about the ultimate end or purpose of government. Critics seem to want "responsive" government;[15] while in contrast Article V is designed for a system that prevents usurpation of the constitutional forms by either the few or the many. The Founders sought to avoid tyranny in any guise whether it was tyranny of the few or tyranny of the majority. Towards this goal they created a system in tension. The tension provided that *the many* restrains the power and machinations of *the few* via elections and democratic accountability; while the power of *the few* is given some shelter from the passions of *the many* via constitutional and institutional restraints on popular will—such as representation along with long and staggered legislative terms—all of which seek to foster deliberation. What the early Progressives sought to do was to empower the will of *the many* against *the few* in an effort to resolve that tension in favor of the impulses of the people. What the later New Deal Progressives did was to empower *the few* (whether in the executive branch or the courts) in the name of *the many* by abandoning the forms that sought to include the people in the deliberations with about constitutional amendment. So in the end, both of the Progressive models err in both extremes; they either indulge the excess of *the many* at the expense of *the few* or they indulge the usurpation of *the few* in the name of, and perhaps the expense of, *the many*; all in the name of "responsive" government. What they fail to consider in all of this is the Founders' reliance on moderation that sought to channel the will of both *the few* and *the many* through constitutional forms and formalities such that neither potentially destructive impulse is given full measure.

If "responsiveness" is the ultimate end of government then there is no need to bind the people in any way. Indeed, if one changes the purpose of government from the preservation of the natural rights of citizens to the mere responsiveness, then the logic of Article V collapses; in fact the logic of written constitutionalism collapses. In opting for impulsive non-deliberative forms of national referendums, they do so at the expense of more prudent and moderate deliberative institutions that Americans have used for centuries. Or they abandon the clear constitutional forms of Article V by opting for radically informal adaptive models of change that hide constitutional alterations in the ambiguous and opaque nature of legal precedents, presidential orders, and congressional legislation. In all of these efforts critics claim to be acting in the name of progress. Now this may perhaps be progress, but it is clear that the Founders would have not have viewed it as such, nor might most American citizens who still seem to cherish their natural rights and who also seem to still find vigor and value in a written Constitution and Article V.[16]

Perfecting the Constitution

In the end, Article V has served as a perfecting mechanism of the Constitution since its inception. Surely true "perfection" will ever prove illusory, yet it is clear that the Founders often referred to Article V as a means of addressing discovered imperfections in the Constitution, and Americans, for generations, have continued to use it for that purpose. Article V has allowed the American people to continue to perfect their constitution over time without resorting to the danger and instability of replacing the entire document; it has also allowed amendments that perfect or improve the document while preventing disastrous or controversial additions. In general its supermajority consent requirements have prevented the Constitution from being captured by narrow or unwise majoritarian impulses of any given moment.

Despite claims of Article V's inadequacy, both the political class and the populace have not lost faith in Article V, nor have either ever fully embraced judicial adaptation.[17] Political actors on both sides of the partisan aisle find the promise of Article V as useful as ever. For example, the left has sought amendments to the Constitution that would end the Electoral College or that would overturn the Supreme Court's *Citizens United v. Federal Election Commission* decision. In contrast, amendment proposals from conservatives have focused on school prayer, balanced budgets, pro-life measures, and upholding traditional marriage. While such efforts have not yet proven successful, the repeated and continued attempts at Article V amendment by both sides of the political spectrum show that it still offers hope of perfecting the Constitution to all comers. Their lack of success, as we have seen, is not evidence of the difficulty or rigidity of Article V, rather it serves as evidence that the amending process demands that reformers must do the long term hard work of assembling political coalitions that will support the constitutional change they desire. If the history of Article V is any indication, controversial measures such as some of these listed above will find it very difficult to produce the supermajorities necessary to meet Article V requirements or it may take decades of public debate before public opinion is ready to amend the fundamental law in such a manner. Spirited partisans and critical scholars often forget that Article V is a recognition of consensus, not necessarily a means of achieving it. In seeking to change the Constitution, conservatives and liberals alike would do well to win the hearts and minds of fellow citizens over time rather than seeking shortcuts around Article V. Only a firm grounding in supermajority public opinion will ensure that their proposals meet the Article V standards for inclusion in the Constitution and will likewise ensure levels of public support that will allow such changes to endure over time.

Proposals for Article V amendments also continue to be quite popular among the political class. In fact, since the 106th Congress (1999-2000) through the 111th Congress (2009-2010) 438 proposals for amendment have been introduced into Congress.[18]

In the end, scholars and citizens alike should take care to fully assess Article V, and its contributions to American Constitutionalism, before endorsing radical departures from its procedures for legitimate amendment. While it is the natural right of American citizens to alter governmental forms, such alterations should be done with the same "reflection and choice" that was utilized in their creation. Likewise, critics might do well to spend less time tearing down the republican form of Article V and would be better served by engaging in the democratic process of deliberation and coalition building, the hallmarks of American politics.

Yet the question still remains as to whether or not Odysseus will be unbound; whether over time through decay or usurpation, Article V will ultimately be rejected as the sole authoritative means of amending the Constitution. If our written Constitution is essential to preserving ordered liberty and natural rights, by binding both the rulers and the ruled to legal forms and formalities, and if Article V is an essential form that is vital in maintaining a written constitution, then it would follow that the preservation of Article V is crucial to perpetuating our political institutions and maintaining our "temple of liberty."[19] As one critic correctly points out, the abandonment of formal amendment leads inexorably to an abandonment of "rule of law" constitutionalism.[20] While he views this abandonment as progress, it is likely that many citizens would see this as a deep loss.

The American people, much like Odysseus, have chosen to bind themselves under Article V and the Constitution for prudent and wise reasons. While it does bind them against their own temporary delusions, it also empowers them to act collectively with clarity, order, and effectiveness. It is a truth in human affairs that often self-imposed restraint is, in itself, an empowering act that displays wisdom and channels scarce energy towards more productive and stable pursuits. Yet, as we have seen, despite Article V's pedigree and effectiveness, legal elites charged with a crucial role in maintaining the polity's commitment to a written Constitution—like the crew in the Odyssey was charged with maintaining the bindings—are debating what to do. If legal elites, over time, persuade the American people to no longer believe that the "song of the sirens" leads to destruction, and they reject the binding nature of Article V and the Constitution, then they sail in those turbulent waters at their own peril and against the evidence and advice of history. Put another way, if legal elites are convinced to ignore Article V, or if the American people, as the sovereigns of the Constitution, are persuaded to untether themselves from Article V—and by extension to slowly unleash themselves from the binding nature of the Constitution—then they will likely find themselves subject to the very same chaos and instability that the Constitution was designed to restrain. If instead, Americans listen to the wisdom of their Founders by exclusively adhering to the Article V amendment process, then Article V can continue to empower them in perfecting and preserving their written Constitution. In turn, their written Constitution can continue to uphold a state of ordered liberty that will allow Americans to pursue their happiness and secure their natural rights, both for themselves and for generations yet unborn.

Notes

1. George Washington, *Farewell Address*, 1796, Yale Law School Avalon Project, http://avalon.law.yale.edu/18th_century/washing.asp (accessed December 20, 2012).

2. Elliot, *Debates*, II: 118; Jarvis contributed this utterance at the Massachusetts Ratifying Convention.

3. While it is not clear where or when Orwell said or wrote this, it is a well-known quote widely attributed to Orwell.

4. George Washington, *Farewell Address*, 1796, Yale Law School Avalon Project, http://avalon.law.yale.edu/18th_century/washing.asp (accessed December 20, 2012).

5. Americans have largely used local state power responsibly to reflect local and regional values and preferences successfully since the founding era. Federalism did earn a "bad name" so to speak when Southern states used their local power to preserve the unconscionable violation of civil and natural rights of black citizens. However, this historical misuse of federalism should not undermine the positive use of local power more generally. It seems reasonable to allow California to have laws different from Iowa, or New York to have laws different from Oklahoma. Laws that reflect local choices and local values allow the average citizen to have much more of a voice in how government interacts with their lives. It is also worthy of note that since the "Jim Crow" era local power has become a venue for ethnic minorities to exert power over their own communities; one need look no further than the existence of many Black, Latino, and Asian mayors, city council members, and governors show to see that federalism can provide voice to a wide array of political insterests.

6. See Charles Evans Hughes (then governor of New York, later the Chief Justice of the Supreme Court) as quoted in Ralph Rossum and Alan Tarr, *American Constitutional Law: The Structure of Government, Volume I*, 8th ed. (Boulder, CO: Westview Press, 2010), 2; And see Franklin Delano Roosevelt, Fireside Chat, March 9, 1937, accessed at The American Presidency Project, UC Santa Barbara, http://www.presidency.ucsb.edu/ws/; (accessed on September 23, 2011).

7. See chapter 7.

8. Bessette, *Voice of Reason*, 35.

9. *Federalist No. 10 and No. 63* respectively.

10. For a full accounting of this argument see Bessette, *Voice of Reason*, 49-55.

11. Again see *Federalist* No. 51 for this point.

12. Bessette, *Voice of Reason*, 31.

13. Sanford Levinson, "Our Imbecilic Constitution," *New York Times*, May 28, 2012.

14. See chapter 6, 154.

15. Even if it is driven by elites discerning the public voice.

16. Since 1789 there have been over 11,000 bills submitted to Congress that sought Article V amendments to the Constitution. See United States Senate Website. http://www.senate.gov/pagelayout/reference/three_column_table/measures_proposed_to_amend_constitution.htm (accessed August 24, 2012).

17. Even an open advocate of Judicial adaptation admits as much; see Sanford Levinson, *Our Undemocratic Constitution,* 163.

18. United States Senate Website. http://www.senate.gov/pagelayout/reference/three_column_table/measures_proposed_to_amend_constitution.htm (accessed August 24, 2012). Even if some politicians might find amendment proposals to merely be an effective way to show their support for a given issue (rather than a serious proposal) their practice of making such proposals in such numbers suggests that the voters respond to such efforts positively.

19. Lincoln refers to the "temple of liberty" in his Lyceum speech.

20. See Stephen Griffin in Levinson *Responding to Imperfection*.

Bibliography

Ackerman, Bruce. *We the People: Foundations.* Cambridge, Massachusetts: The Belknap Press, 1991.

———. *We the People: Transformations.* Cambridge, Massachusetts: The Belknap Press, 1998.

———. "Higher Lawmaking" in Sanford Levinson, ed. *Responding to Imperfection: The Theory and Practice of Constitutional Amendment.* Princeton, New Jersey: The Princeton University Press, 1995.

Adams, Willi Paul. *The First American Constitutions: Republican Ideology and the Making of the State Constitutions in the Revolutionary Era.* Chapel Hill, North Carolina: The University of North Carolina Press, 1980.

Allen, W.B. *George Washington: A Collection.* Indianapolis: Liberty Fund, 1988.

Amar, Akhil Reed. "The Consent of the Governed: Constitutional Amendment Outside of Article V." *Columbia Law Review,* Mar. 1994, 457-508.

———. "Philadelphia Revisited: Amending the Constitution Outside Article V." *The University of Chicago Law Review,* Autumn, 1988, 1043-1104.

———. "Popular Sovereignty and Amendment" in Sanford Levinson, ed. *Responding to Imperfection: The Theory and Practice of Constitutional Amendment.* Princeton, New Jersey: Princeton University Press, 1995.

Ames, Herbert. *The Proposed Amendments to the Constitution of the United States During the First Century of its History.* New York: Burt Franklin, 1970; reprint of 1896 edition.

Bailyn, Bernard. *The Ideological Origins of the American Revolution.* Cambridge, Massachusetts: Belknap Press, 1967.

Barber, James David. *The Book of Democracy.* Prentice-Hall, 1995.

Baumgartener, Frank R. et al. "Punctuated Equilibrium in Competitive Perspective." *American Journal of Political Science,* Jul. 2009, 603-620.

Belz, Herman. *A Living Constitution or Fundamental Law?: American Constitutionalism in Historical Perspective.* Lanham, Maryland: Rowman & Littlefield Publishers, Inc., 1998.

———. "Lincoln's Construction of the Executive Power in the Succession Crisis." *Journal of the Abraham Lincoln Association.* Winter, 2006, 13-38.

Benedict, Michael Les. *The Blessings of Liberty: A Concise History of the Constitution of the United States.* Lexington, Massachusetts: D.C. Heath and Company, 1996.

Berns, Walter. *Taking the Constitution Seriously.* New York: Simon & Schuster, 1987.

Bernstein, Richard B. with Jerome Agel. *Amending America.* New York: Times Books-Random House, 1993.

Bessette, Joseph M. *The Mild Voice of Reason: Deliberative Democracy and American National Government.* Chicago: The University of Chicago Press, 1994.

Bloom, Allan. "Justice John Rawls vs. the Tradition of Political Philosophy." *The American Political Science Review,* Jun. 1975, 648-662.

Borgeaud, Charles. *Adoption and Amendment of Constitutions in Europe and America.* New York: Macmillan and Co., 1895.

Bryce, James. *Constitutions.* New York: Oxford University Press American Branch, 1901.

———. *The American Commonwealth,* 2 Vols., 3rd ed. New York: Macmillan, 1906.

Caresse, Paul O. "Judicial Statesmanship, the Jurisprudence of Individualism, and Tocqueville's Common Law Spirit." *The Review of Politics,* Summer 1998, 465-495.

Ceaser, James W. *Liberal Democracy & Political Science.* Baltimore: Johns Hopkins University Press, 1990.

Colucci, Frank J. "Review: Taking Doctrine Seriously." *The Review of Politics,* Winter 2005, 168-170.

Croly, Herbert David. *Progressive Democracy.* New York: The Macmillan Company, 1914.

Dellinger, Walter. "The Legitimacy of Constitutional Change: Rethinking the Amendment Process." *Harvard Law Review,* Dec. 1983, 386-432.

Diamond, Martin. "Democracy and the Federalists: A Reconsideration of the Framer's Intent." *The American Political Science Review,* Mar. 1959, 52-68.

Dinwiddie, Courtney. "The Present Status of Child Labor." *Social Science Review,* Sept. 1939, 431-439.

Dow, David. *The Plain Meaning of Article V.* In Sanford Levinson, ed. *Responding to Imperfection: The Theory and Practice of Constitutional Amendment.* Princeton, New Jersey: Princeton University Press, 1995.

Durbin, Thomas M. *Amending The U.S. Constitution: by Congress or Constitutional Convention.* Congressional Reasearch Service. May 10, 1995.

Eden, Robert. "Tocqueville on Political Realignment and Constitutional Forms." *The Review of Politics,* Summer 1986, 349-373.

Fisher, Sidney George. *The Trial of the Constitution.* New York: Da Capo Press, 1972; reprint of J. B. Lippincott & Co., 1862.

Fox, Muriel. "Why Ratify the Child-Labor Amendment?" *Junior-Senior Highschool Clearing House,* Mar. 1936, 419-423.

Gerber, Scott Douglass. *To Secure These Rights: The Declaration of Independence and Constitutional Interpretation.* New York: New York University Press, 1995.

Gillman, Howard. *The Collapse of Constitutional Originalism.* Studies in American Political Development. 11 (Fall 1997), 191-247.

Griffin, Stephen. "Constitutional Theory Transformed." *The Yale Law Journal,* Jun. 1999, 2115-2163.

———. *Constitutionalism in the United States: From Theory to Politics.* In Sanford Levinson, ed. *Responding to Imperfection: The Theory and Practice of Constitutional Amendment.* Princeton, New Jersey: Princeton University Press, 1995.

Grimes, Alan P. *Democracy and the Amendments to the Constitution.* Lexington, Massachusetts: Lexington Books, 1919.

Hall, Kermit, L. "[Untitled]" *The American Political Science Review,* Jun. 1993, 503-504.

Hamilton, Alexander, James Madison, and John Jay. *The Federalist Papers.* Ed. Clinton Rossiter. New York: Mentor, 1961.

Higgins, Hennery Bournes. "The Rigid Constitution." *Political Science Quarterly,* Jun, 1905, 203-222.

Horowitz, Morton J. *The Transformation of American Law 1870-1960.* Oxford: Oxford University Press, 1992.

Huckabee, David C. *Ratification of Amendments to the U.S. Constitution.* Congressional Research Service. September 30, 1997.

Hyneman, Charles S. and Donald S. Lutz. *American Political Writing during the Founding Era 1760-1805.* Indianapolis: Liberty Fund, 1983.

Kelly, Alfred H., Winfred A. Harbison, and Herman Belz. *The American Constitution Its Origins and Development: Volume I.* New York: W. W. Norton & Company, 1991.

———. *The American Constitution Its Origins and Development: Volume I.* New York: W. W. Norton & Company, 1991.

Kessler, Charles R. ed. *Saving the Revolution: The Federalist Papers and the American Founding.* New York: The Free Press, 1987.

Kosar, Kevin R. *Regular Vetoes and Pocket Vetoes: An Overview.* Congressional Research Service. #RS22188, July 18, 2008.

Kramer, Larry D. "Constitutionalism, circa 2004." *California Law Review,* Jul, 2004, 959-1011.

Kruman, Marc W. *Between Authority & Liberty: State Constitution Making in Revolutionary America.* Chapel Hill, North Carolina: The University of North Carolina Press, 1997.

Kyvig, David. *Explicit & Authentic Acts: Amending the U.S. Constitution 1776-1995.* Lawrence, Kansas: University Press of Kansas, 1996.

———. "The Road Not Taken: FDR, the Supreme Court, and Constitutional Amendment," *Political Science Quarterly,* Autumn 1989, 463-481.

Lazare, Daniel. *The Frozen Republic: How the Constitution Is Paralyzing Democracy.* New York: Harcourt Brace, 1996.

Leuchtenburg, William E. "FDR's Court-Packing Plan: A Second Life, A Second Death." *Duke Law Journal,* Jun-Sep. 1985, 673-679.

———. *The Supreme Court Reborn: The Constitutional Revolution in the Age of Roosevelt.* Oxford: Oxford University Press, 1995.

Levinson, Sanford, ed. *Responding to Imperfection: The Theory and Practice of Constitutional Amendment.* Princeton, New Jersey: Princeton University Press, 1995.

———. *How Many Times Has the United States Constitution Been Amended? (A) <26; (B) 26; (C) 27; (D) > 27: Accounting for Constitutional Change.* In Levinson, Sanford, ed. *Responding to Imperfection: The Theory and Practice of Constitutional Amendment.* Princeton, New Jersey: Princeton University Press, 1995.

———. *Our Undemocratic Constitution: Where the Constitution Goes Wrong (and How We the People Can Correct It).* New York: Oxford University Press, 2006.

Lovell, George I. "Keith E. Whittington, Constitutional Construction: Divided Powers and Constitutional Meaning." *Ethics,* April 2011, 655-658.

Lutz, Donald. *The Origins of American Constitutionalism.* Baton Rouge: Louisiana State University Press, 1998.

Manning, Jennifer. *Congressional Statistics: Bills Introduced and Laws Enacted 1997-2004.* Congressional Research Service, Report 96-727. January 13, 2005.

Martens, Allison M. "Reconsidering Judicial Supremacy: From the Counter-Majoritarian Difficulty to Constitutional Transformations." *Perspectives on Politics,* Sep. 2007, 447-459.

McDonald, Forrest. *E Pluribus Unum: The Formation of the American Republic 1776-1790.* Indianapolis: Liberty Fund, 1979.

McDowell, Gary L. "Coke, Corwin and the Constitution: The 'Higher Law Background' Reconsidered." *The Review of Politics,* Summer 1993, 393-420.

McIlwain, Charles Howard. *Constitutionalism: Ancient and Modern.* Indianapolis: Liberty Fund, 2008.
McKenna, Marian C. "Prelude to Tyranny: Wheeler, F.D.R., and the 1937 Court Fight." *Pacific Historical Review,* Nov. 1993, 405-431.
Morgan, Edmund S. *Inventing the People: The Rise of Popular Sovereignty in England and America.* New York: W. W. Norton & Company, 1988.
Musmanno, M.A. *Proposed Amendments to the Constitution.* Washington, D.C: Government Printing Office, 1929.
Orfield, Lester. *The Amending of the Federal Constitution.* Ann Arbor, Michigan: The University of Michigan Press, 1942.
Palmer, Matthew S. R. "Using Constitutional Realism to Identify the Complete Constitution: Lessons from an Unwritten Constitution." *The American Journal of Comparative Law,* Summer 2006, 587-636.
Peterson, Merrill D. *The Portable Thomas Jefferson.* New York: Penguin Books, 1975.
Reid, John Phillip. *The Constitutional History of the American Revolution: The Authority to Legislate, No. 3.* Madison, Wisconsin: The University of Wisconsin Press, 1991.
———. *Constitutional History of the American Revolution: The Authority of Law, No. 4.* Madison, Wisconsin: The University of Wisconsin Press, 1993.
Rossum, Ralph A. and Gary L. McDowell, ed. *The American Founding: Politics, Statesmanship, and The Constitution.* Port Washington, NY: Kennikat Press, 1981.
Schaefer, David Lewis. "'Moral Theory' versus Political Philosophy: Two Approaches to Justice." *The Review of Politics,* Apr. 1977, 192-219.
Simmons, Charlene Wear. "California's Statewide Initiative Process." *California Research Bureau, California State Library,* May, 1997.
Smith, J. Allen. *The Spirit of American Government-A Study of the Constitution: Its Origins, Influence, and Relation to Democracy.* London: Macmillan & Co, 1907.
Smith, James Barclay. "A Child Labor Amendment Is Unnecessary." *California Law Review,* Nov. 1938, 15-47.
Stoner, James R. Jr. "Common Law and Constitutionalism in the Abortion Case." *The Review of Politics,* Summer, 1993, 421-441.
———. "Religious Liberty and Common Law: Free Excersise Exemptions & American Courts." *Polity,* Autumn, 1993, 1-24.
Strauss, David A. "The Irrelevance of Constitutional Amendments." *Harvard Law Review,* Mar. 2001, 1407-1505.
Thomas, George. "Recovering the Political Constitution: The Madisonian Vision." *The Review of Politics,* Spring, 2004, 233-256.
Tocqueville, Alexis. *Democracy in America.* J.P. Meyer ed. Harper Perennial, 1969.
Tushnet, Mark. "[Untitled]." *The Journal of Interdisciplinary History,* Autumn 2000, 290-291.
United States Constitution, Article V.
Vile, John R. *The Constitutional Amending Process in American Political Thought.* Westport, Connecticut: Praeger, 1992.
———. *Contemporary Questions Surrounding the Constitutional Amending Process.* Westport, Connecticut: Praeger, 1992.
———. *Constitutional Change in the United States.* Westport Connecticut: Praeger, 1994.

Watson, Brad C. S. *Living Constitution Dying Faith: Progressivism and the New Science of Jurisprudence.* Wilmington, Delaware: ISI Books, 2009.

Wilson, Woodrow. *Congressional Government.* Boston: Houghton Mifflin, 1885 and 1913.

Whittington, Keith E. "Presidential Challenges to Judicial Supremacy and the Politics of Constitutional Meaning." *Polity,* Spring 2001, 365-391.

———. "Review: Clothed with the Legitimate Authority of the People." *Virginia Law Review,* Dec. 2005, 2033-2043.

———. "The Road Not Taken: Dread Scott, Judicial Authority, and Political Questions." *The Journal of Politics,* May, 2001, 365-391.

Wood, Gordon S. *The Creation of the American Republic, 1776-1787.* New York: W. W. Norton & Company, 1969.

About the Author

Darren Patrick Guerra is Associate Professor of Political Science at Biola University. He formerly taught at Vanguard University of Southern California. His areas of teaching and research are American Politics, Public Policy, Constitutional Law, and Political Philosophy.

www.ingramcontent.com/pod-product-compliance
Ingram Content Group UK Ltd.
Pitfield, Milton Keynes, MK11 3LW, UK
UKHW041125071026
15587UKWH00009B/220

9 780739 168387